Nebraska Symposium on Motivation, 1972, is Volume XX in the series on CURRENT THEORY AND RESEARCH IN MOTIVATION

nebraska symposium on motivation
1972

James K. Cole and Donald D. Jensen, Editors

Robert Bigelow
Reader in Zoology
University of Canterbury, New Zealand

Robert B. Cairns
Professor of Psychology
Indiana University

John P. Flynn
Professor of Anatomy
Yale University School of Medicine

Ronald R. Hutchinson
Director of Research
Fort Custer State Home, Augusta, Michigan

John B. Calhoun
Chief, Section on Behavioral Systems
National Institute of Mental Health

Dan Olweus
Professor of Personality Psychology
University of Bergen, Norway

university of nebraska press
lincoln
1972

UNP *Publishers on the Plains*

Copyright © 1973 by the University of Nebraska Press
International Standard Book Number 0–8032–0614–3
Library of Congress Catalog Card Number 53–11655
Manufactured in the United States of America

Contents

Introduction

In recent years the *Nebraska Symposium on Motivation* has been organized according to psychological themes, in contrast to the earlier volumes, which included papers having only the common denominator of motivation as a relevant issue. Some of these papers critically evaluated the amorphous validity of motivation as a unifying theme. Last year the symposium included two themes, each represented by three papers: nonverbal communication and developmental psychology.

The current volume, for the first time, is organized entirely around one common theme, aggression. It includes research on both human and animal aggression and one paper which develops a theoretical focus for the evolution of aggression in man.

For this symposium, Professor Robert Bigelow's paper, "The evolution of cooperation, aggression, and self-control," constitutes a unique departure from the "current research" emphasis usually found in symposium papers. Professor Bigelow, author of *The Dawn Warriors: Man's Evolution toward Peace*, considers the problem of human evolution and develops a conceptual framework which attempts to interpret evolutionary data and the relationship of evolution to both aggression and the factors which inhibit aggression—cooperation and intelligent self-control. His theory emphasizes both the need for aggressive group behavior in early humans and the capacity to control potential aggressive behavior. The ability of groups to respond effectively against threat was due in part to the development of within-group self-control. Professor Bigelow questions the assumption that intergroup competition was inconsequential during prehistoric times; for some authorities, man was the peaceful "noble savage." Professor Bigelow rejects the conclusiveness of this assumption and hypothesizes that intergroup competition, if not intrahuman violence, was an important and primary characteristic of prehistoric man. Intergroup competition can account for the evolution of hunting and of the inability of other primates to keep pace with man. Furthermore, the requirement of self- and group control over behavior argues against a blind or uncontrollable "aggression-instinct." According to Bigelow's theory, aggression is not a necessary, inborn characteristic of man, and warfare is not an uncontrollable manifestation of inborn propensities. In rejecting both a "purely cultural" or conditioned motivation for warfare and a blind, innate "instinct," Bigelow states that cultural evolution is a natural result of biological evolution. Biological evolution has created an enormous, complex brain in man which has the capacity to control and regulate aggressive potentialities and to establish and maintain social communication and cooperation—even on a global scale. Part of the evolutionary consequences has been the ability to learn from experiences and the ability to adjust to novel situations. As brains grew in size and complexity, they developed great capacities for processing information to understand not only the past and present, but also to predict the future.

Finally, Bigelow's theory offers considerable hope for the future of mankind. Man has not inherited an uncontrollable "instinct" for war. If our brains were indeed fashioned by selective forces of warfare, they were also developed to conquer war.

The primary concern for Professor Robert Cairns is an ontogenetic analysis of injury-producing and punitive behaviors in young humans and animals. His paper emphasizes a comparative approach with an ontogenetic resolution in which social learning and ontogenetic events are synthesized in understanding these behaviors. The paper focuses on the concept of aggression and the ontogenetic perspective, experiments and observations on the establishment of fighting and punishment from that perspective, and the issues of comparative generalization. Professor Cairns outlines the major controlling events for fighting and punishment— self-produced events, intraorganismic states, and contextual events —and points out that stimulus analyses alone cannot explain the behaviors since the developing organism must be understood. From this perspective, Professor Cairns explores an ontogenetic analysis of the development of violent mice. The importance of the ontogenetic approach was clearly substantiated since training was not necessary to establish fighting behavior, while the method of rearing was found to be the primary effect. It is clear that the maturation of the necessary sensory and motor structures is necessary to establish the behaviors. The fact that rearing conditions that preclude exposure to fighting facilitate the establishment of the behaviors is partially explained by a spiraling interchange, where the behavior of at least one member of a pair becomes increasingly more intense and provocative, resulting in feedback events. Conspecific "taming" is linked to the clumping and huddling behavior of the species. Isolation rearing increases reactivity to physical stimulation and odor, predisposing the animal to escalating sequences that terminate in attacks and counterattacks. Thus, establishment of attack behaviors and social interchanges is bidirectional, and the biological states of the individual are significantly modified by social interaction in ontogeny. Although learning is not necessary to establish attack behavior, it does influence its generalization, control, and suppression. In a comparative analysis with mammalian young, it is also apparent that attack behaviors can be established in the absence of specific training experiences, and bidirectionality of events is important in the establishment or control of the behaviors. Professor Cairns underscores the necessity for dyadic, ontogenetic analyses of aggression in children. The interchanges in the developing life simply cannot be ignored; as he states, "Bo Bo dolls do not fight back." Furthermore, as in animals, pain-producing responses may be adaptive.

Professor John P. Flynn's research attempts to determine the neural basis of attack behavior. More specifically, the primary behaviors that are observed are the behaviors of a cat that ensue when a rat (attack object) is present and attacked. These behaviors include approaching the attack object, striking at it, placing a paw on it, lunging, and biting. Attack behaviors and reflexes which are an important part of attack behavior when the attack object is present are elicited through electrical stimulation of the attack sites in the brain. Stimulation imposes a pattern of excitability on the nervous system, and attack sites are identified as patterning mechanisms. Patterned reflexes are those reflexes present during stimulation but otherwise not ordinarily present. The experimental data suggest that these patterned reflexes are close to the final act of biting or striking. The patterning mechanism that brings about the attack behavior has a temporal pattern, it is localized (strongest at the site of stimulation), and its influence has directional characteristics. The behavior elicited by stimulation is less important than the locus of excitation. These findings argue against the arousal of a simple drive which is accountable for the behavioral data.

Professor Ronald R. Hutchinson identifies two principal classes of environmental causes of aggression: (a) events antecedent to aggression, and (b) events subsequent to aggression which influence future aggression. Two major types of antecedent events are presented. The first type involves the onset or increase of noxious stimuli or other stimuli which have been paired with such stimuli. The second type is the offset or decrease of positive stimuli or previously neutral stimuli paired with these stimuli. Professor Hutchinson reviews the empirical data for these classes of events which generally establish these classes across species as they relate primarily to attack behavior. The temporal and intensive character of attack behavior and the strength of attack behavior are related to these events. Two classes of subsequent stimuli which alter future attack behavior include the onset or increment of positive stimuli or paired neutral stimuli and the reduction, termination, or continued absence of noxious stimuli. Professor Hutchinson points out that although both antecedent and subsequent classes of events can cause aggression, the behaviors produced are fundamentally different. Behavior display reflecting anger is associated with antecedent events, but emotional arousal is often not associated with subsequent-event classes.

In the first part of his paper, Professor John B. Calhoun proposes that all major attributes of an animal—motivation, drive, mood, stereotypy, emotion, and personality—can be defined by five probability functions which account for the character of behavior over time in a constant environment. p' is a duration terminator probability for a behavioral state. It designates the probability of a behavioral state terminating in a unit of time and is constant throughout the unit of time. Duration of the behavioral state increases with decrements in p', and functioning of p' alone leads to a negative exponential equation describing the number of behavioral states. p_i is a behavioral state duration inhibitor probability. p'' is a behavioral state prolonger probability. p_i is the probability of reducing p' from an elevated level to its normal value, and p'' becomes functional when a need arises for an increase in duration. In the absence of external disruptive stimuli, duration of a behavioral state is solely governed by these three probabilities. $\hat{p}$ is the probability of initiating a behavioral state given an ongoing state has terminated. Every state has a unique $\hat{p}$ and this probability is subject to limitation by an environmental context. p_k is the concatenator probability. When behavioral states are repetitive over some extended period of time, the functioning of a positive concatenating probability will thereafter enhance the likelihood of the persistence of this concatenation.

The second part of Professor Calhoun's paper reviews the behavioral state of aggression from the perspective of these five probability functions. The analysis is based on the behavior of wild and domesticated strains of mice and rats that were members of socially organized groups. Situations and contexts for aggression and deviant reactions include exposure to a strange environment, invasion of personal space, locomotor activity and alertness (social velocity), stimulus deprivation and limitations of behavior, and social rejection. The establishment of extreme or deviant patterns of aggression are discussed, including the use of social and physical settings, and the importance of vitamin A. Perhaps one of the more interesting groups of mice studied by Professor Calhoun was a group he called "the beautiful ones." This group has excellent pelage and physically appear in excellent condition. However, maturation of complex behavior was apparently impaired by reduced intensity and duration of social intercourse which occurred when group size increased above an optimum-sized social group. The "beautiful ones" do not engage in aggression or breeding.

Professor Dan Olweus's paper on personality and aggression emphasizes the author's conceptual scheme for the determination of aggressive responses within the context of a general scheme for the organization of psychological theories and their elements. The scheme is depicted as a truncated pyramid consisting of low levels of generality which are the levels of observable variables and progressing to high levels of generality which are the levels of theoretical concepts. Professor Olweus then focuses on the aggressive response, or any act or behavior that involves, might involve, or aims at the infliction of injury or discomfort, including manifestations of feelings or inner reactions which have this aim. Short-term causation of the aggressive response and the development of more stable aggressive reaction tendencies are briefly examined. Like Bigelow, Olweus does not accept an instinct theory as an explanation for the motivation of aggression. Frustration, threat, and attack appear to be primary instigators for aggression, although aggression-inhibitory tendencies may also be elicited. Long-term or stable aggressive tendencies appear to be related to child-rearing practices, aggressive or nonaggressive models during childhood, and the presence of frequent or severe frustrations.

Professor Olweus's conceptual scheme for the determination of aggressive responses emphasizes classes of variables consisting of aggressive tendencies and inhibitory tendencies as well as situational and habitual components, which constitute an interactive system leading to aggressive responses. The conceptual scheme is then applied to a study of the relationship between projective test data and aggressive behavior in an interpersonal situation involving adolescent boys. Two hypotheses were derived from the scheme and were tested. The first hypothesis predicted a positive relationship between aggressive responses in a projective test and overt aggressive responses for boys with low aggression-inhibitory tendencies. The second hypothesis predicted a negative relationship between aggressive responses in the projective test and overt aggressive responses for a group with high aggression-inhibitory tendencies. Both hypotheses were strongly supported. The results confirm the pattern effects implied by the conceptual scheme and the importance of extracting components in the model to predict behavior (e.g., the correlations for the combined groups are close to zero). A linear method of analysis is inadequate, while moderator effects (i.e., when relationships between variables are dependent on the level of some other variable) are important.

Professor Olweus outlines the development of his multifaceted aggression inventory, including the results of two factor analyses. He concludes his paper with an overview and some general implications, with a particular emphasis on the individual-versus-situation controversy. Both situational components and central tendencies are important components. Furthermore, at least two central tendencies and their interaction appear to be primary determinants, suggesting the inadequacy of a single trait of aggressiveness to explain aggressive response potentialities.

We are planning to continue the thematic approach next year by devoting the entire volume to a theme which we feel will be particularly timely following the current presentation on aggression. Next year the symposium will emphasize human sexuality. Professor Richard Dienstbier, Department of Psychology, University of Nebraska–Lincoln, will serve as coeditor.

The symposium has been continuously supported by the Clinical Psychology Training Grant provided by the National Institute of Mental Health. The University of Nebraska has also graciously provided support. All of us associated with the *Nebraska Symposium on Motivation*, including students and faculty at the university, wish to express once again our gratitude for this support.

JAMES K. COLE
Associate Professor of Psychology

The Evolution of Cooperation, Aggression, and Self-Control

ROBERT BIGELOW

University of Canterbury, New Zealand

In 1966 Sir Macfarlane Burnet said this about the problem of human evolution: "Just how the human brain grew so very rapidly over the last million years to its present size and complexity we do not know. Under the circumstances, a larger and more effective brain was an evolutionary necessity—so it developed. That is really all we can say."

Under what circumstances was a more effective brain an evolutionary necessity? We will not understand human evolution until we can answer this question. It is, of course, important to describe and illustrate fossil bones and man-made artifacts and to date them with potassium-argon and other techniques. Without a foundation of accurately analyzed evidence scientific interpretation is impossible. But the facts do not interpret themselves. Cortical activity in human brains must correlate the scattered facts and try to interpret their relationships. This is sometimes called speculation, but without it there would be no science and no growth of human understanding. Scattered evidence is "out there" in the universe surrounding us, but the means of interpreting it lies inside the human body. The evidence is incomplete, but there is more of it than we have realized. Most of our confusion is not due to lack of evidence. It is due primarily to difficulties in perceiving the significance of the evidence we already have. We must, of course, continue to gather facts—but the mere collection of evidence will not in itself lead to fuller understanding. It could actually lead to greater confusion, for there are limits to the volume of evidence our brains can process. No matter how voluminous the evidence before us may become, our major task will be to interpret that evidence and to reinterpret it as our understanding grows.

In this paper I will consider the problem of human evolution, and some of the conceptual difficulties which I believe to be a major barrier between us and a fuller understanding of ourselves. I believe that much of our present confusion is due to very ancient, and erroneous, assumptions which continue to influence our approach to the problem of human behavior in very subtle ways. I will consider possible relationships between genes, brains, communication, cooperation, competition, inherited propensities, learning, and self-control. I make no claim that my views are indisputable, but I do contend that they are based on evidence, and that they warrant serious consideration as a promising approach to future study.[1]

The fossil evidence of human evolution is still meager and anthropological opinion is still divided on many issues. But certain important aspects of the problem are now reasonably clear. We know, for example, that the hands, feet, teeth, pelvis, and erect posture of our ancestors were distinctly hominid when their brains averaged only a third the size of ours. The crucial transformation in human evolution was a threefold increase in the size of the brain. This great evolutionary change took place very rapidly. Even three million years is a brief span of time for the profound genetic reorganizations required for such a remarkable transformation of such a complicated structure. The human brain is not only very complex in itself, but is also intimately related to the functioning of the entire body. And the evidence we have suggests that the rate of this change was actually accelerated during later stages of the process. We therefore know that smaller-brained humans were at a strong selective disadvantage during the Pleistocene. It is important to

1. Alexander (1971) has formulated a very similar theory of human evolution. Dr. Alexander and I had previously worked together on the speciation of field crickets and had published a joint paper on this problem. We did not, however, become aware of our common interest in human evolution until 1968, several months after Dr. Alexander's manuscript had been submitted for publication, and months after my book, *The Dawn Warriors*, was in the hands of publishers. Our very similar arguments were derived quite independently.

remember that selection could favor larger brains only by acting against smaller ones.

Since the increase in brain size was rapid, the selective force must have been powerful. We know this powerful selective force was concentrated on the lines that led to modern man. Within no other primate species were smaller-brained individuals under such a severe disadvantage. The brain of *Homo erectus* was more than twice as large as the brain of a modern chimpanzee—yet *Homo erectus* is extinct while chimpanzees are still alive. This powerful, distinctively human selective force seems to have been generated within the human line itself—and since the brain functions as a social instrument, the selective force seems to have been related to distinctively human social interactions. We cannot, of course, be certain, but we have here some promising clues from which those crucial circumstances might be reconstructed.

We also have vast quantities of evidence from anthropology, ethology, psychology, history, and other fields waiting to be correlated, compared, and reevaluated. Recent advances in population genetics, including studies of human populations, have made it possible to account for the continual re-creation of genetic variation required for such a rapid and extensive evolutionary change. We are in a very good position to formulate a preliminary explanation of "just how the human brain grew so very rapidly," and we can do so without discarding skepticism or humility.

In recent works (Bigelow, 1969, 1971, 1972) I considered intergroup competition as a selective force and proposed a theory of human evolution. I will restate the theory here and then consider some of its implications, emphasizing those related to the evolution of intelligence and self-control.

THE THEORY

Very briefly, the theory assumes that early humans, like other primates, lived in social groups. The primary biological advantage of social life was protection of the young. Social cohesion within a given group was achieved through communication, which required an ability to interpret postures, sounds, and other signals. This capacity was provided by brains, which developed only through complex interactions of genes. There was thus a direct link between genes, brains, interpretation, communication, cooperation, and reproductive success. The members of each social group cooperated for defense against lions, leopards, and other external threats. This required both a potential for aggressive group response and a capacity to control this aggressive potential during encounters between individuals within the group.

Early human groups competed occasionally with other human groups (for territory and for mates), but such competitions tended to weaken both contending groups, leaving them vulnerable to lions and leopards. Natural selection thus held intergroup competition below certain levels during the earlier stages of human evolution. Such competitions did, however, take place—and when they did, success was determined largely by capacities for aggressive and intelligent group response, which of course required cooperation within each of the contending groups.

As brains and social capacities gradually evolved, the ability to deal with nonhuman predators increased accordingly. More intergroup competition was possible without seriously eroding defenses against lions and leopards. Each increase in the level of intergroup competition placed a greater disadvantage on groups with the least effective cooperation, communication, self-control, brains, and genes. On the average, the most cooperative, intelligently self-controlled groups prevailed in territorial and other intergroup encounters. *They themselves* were the source of the selective force which banished less cooperative groups to deserts and other inhospitable areas. The circumstances which favored ever more effective brains were thus built into the species itself. With each genetic advance in mental capacities in one area, the force of selection against less advanced groups in other areas became more severe. Waves of progressively more advanced groups diffused outward from the more fertile areas (for which competition was most intense) and placed increasingly severe pressures on peripheral groups whose levels of cooperation were inadequate for effective self-defense.

As capacities for intelligent self-control increased, so did levels of intergroup cooperation. Cooperation with former enemies requires great self-control and an ability to perceive the longer-term advantages of suppressing local feuds in order to unite against more powerful and more complex external threats. Humans with inferior abilities to see beyond their local feuds were therefore placed at a greater selective disadvantage with every increase in the levels of intergroup cooperation in other regions. Ever larger and more effective brains became an evolutionary necessity because the "growing points" within the species not only continued to apply the selective force, but did so with ever increasing power. As human mobility increased, the rate of diffusion of the growing points, and the corresponding rate of removal of less advanced elements, increased accordingly. Continued over several million years, at accelerating rates, this positive-feedback social interaction trebled the average size of the human brain.

The selective force was largely self-contained, not only within the human species as a whole but also within each major component of the species. The vast majority of the intergroup interactions were between more or less closely related human groups. But though they were closely related, these competing groups were very diverse genetically. Any species that is characteristically subdivided into many small, relatively isolated groups will be diverse genetically. Inbreeding will tend to increase uniformity within each group, but in combination with isolation and random drift this will actually increase the range of genetic diversity between groups. Such a breeding structure will provide selection with a great diversity of complex genetic constellations, or *systems*, upon which to act—and human brains are produced by very complex systems of interacting genes. There is a growing body of evidence which suggests that Sewall Wright's "genetic drift" (in the broad sense) has been a particularly significant factor in human evolution. (See: Wright, 1931, 1932, 1970; Cavalli-Sforza, 1969; Neel, 1970; Muller, 1957).

Local genetic diversity was continuously maintained at levels adequate for rapid genetic response to the accelerating forces of natural selection within each region. Interracial, and even inter-specific, interactions took place—but they played a relatively minor role in human evolution. Even if no interactions whatsoever had taken place between inhabitants of widely separated regions, both the genetic diversity and the intensity of intergroup interactions within each major region were adequate for rapid evolution-ary change. Rates of evolution were not, of course, precisely equal in all major regions. Relict populations of advanced australopithe-cines probably coexisted for a while with early forms of *Homo erectus*. The struggle was not, however, primarily interracial.

Since success in intergroup competition was determined mainly by capacities for cooperation and intelligent self-control, the result of the selective process was *not* an increasingly uncontrollable "aggression instinct." At all stages the effectiveness of aggressive group response to external threats was due to the effectiveness of self-control within the group—particularly when the contending groups were large conglomerates of recently interhostile components. Discipline and intelligent self-control have always been decisive factors in intergroup competition. Capacities for self-control are provided by the actual physical structure of the brain, particularly the cerebral cortex. The result of human evolution was not an array of bodiless "instincts," but a network of physical nerves and endocrine organs. As this physical organization became more complex and efficient it provided greater capacities for learning from experience, for the repression of emotional drives, and hence for more intelligent self-control. Human capacities for learning, communication, government, science, and art are products of biological evolution, just as running, or any other manifestation of animal behavior, is an expression of the biological potential of interacting muscles, bones, and nerves.

Prehistoric Peace and Hunting

Certain anthropologists, archaeologists, and historians assume that intergroup competition was inconsequential during prehistoric times. Their works imply that war was more or less unknown until the dawn of history. Not all authorities hold such views, but those who do are influential. Hand-axes, arrowheads, and spearheads are usually regarded as tools or hunting implements rather than as weapons of primitive warfare. It is, of course, extremely difficult to prove that such implements were *not* used against other humans (as well as for hunting, etc.), but those who take prehistoric peace for granted do not accentuate this difficulty. They circumvent it by demanding unequivocal proof that prehistoric weapons *were* used against other humans. This forces those who recognize the possibility of prehistoric warfare into a defensive attitude—and distracts attention from the difficulty of establishing several million years of worldwide prehistoric peace as an incontestable "scientific fact." The use of primitive weapons for killing other humans by Australian aborigines, African Bushmen, Amazon Indians, Eskimos, and other peoples living at hunting-and-gathering cultural levels is either disregarded or explained away as due to corrupting influences from more advanced societies.

Attempts to prove "absolutely" that prehistoric men either did or did not kill other prehistoric men can only be exercises in futility. We cannot resurrect the Pleistocene or transfer ourselves backward through time and observe the behavior of prehistoric men directly. Even if we could it would be difficult to convince those who do not wish to be convinced. Overwhelming evidence of warfare during historical times has failed to alter the views of those who believe that man is basically a peaceful "noble savage."

There is evidence which, though it cannot prove prehistoric violence absolutely, does suggest strongly that early humans did kill other humans. Roper (1969) made a careful survey of the evidence for intrahuman killing during the Pleistocene, and the bones of about 56 out of the approximately 169 pre–*Homo sapiens* individuals showed injuries which one or more specialists attributed to intrahuman violence. Evidence suggesting violence exists in a remarkably high proportion, over 34%, of this sample. The sample contained about 36 australopithecine individuals, of which about 20, over 55%, showed evidence suggesting intrahuman violence. Even if only a fraction of these claims are justified, intrahuman violence cannot be ignored as a factor in human evolution. Roper lists some 50 claims of violence and 17 published counterarguments. The issue here is not whether claims of violence can be either proved or disproved unequivocally. Such disputes are a diversion from the fact that specialist opinion is divided, and hence that prehistoric *nonviolence* cannot be taken for granted as a well-established scientific fact.

Faced with such evidence, we sometimes go to impressive lengths in our attempts to explain it away. A hole in a fossil skull may have been due to a rock that fell from the roof of the cave while the man was asleep; he may have stumbled and bumped his head against a sharp projection which happened to be about the size and shape of a prehistoric hand-axe; one anthropologist has even suggested to me that chimpanzees may have been throwing stones for fun and happened to hit prehistoric men by mistake. Almost any alternative explanation will do—the aim is to show that such alternative explanations are possible, and thus that violence cannot be proved absolutely. The onus of unequivocal proof is being transferred to those who recognize the possibility of prehistoric violence, with the implication that unless violence can be proved absolutely it should not even be considered as a possibility. Nonviolence, on the other hand, is taken for granted without proof.

Intrahuman violence is also excluded by defining the term more narrowly. Roper, for example, interprets indications of violence on certain neanderthaloid bones as follows: "Intraspecific aggression cannot be definitely assumed, however, because of the fact that Neanderthaloids and *H. sapiens* may have been living in the same area contemporaneously." Can we exclude the killing of neanderthaloids by *Homo sapiens* from the category of intrahuman aggression? Some anthropologists now refer to Neanderthal man as *Homo sapiens neanderthalensis*. But however we classify him it is clear that he was human, and the term *intrahuman killing* means the killing of humans by other humans. Certain anthropologists recognize the likelihood of violent interactions between Neanderthal man and *Homo sapiens*, and then say it was "almost certain" they did not fight battles to the death—*Homo sapiens* may have merely "got the game first" (Howells, 1967). This implies that Neanderthal man starved peacefully while *Homo sapiens* ate his food. We are surely entitled, without demanding unequivocal proof of this explanation, to expect a careful evaluation of its *likelihood* before assuming it can be taken for granted as "almost certain."

Difficulties in assessing the role of intergroup competition in human evolution are due mainly to our very strong reluctance to face the facts, not to a scarcity of evidence. There is overwhelming evidence of man's potential for violence, and this may be precisely why it frightens us. We live in the shadow of the Nazi gas chambers, under a nuclear umbrella, surrounded by rising crime rates, riots, wars, and threats of wars on every continent. But in the face of such evidence it may be unwise to comfort ourselves with the belief that prehistoric man was strikingly different from us. There is evidence suggesting that he was no more peaceful than we are. The relatively sudden disappearance of Neanderthal man coincides with the appearance of *Homo sapiens* in western Europe, and we cannot ignore the very obvious implications of this coincidence. Nor can we ignore those perplexing injuries on fossil skulls, or the prevalence of violent interactions between surviving hunters and gatherers (when they are living beyond the reach of modern law-enforcement agencies). And we cannot brush aside the evidence of five thousand years of history as irrelevant. We cannot evade this evidence on the grounds that we cannot yet be "absolutely certain" of what it so strongly implies. We must, indeed, refrain from closing our minds around "certainty" if we wish to pursue an open-minded, scientific inquiry. And we must remember that intergroup competition may have played a very significant role in human evolution even when it did not lead to actual killing.

It is often assumed that prehistoric human groups were widely dispersed and only rarely met one another. This was very likely so, in a relative sense. People who live in teeming cities naturally regard a few million people scattered over much of Africa and Eurasia as very widely dispersed. But we cannot assume that prehistoric human groups were always *evenly* dispersed. Flies congregate around decaying carcasses and other rich concentrations of food. Our hominid ancestors were more intelligent than flies and were able to perceive that some areas were more amenable than others to their way of life. They were surely intelligent enough to avoid deserts and mountain tops in favor of rich grasslands teeming with herds of game. Had there been no intergroup competition, one would expect fertile areas to have been very densely populated while more inhospitable regions were virtually uninhabited. It is unlikely that intelligent human groups would have left fertile areas voluntarily in order to take up permanent residence in deserts. It is most unlikely that they would have starved peacefully while the other groups were "getting the game first." If they were at all like modern humans, strong persuasion would have been required in order to induce them to leave a land of milk and honey for a wilderness. Lions and leopards could not have driven them out of their territories—but it is highly likely that other human groups could have done so. Intergroup dominance hierarchies are known in rhesus monkeys (Southwick, Beg, & Siddiqi, 1965) and in other primates; intergroup dominance hierarchies could well have existed in the case of early humans. It is therefore unreasonable to assert that early humans did *not* compete, group against group, for the most desirable territories. Whether or not these intergroup competitions resulted in wholesale slaughter, they would have had evolutionary effects. Groups trying to survive in deserts would have had less reproductive success, on the average, than groups living in food-rich areas. Wide dispersal over both rich and poor areas could have been maintained as an outcome of intergroup competition, but what other force could have kept them so widely dispersed?

We cannot assess prehistoric population densities from those prevailing among surviving hunters and gatherers today. Modern hunters and gatherers live on poor land because other people are firmly established on all the better land. When European and Bantu peoples invaded South Africa from the south and the north, Bushmen and Hottentots were living *outside* the Kalahari desert. American Indians, Australian aborigines, and many other peoples were driven forcefully from land that Europeans coveted. During prehistoric times the more fertile regions were not guarded by men with rifles or machine guns. Humans were free to hunt and gather anywhere, provided they were not driven away by other hunters and gatherers. They were intelligent enough to recognize good land, and human enough to covet good land. Upon what grounds, then, can we assume they did not compete for it, group against group?

Hamburg (1972) has briefly and accurately reviewed my book, *The Dawn Warriors*, and concluded that "this suggestion of Bigelow's regarding the eliciting of intergroup hostility in 'population hot centers' raises the question of whether the biological nature of early man was in some way susceptible to these environmental conditions." Hamburg then proceeds to note the discovery of ethologists that among the environmental conditions most conducive to severe aggression in many species of birds and rodents is the crowding of strangers, especially near such valued resources as food or mates. He goes on to say that his own and others' observations of chimpanzees, baboons, and rhesus macaques are quite consistent with this concept, and suggests: "It may well be that millions of years of vertebrate and primate evolution have left the human species with many legacies, one of which is a readiness to react fearfully and aggressively toward strangers, especially when crowded in with them, competing for valued resources."

It is widely assumed that hunting was more important than intergroup competition in human evolution. Successful hunting of big game with primitive weapons requires communication and cooperation, which in turn requires brains. (This does not, of course, apply to small game which can be taken by individuals hunting alone.) Hunting is a less disturbing activity than warfare. But is it likely that failure to bring down big game led to starvation on a scale that can account for a threefold increase in average brain size during the Pleistocene? Baboons and chimpanzees survived without becoming big-game hunters. Surviving human hunters and gatherers do not by any means rely entirely on big game. Can we, then, assume that *Homo erectus* became extinct because he failed to "get the game first"? And can we assume that Neanderthal man followed him into extinction for the same reason? How did the capacity for big-game hunting evolve in the first place?

One of the most effective ways to ensure getting the game first is to keep other humans off the hunting grounds. Intergroup competition is therefore likely to have been a primary factor in successful hunting. Intergroup competition takes place between living nonhuman primates who do not depend on hunting for their subsistence. Washburn and Hamburg (1968) believe that intergroup aggression in primates has been greatly underestimated. It is therefore likely that early human groups competed long before they became big-game hunters. Even the best-fed infants had to be protected from lions and leopards, before as well as after other human groups became the greatest threats to their survival. Intergroup competition can account for the evolution of the capacity for big-game hunting, since ever increasing capacities to conquer other humans would lead naturally to an ability to conquer big game. But can big-game hunting account for the evolution of the capacity for big-game hunting? And can hunting alone account for the extinction of *Homo erectus* and Neanderthal man?

Intergroup competition can account not only for the evolution of hunting and of modern cultural capacities, but also for the failure of other primates to keep pace with man. Just as lions and leopards applied a brake during early stages of human evolution, so hominids applied a brake on the evolution of other primates. As long as they are not serious threats to human survival, other primates are tolerated—up to a point. They are driven away from vegetable patches, hunted for food, and observed for amusement while confined in cages. A few of the smaller species are allowed to roam free in human cities. We do not, however, allow chimpanzees, gorillas, and orangs to wander freely through our cities—or to enter schoolrooms and nurseries—unless they are kept well under control. The primate species that resemble us most closely are not permitted to roam at large through habitats favored by man. They are now rather strictly confined to remote jungles in which very few humans care to live, and the shape of their feet suggests they have been so confined for a very long time. The more closely other animals come to resemble man, the less likely it becomes that man will tolerate them. *Homo sapiens* is not a particularly tolerant species unless he has other animals firmly under his own control. He is particularly intolerant with other animals very like himself, as the bloody wars of history so copiously testify. There was a time when two or more hominid species coexisted—for a while—but those species failed to survive. For more than thirty thousand years there has been room for only one hominid species on the earth. If *Homo sapiens* should disappear, without harming any other primate species, something very similar to the bloody course of human evolution would probably be repeated. All the required biological foundations now exist in other species. But while *Homo sapiens* and his descendants continue to dominate the earth, none of these other species will be allowed to evolve very far in a hominoid direction. Unless we ourselves take prompt action, the few remaining species of nonhuman anthropoids will soon become extinct. They all clearly lack the ability to save themselves. They cannot successfully compete with us, and their only hope is to cooperate (on our terms), as dogs and cows and horses do.

THE "INSTINCT" CONCEPT

It is generally taken for granted that if warfare played a major role in human evolution, then we must be driven by a blind, and more or less uncontrollable, aggression instinct. In one way or another this is assumed (consciously or unconsciously) by proponents of both sides in the aggression controversy. Attempts to evade, deny, or explain away evidence of aggression in prehistoric man and in nonhuman primates are due very largely to an underlying conviction that if we accept such evidence we must then agree with those who claim that aggression is "normal, inborn, necessary." If it were not for such conceptions of the meaning of *innate*, I doubt that so many otherwise reasonable people would go to such remarkable lengths to conceal or deny the evidence.

The old nature-nurture controversy has yet to be resolved. Many leading ethologists and psychologists have discarded the archaic either-or approach to the instinct problem (see, for example, Crook, 1968; Berkowitz, 1969; Hinde, 1960, 1970; Freeman, 1971). But many anthropologists and sociologists are still influenced by older points of view.

The belief that our aggressive reactions must be *either* biological (in the sense that they are therefore blind and uncontrollable) *or* cultural (in the sense that they are therefore unrelated to biology) is stated or implied in widely circulated books. Montagu (1968), for example, claims that "everything a human being does as such he has had to learn from other human beings." Only a few of those who join Montagu in opposing the views of Ardrey, Lorenz, and Storr (1968) would go to this "cultural" extreme, but a large proportion of Montagu's readers do accept this point of view. On the opposite side, Ardrey (1968) sees human aggression as "normal, inborn, necessary." Even when authors do not intend to imply that inborn propensities are uncontrollable, their readers tend to draw this conclusion—and the implication of the authors is sometimes very strong indeed. Ardrey (1966), for example, asks:

> Was my response to Pearl Harbor innate or conditioned? This is the question we must ask. Was it something I had been born with or something I had been taught? Was it truly a command of genetic origin, an inheritance from the experience and natural selection

of thousands of generations of my human and hominid ancestors? Or was it a display of a cultural heritage to which I had been conditioned during my lifetime?

The old either-or approach stands out here in bold relief. Most of Ardrey's readers have been exposed to a cultural heritage which draws a sharp conceptual dichotomy between man and animal, cultural conditioning and "genetic command." Ardrey's words reinforce this misconception. He could have asked if his reaction to Pearl Harbor was a combination of the innate and the conditioned. Was he born with genes whose commands fashioned a man with a brain that was able to learn a cultural heritage? Was this brain, with all its capabilities, what was inherited from thousands of generations of selection? Could he have responded as he did without that crucial *combination* of genes, brain, and cultural heritage? But Ardrey asked either-or instead of both-and questions and left his readers with even more deeply entrenched either-or misconceptions.

Konrad Lorenz (personal communication) disagrees with Ardrey's strongly either-or approach to the problem of human aggression. But Lorenz (1966) also reinforced this misconception when he emphasized the "spontaneity" of the aggression instinct:

> Knowledge of the fact that the aggression drive is a true, primarily species-preserving instinct enables us to recognize its full danger: it is the spontaneity of the instinct that makes it so dangerous. If it were merely a reaction to certain external factors, as many sociologists and psychologists maintain, the state of mankind would not be as perilous as it really is, for, in that case, the reaction-eliciting factors could be eliminated with some hope of success.

These words were written nearly ten years ago, and Lorenz has modified his views since then. But most of those who read *On Aggression* do not know this, and our culture is permeated with belief in a mysterious something called "instinct." The word *instinct* has been widely used in eighteenth-, nineteenth-, and even twentieth-century literature—and it still conveys ideas with strongly spiritual connotations. Bodies and spirits are still widely regarded as two quite different things, and the conceptual difference between spirits and instincts is far from clear in the popular imagination. The words of Konrad Lorenz strongly reinforce these very old ideas. Given this cultural background, the reputation of Konrad Lorenz, and the current influence of Sigmund Freud, it is not surprising that so many modern thinkers are frightened by the evidence of human history and by the possibility that warfare played a major role in human evolution.

Old conceptions of aggression instincts are being modified by Freudians. At a conference of psychoanalysts held in Vienna in late July and early August, 1971, Anna Freud is said to have recommended a revision of her father's theory of aggression. Through her suggestion that the aim of the aggressive impulse may be dictated by environmental necessities, she may have promoted a major shift in psychoanalytical opinion. It will, however, be some time before such a shift in opinion filters down through psychoanalysts to cultural anthropologists and then diffuses outward through the ranks of educated laymen. In the meantime, many leading authorities will continue to believe that if warfare played a major role in human evolution, then education and social reform can do little or nothing to prevent spontaneous (i.e., blind) eruptions of human violence. Because of this underlying assumption they will continue to cling with unscientific tenacity to the hope that prehistoric man enjoyed a universal peace throughout the Pleistocene. The implications of this assumption are almost as frightening as those of the aggression-instinct concept—for if the neurophysiological organization of our bodies was indeed fashioned by millions of years of prehistoric peace, our ancestors have been insane for five thousand years, and insanity is not a hopeful mental state for the establishment of global peace. This, however, seems to be less frightening than the thought of being inhabited by a spontaneous and almost uncontrollable aggression instinct.

Clarification of this misunderstanding is one of the most important problems of our day, but the task will not be easy. Most of us learn to draw sharp conceptual dichotomies between body and spirit during our early childhood. The habit has been handed down from very ancient times, and it persists in many subtle forms—including the segregation of departments of cultural anthropology from departments of physical anthropology. This ancient mental orientation warrants careful reexamination in the light of evidence that was not available to our remote ancestors.

Primitive societies believe that living movement, and hence animal behavior, is due to an invisible something related to breath. Many languages use the same word for *spirit* as for *breath*, and the two words are related in virtually all languages. The origin of this belief is not really hard to understand. When an animal dies it stops breathing and no longer responds when prodded. Something seems to have gone out of it, and that something was "obviously" its breath, or spirit. This spirit was the source of the animal's movements while it was alive—and hence spirits are the source of all behavior, the Primal Movers of life. Such assumptions were extended to include conceptions of both "good" and "bad" behavior. There were good as well as bad spirits, and all of them were independent of the bodies they inhabited. Sinful and iniquitous behavior was due to evil spirits, and iniquities could be induced to leave human bodies and enter the bodies of animals, as can be seen from the biblical account of the original scapegoat:

> And Aaron shall lay both his hands upon the head of the live goat, and confess over him all the iniquities of the children of Israel, and all their transgressions in all their sins, putting them upon the head of the goat, and shall send him away by the hand of a fit man into the wilderness. [Lev. 26:21]

Another form of these early beliefs is apparent in the parable of the Gadarene swine:

> Then went the devils out of the man, and entered into the swine: and the herd ran violently down a steep place into the lake, and were choked. [Luke 8:33]

Such conceptions have been taught to millions of children and they continue to influence our approach to the problem of behavior in subtle ways. It is significant that old "iniquities" and "devils" were thought to be independent entities which came and went on their own. They left one body and entered another, even when the bodies were still alive. The bodies merely responded to these Primal Movers, and when all the spirits left them, bodies were completely unable to move on their own. This is a very profound conceptual dichotomy between bodies and spirits, and similar ideas still permeate our culture. Many forms of human behavior are still regarded as something more than a "mere" manifestation of bodily function. Although the association of all forms of behavior with the functioning of bodies could hardly be more clear and direct, we still seem to find it remarkably difficult to recognize this obvious association. This difficulty is due more to cultural conditioning than to the obscurity of the relationship itself.

There are interesting similarities between ancient conceptions of spirits and modern conceptions of biological urges. To the ancients, bodies were obviously transient, but spirits were regarded as immortal. Spirits never died. When they left a broken body they could inhabit a younger, better one, or they could drift about on the winds in disembodied form, or fly off to Heaven, Valhalla, or a Happy Hunting Ground. Spirits were immune from the distressing changes to which bodies were so clearly vulnerable. They offered at least a hope of escape from the relentless flow of change which was so alarmingly obvious in the physical world. Everything that man could see (i.e., all the actual evidence) was clearly susceptible to change. But the imaginary spirits were not. Modern conceptions of biological urges differ from these ancient spirit-ideas, but we still think of biological urges as remarkably immutable.

Morris (1967) contends that modern men respond to breasts and lipstick because their four-footed male ancestors were aroused by the hemispherical buttocks and red genital lips of the females. These blatant signals aroused a spontaneous urge to copulate, and the males were presumably unable to function without them. The change from a back-to-front to a face-to-face copulatory position could be accomplished only by the evolutionary trick of shifting the same old signals around from back to front. Morris is clearly assuming here that biological urges are remarkably resistant to biological change. He believes they were handed down in scarcely altered form despite a more than threefold increase in the size of the brain. Although the physical brain was clearly susceptible to biological evolution, the old biological urges were somehow immune from change. "Animal" responses are often discussed as though they were the only aspects of human behavior which could have evolved biologically, and yet they are often regarded as more or less immune from the force of evolution. This is a remarkable inversion of the evolutionary concept: because we have evolved from lower animals, our "animal" responses have not evolved! Without pretending to understand all the complexities of our own cortical activity, we can recognize a similarity here between the old, immutable spirits and new, but more or less equally immutable biological urges.

It is also interesting to note that we confer upon our biological urges the power to sweep us blindly into Armageddon, rather as the devils swept the Gadarene swine into the lake. And modern concepts of the spontaneity of biological urges resemble old conceptions of the motivating properties of ancient devils. The old Primal Movers were regarded as the exclusive source of all movement; bodies were essentially inert and merely responded. They were directed here and there by the whims and wills of the spirits inside them. Modern conceptions of instincts as *sources* of motivation which, without any outward stimulation, *impel* animals to do things are very similar to far more ancient points of view.

Strident either-or disputes as to whether we are or are not innately aggressive reveal the extent to which both sides are still under the influence of highly questionable assumptions. Such disputes are worse than futile because they reinforce the very misconceptions we should be trying to overcome. Our fear of the innate is exaggerated by our misconception of it—and because of our fear we divert attention from the very evidence that can help to enlarge our understanding of how aggression is controlled, in other animals as well as in man.

Contrary to widespread current opinion, other animals do kill members of their own species. Wolves kill other wolves (I. M. Cowan, University of British Columbia, personal communication); lions kill other lions in territorial intergroup encounters (Schenkel, 1966); under certain conditions baboons kill other baboons (Hall, 1968a; Zuckerman, 1932); victorious langur males may kill the offspring of rival males when taking over a group (Sugiyama, 1967; Yoshiba, 1968); struggles between leaders of separate gorilla bands have resulted in the death of one gorilla in at least one instance (Dart, 1961). On the whole, however, animals hold their aggressive tendencies in check. This capacity for self-control is all the more impressive when we recognize the fact that there is really something there to be controlled—something powerful enough to escape control now and then.

The tendency to respond aggressively seems to be particularly powerful in man. It escapes control with alarming frequency, and often with catastrophic force. The potential of our nuclear arsenals is called "unthinkable." This potential exists, here and now, and we will not escape its consequences by refusing to recognize its biological origins. The doctrine that all the wars of history were purely cultural phenomena cannot reduce the impact of a bullet or a nuclear explosion. We will have to cope with human tendencies for violence whether we call them cultural or biological. But if we recognize the obvious fact that we are animals, that every nerve and muscle in our bodies, including the cerebral cortex, is a biological structure which evolved in response to natural selection, we will be in a better position from which to approach the problem of controlling human violence with greater understanding and intelligence. Other animals show aggressive tendencies, and they also control these tendencies. Understanding how they do it will not immediately solve the problem of how we must learn to do it, but it might at least help.

It might be helpful also to recognize the very impressive capacities for self-control which already exist in us. Cultural evolution has not thrown *all* our biological equipment out of adjustment. Hundreds of millions of people learn to restrain their aggressive tendencies during childhood and keep them under control throughout most of their lives, often despite severe provocations. Other animals also learn to control their aggressive tendencies. The capacity to learn social behavior, including the control of aggression, is not confined to man and is not a purely cultural phenomenon. Cultural evolution is a natural result of biological evolution. Our problems have become more complex, but they are not completely new. Our remote ancestors were learning to control aggressive tendencies long before they became what we now call human. And we have an enormous volume of circumstantial evidence which suggests, very strongly indeed, that the problem of war was a familiar one to Neanderthal man, and probably also to Peking man and *Australopithecus africanus*.

We are not the first animals whose "natural urges" have been repressed by authoritative social organizations. Our children are not the first children to have thrown tantrums when not allowed to have their own way. Baboons force other baboons to repress their sexual and other urges. Young male Australian aborigines are forced to capture wives from other bands before they can indulge their sexual urges. "Noble savages" do not live in a state of unfettered freedom, indulging their biological urges whenever they feel inclined. People living in primitive societies impose very powerful taboos on one another. They scarify each other's flesh with the same "brandmarks." They tear teeth from the mouths of adolescent boys. They cut fingers from the hands of little girls. They view deviations from the tribal norm with dark suspicion. If we could be spirited back to prehistoric times we would probably sorely miss the indulgence of societies we now call repressive. Our problem may be the reverse of what we think it is. Instead of being the first victims of "unnatural" repressions we may be one of the most spoiled of all generations of humans—especially those of us who pity ourselves because we are "forced" to wallow in unprecedented affluence and social freedom.

Since man is the only animal who deliberately kills other members of his own species in large numbers, we conclude that something has gone wrong with human evolution. We forget that evolution is a process which has never been directed by human fears and morals. We overlook the fact that the bloody wars of history have been accompanied by an enormous increase in human numbers. Reproductive success is the final arbiter in evolution, and from an evolutionary point of view nothing has gone wrong with the evolution of the most successful mammalian species on earth—apart from a possible surfeit of success. Something may go very wrong in the near future, but we are referring here to the recent past.

We approach the problem from an anthropomorphic rather than an evolutionary point of view. Because we value peace we assume that the natural checks and balances which in other species control and inhibit attacks on conspecifics are out of adjustment in man. We conclude that unnatural cultural and technological innovations are distorting our natural biological urges. It is, of course, true that our prehistoric ancestors were never overcrowded in polluted city ghettos, never worked in factories and offices, and threatened each other with hand-axes rather than hydrogen bombs. The forces of selection which fashioned our ancestors differed from those surrounding us today. But we forget that the forces of selection that were striking *Homo erectus* differed from those which had fashioned *Australopithecus africanus*. Had the forces of selection remained constant, the rate of human evolution would not have accelerated during the more recent stages of the process. Our hydrogen bombs are not supernatural, nor are they artificial. Our houses and cars and drugs are also very real. In what sense, then, can we call them unnatural?

In earlier days, human inventions were regarded as the productions of distinctively human thoughts. It was assumed that these thoughts were derived from a supernatural source. Most of us no longer hold such views, but we are not completely free from their influence. We rarely ask each other what we mean when we refer to our culture as unnatural. But if we exclude supernatural connotations our culture is unnatural only in so far as it is novel. Overcrowded cities, factories, and television screens are new. They played no part in human evolution during the Pleistocene. But the creation of novelty itself is far from new; it has always been the very essence of the evolutionary process.

Long before human technology began to pollute the air and water, land connections between North and South America were reestablished and a host of predators moved south along the new isthmus. These predators were new to South America. They had played no part in the evolution of the giant sloths and other species upon which they began to feed. From the viewpoint of the giant sloths these new predators were as unnatural as our own cultural innovations now seem to us. But the new selective forces which arrived with these new predators were forces of natural selection. In this evolutionary sense our cars, houses, and bombs are as natural as the nests of birds, beaver dams, or any other results of animal behavior. The human cerebral cortex is itself a natural result of natural selection, and the results of its activities are as natural as the results of the activities of those predators which descended into South America so long ago. Our brains may well create conditions that we cannot endure. There are limits to the rate at which we can adjust our behavior to novel conditions. But this would not be unnatural in an evolutionary sense. This would not be the first time a species became extinct through its failure to respond adequately to novel conditions. Extinction has been a rule rather than an exception in evolution. Without it the concept of natural selection would be meaningless.

There may, however, be hope for us. Our nerves and muscles may not have been designed for a life of gentle, Edenic peace. We may possess biologically evolved networks of nerves which can deal with threats of war by the age-old method of suppressing local feuds. We may not be the first unfortunate animals who have ever had to deal with "unnaturally" novel conditions, but rather the first animal species to establish and maintain social communication, cooperation, and intelligent self-control on a truly global scale.

Self-control and Intelligence

A significant relationship between aggressive and nonaggressive behavior is apparent in the structural and functional organization of the vertebrate nervous system. Neural and other organ systems act as a single organized whole in the coordination of body movements. Neural coordination is achieved through reciprocal excitations and inhibitions of antagonistic systems. Emotional reactions are organized into definite patterns of response in the hypothalamus, but the hypothalamus is itself strongly influenced by the cerebral cortex. Decorticate animals respond aggressively to very slight provocations, but their attacks lack coordination and the aggressive emotional state quickly disappears when the stimulus is removed. Decorticate dogs snap savagely at the air directly before them in response to a mild pinching of their tails, but they stop snapping as soon as the tail is released. The normal cortex restrains aggressive reactions, but if provocation reaches certain levels the cortex not only permits the release of aggressive response but also provides it with direction and effectiveness. Partially decorticate animals, in which cortical components of the limbic system are intact, do not respond aggressively. Even severe provocation produces no aggressive response. Part of the cortex clearly inhibits aggressive response while other cortical areas provide direction to its release. The two areas interact in normal animals, and through this interaction aggressive response is restrained and controlled, or released and directed, according to the nature, persistence, and intensity of the pattern of provoking stimuli (Morgan, 1965; Dethier & Stellar, 1970).

The presence of this intimate relationship between aggressive and nonaggressive response, built into the very structure of the nervous system, is highly significant. It is also important to note that the mammalian cerebral cortex (which in humans is the source of culture and technology) plays a vital role in the intelligent control of aggressive emotional states. Ineffectual snapping at the air is unintelligent, and so is a lack of response to severe provocation—but restraint due to past experience, a warning growl, or a sudden coordinated whirl of the body followed by an effective (yet restrained) bite are intelligent responses. There is a degree of intelligence even in such apparently instinctive behavior.

Intelligence appears with the ability to learn from experience. This ability is favored by selection because evolution is never really static. Novel situations may appear very suddenly in the experience of individuals—as when a dodo looked up and saw a man for the first time. The ability to adjust behavior quickly may then be favored by selection. Old behavioral responses, however effective they were in the familiar but obsolete past, may be rendered dangerous by the new, "unnatural" conditions. Varying degrees of such capacities for behavioral flexibility are conferred by the cerebral cortex. The cortex tends not only to adjust behavior to the individual's own particular past experience, but also to readjust it as experience changes. Cortical capacities are, of course, limited. Certain novel situations pose problems which even the most intelligent animals, despite (and in part because of) all their past experience, are unable to solve.

All intelligent behavior is inextricably interwoven with emotional states. These emotional states are due in part to chemical constituents of blood, in part to inherited structural features of the nervous system. Hunger and thirst and the effects of testosterone on neural tissue are not in themselves intelligent, and the basic structure of the entire nervous system is determined in advance by the interactions of genes with environments immediately surrounding them inside the body cells. All intelligence, including the whole of human culture, is vitally dependent on these basic biological interactions.

Their influence on behavior is so pervasive, profound, and fundamental that we cannot hope to understand ourselves if we ignore
them. But the cerebral cortex nevertheless coordinates, inhibits, and
controls this nexus of antagonistic biological interactions. Its ability
to do so is limited by structural and chemical inadequacies as well
as by inadequate experience, but it nevertheless influences the
medley of internal stimuli while it in turn is being influenced by
them. The result of these reciprocating interactions (the overt behavior we observe) is a coordinated whole in which we can often
recognize a degree of what we call intelligence. We cannot segregate
"intelligent" from "instinctive" components of behavior any more
than we can attribute one property of water to hydrogen and another
to oxygen. Reciprocal interactions are the very essence of both
behavior and the properties of water. Without them neither water
nor behavior could exist. These interactions are what we must try
to understand, and we distract attention from them when we
dissociate learned from "instinctive" behavior, or culture from
biology.

The primary function of animal brains is self-control. Degrees
of self-control achieved and the effectiveness of the resulting co-
ordinations of behavior are limited and variable. But biological
evolution has not been confined to the creation of bones and muscles
and blind biological urges. Intelligence and social cooperation are
not the results of a cultural evolution which is somehow distinct
from biology. Laws and social customs are not unnatural impositions
from a source somewhere outside biology. They arise from interactions between the cerebral cortex and other parts of a single body,
and from interactions between the brains and eyes and ears and
vocal cords of different bodies. They are biological results of biological behavior.

Other animals control and restrain their aggressive urges, and
with our own more elaborate biological equipment, we should be
able not merely to emulate but to excel their achievements. In
order to do so we must learn to study aggressive behavior as an
integral part of a reciprocally interacting complex, rather than as
a presumably independent thing in itself. Ethologists have noted
that threat postures may quickly alternate and intergrade with
submissive or courtship postures. In higher mammals a given

posture often expresses both fear and aggression simultaneously. In higher primates these postural displays include facial expressions. Tendencies for "fight" and "flight" are intermingled and coordinated. The association between aggressive and nonaggressive behavior is so intimate that purely aggressive behavior is often hard to recognize, and hence to define. Consequently, many ethologists no longer refer to territorial and other confrontations between conspecifics as aggressive encounters. They use the more comprehensive term *agonistic*, which refers simultaneously to both aggressive and nonaggressive tendencies (Scott & Fredericson, 1951; Manning, 1967; Hinde, 1970; Eibl-Eibesfeldt, 1970). The association between opposing tendencies which appears in overt behavioral interactions corresponds with what is known about the structural and functional organization of the nervous system.

We can now at least begin to understand the reasons for the incorporation of such antagonistic neural systems into the brain, and for the manifestations of such conflicting tendencies in overt behavior. Animals live in complex environments which contain not only food, shelter, and mates but also predators, rivals, and other hazards. When they leave concealed places to find food many animals expose themselves to such hazards. If they do not do so they will starve, but if they ignore potential dangers when they venture forth they may come to an even more abrupt end. The manifestation of such opposing tendencies can be recognized in animals approaching food in exposed places. Reproductive success is the final arbiter in evolution, and therefore animals who succeed in finding mates tend to leave the most offspring. Animals often compete for mates, and the competitions may lead to fights, and hence to injuries. Injured animals leave fewer offspring, on the average, than uninjured animals. Forms of behavior which reduce the likelihood of injury are therefore favored by selection—but refusal to compete is not favored. Reproductive success thus requires an effective balance between opposing tendencies, which means that it requires self-control.

Social Life and Self-control

The degree of behavioral flexibility required for success in agonistic encounters depends largely on the intelligence of an animal's adversary. In the case of higher primates the behavior of an adversary is often disturbingly flexible and hard to predict. The influence of unlearned, inherited structural organization is strong in all animals, including primates, but in higher primates this internal organization confers an unusual capacity for rapid learning from experience. The primate cerebral cortex is particularly influential in the coordination of chemical and other internal influences. Intelligence is therefore a very important factor in agonistic confrontations between higher primates, and it is for this reason that the aptitudes and facilities of the human brain have never been far in excess of what was needed at any one time. Human brains have always had to contend with other human brains. We sometimes overlook this vital aspect of primate behavior when we consider the problem of human evolution. All higher primates are profoundly social animals, and agonistic interactions are a prominent feature of primate social life. Every agonistic interaction is a test of the effectiveness of cortical control over a medley of internal stimuli. And reproductive success is enhanced by success in these social encounters.

It is interesting to note that only a decade ago prominent authorities on human evolution were just beginning to realize the significance of primate social life. Dobzhansky (1962), for example, believed that it was "possible though not certain that some of the australopithecines hunted not singly but in bands." Note that social interaction was attributed only to "some" of these early humans, and then only for the purpose of hunting. When not hunting, were they scattered "singly" over the dangerous Pleistocene savanna? Such views have been rendered obsolete by field studies of a wide variety of primate species. Nonhuman primates rarely *hunt* in bands, but they are born into highly integrated social groups and live out their lives in nearly constant social interaction with very well known members of their own social group. It is therefore most unlikely that early humans differed from other primates in this respect. It is also unlikely that they could have survived without the protection social life confers.

It is now clear that one of the primary biological advantages of primate social life is the protection of the young. Reproductive success is the most essential criterion for biological success in an evolutionary sense. Members of a given primate group cooperate to counter external threats. This is particularly noticeable in species that live in the open. Baboons, for example, cooperate to repel lions and leopards. An isolated female baboon, encumbered by an infant, is relatively easy prey for a leopard—but while she remains within her social group, both she and her infant are relatively safe. Even a mature male baboon would be vulnerable to leopards on his own, but three or four large males can "persuade" lions or leopards to withdraw.

The primate social group, like the nervous system, functions as a coordinated whole. It provides an "internal" environment within which the young can mature slowly in reasonable safety. The slow rate of maturation, coupled with the complexity of the primate brain, permits an extended period of learning. This learning is applied primarily to the complex social interactions which provide cohesion to the group. When a lion or a leopard is encountered the group can then respond effectively as a unit. The capacity to repel lions requires a strong potential for aggressive action, but this cannot be realized without internal cohesion—which requires restraint during internal encounters between fellow members of the group. At a somewhat higher level of complexity, we thus have a system of opposing but interdependent tendencies not unlike those contained within the nervous system of an individual. Both the capacity for aggressive action and the ability to repress, control, and direct it are required simultaneously. Neither would be effective without the other. The two apparently opposing tendencies are profoundly interdependent components of a single interacting system. The functioning of this system depends on the survival and development of flexible brains which are able to learn the complexities of social behavior required for controlled and effective group action. Both the physical development and the training of such brains requires time, and until they have matured, these developing brains require protection. The potential disadvantage of slow maturation, like the potential disadvantage of aggressive tendencies, must be countered. Aggressive capacities counter the disadvantage of slow maturation and are themselves controlled by the extended learning period which slow maturation confers. The components of this interacting system cannot be understood in isolation. They must all be related to the whole of which they are dependent parts. Such interacting systems are very complex, and their overall effects often differ profoundly from the separate properties of their individual components. They are, however, the very essence of life and evolution. And no level of complexity is beyond the reach of natural selection—least of all human culture, which is now one of the most powerful of all selective forces.

Control of aggression within a primate group is achieved primarily through a dominance hierarchy. In most groups, order is maintained by hierarchies which depend ultimately on the power of males. Male dominance is probably the most important influence on social cohesion in all the primarily ground-living monkeys which have so far been studied in the field (Washburn & Hamburg, 1968; Jay, 1965). Levels of aggression within groups tend to be minimal under a strong dominance hierarchy, and the frequency of severe bites (which sometimes lead to death) increases sharply after a dominant male has been removed (Washburn & Hamburg, 1968). Groups of gray langurs often seek other groups, sometimes going far beyond their home range, in order to engage them in intergroup conflicts—and these animals are noted for lack of aggression *within* a given group (Ripley, 1967). The prevalence of dominance hierarchies in primates is very well established, and their function in the maintenance of internal peace is widely recognized.

Dominance hierarchies are not static, and the social rank of primate individuals is not determined in advance as are the castes of termite colonies. All social groups resemble living bodies in that old and worn-out individuals, like old and worn-out cells, are constantly discarded and replaced. But in primates, individuals must *learn* their place in the group, and *relearn* it as the social constitution alters with the flow of aging, birth, and death. The importance of learning in primates has been emphasized by Washburn and Hamburg (1965) and others. Novel conditions, in the form of new social relationships, are continuously re-created, and yet attempts to retain the old order provide a degree of continuity. Despite an endless struggle between the generations there must always be effective cooperation when powerful predators are encountered. Each new dominance hierarchy is formed gradually on the foundation of its predecessor. The old pass on their learning to the young, and the young are often quick to take advantage of their elders' mistakes. Social organization is also altered by newly learned responses to environments external to the group. Baboons, for example, become very tame in protected areas—yet group behavior alters quickly if an individual baboon is shot. Regional populations of baboons differ considerably in habits and social organization (Hall, 1967), which indicates capacities for flexibility of social as well as individual behavior. This seems to be an embryonic form of "cultural evolution."

Each new dominance hierarchy is both established and maintained through frequent agonistic interactions between individuals. As some individuals grow stronger while others age, subtle changes appear in the form and the results of these encounters. Interactions between dominant males are observed by other members of the group, and the gradual decline of a leader's status may be noted by males who have not yet seriously threatened him. Social status does not depend entirely on the separate results of isolated interactions. The primate group is a coordinated whole. Primate brains can correlate and recall complex patterns of information—and it can be important, even for monkeys, to avoid losing face. Agonistic interactions are not confined to pairs of individuals. Several young males may cooperate during encounters with a rival male. Groups of females may cooperate to repel a powerful male they all dislike. Dominance is not achieved by size and brawn alone. Successful leaders learn when and how and whom to threaten, which other males are potential supporters, what and how much to tolerate.

Dominance relationships are not planned in advance, and the social organization of nonhuman primate groups is not laid out in detail on paper. The unwritten "laws" develop naturally from the continual flow of social interaction. Basic emotional drives are involved, but the end result is very strongly influenced by learning and by intelligent self-control. Primates repress their basic drives. When they are thirsty, baboons wait until the group moves as a unit to the drinking place. Hamadryas baboons do not attempt to copulate with the females of another male's "harem" even though their own females remain unreceptive for as long as 2 to 6 months (Kummer, 1968). Self-control is clearly apparent in primate behavior, and it is strongly influenced by cortical activity.

Success in agonistic encounters favors reproductive success. Dominant male baboons often maintain exclusive rights to certain females during the full estrus period (when the females are most likely to conceive). Capacities for intelligent self-control favor the achievement of social rank, and high social rank favors reproductive success. There is thus an intimate relationship between genes (which interact to form biological brains) on the one hand, and social cooperation on the other. Although living monkeys and apes are not our ancestors, certain significant features of their social life are highly relevant to the problem of the evolution of human social capacities. All human political, cultural, and technological achievements are products of biological systems which have been produced by natural selection.

The basic features of all human social and political organizations can be discerned in the social organizations of nonhuman primates. In humans, as in monkeys, the maintenance of peace *within* a given group is achieved through a dominance hierarchy. The differences involve degrees of complexity, not any fundamentally distinct attributes peculiar to humans alone. Large modern nations have elaborately organized law-enforcement agencies; their laws are enforced, if necessary, by policemen. Nonhuman primate social groups do not contain uniformed policemen, but order within them also depends ultimately on the power of males. In their modern form, human police organizations are a relatively recent development. The metropolitan police force of London was established in 1829 by Robert Peel (after whom the policemen were called "bobbies"). In earlier days internal order was maintained through other organizations, based ultimately on the king's army. More primitive human societies, even today, have no uniformed police forces, but order is still maintained primarily through the power of males. Internal disputes are usually settled by various forms of duels, with clubs or other weapons. (The most lethal weapons were used in eighteenth-century France, Britain, Germany, and other European nations.) These duels were, and are, subjected by custom or law to certain rules which served to reduce the rate of destruction of valuable fighting males. The Yanomamo of Venezuela use 10-foot clubs and each opponent allows the other to hit him on the head. The scalps of older men "are almost incredible to behold, covered as they are by as many as a dozen ugly welts" (Chagnon, 1967a, 1967b). During these encounters the headmen stand by with drawn bows in an attempt to prevent the participants from losing control of their aggressive emotions, and such attempts to repress excessive aggression are partially effective even though the duels do sometimes lead to free-for-alls which may produce fatalities.

We have here a control system at a higher level which tends to reinforce the control systems built into the nervous systems of the competing individuals. This is not a purely cultural innovation peculiar to man. Dominant male monkeys also reinforce the control systems built into the brains of lower-ranking monkeys. Similar controls were also imposed from above on the more lethal European duels, but here the purpose was mainly to prevent one opponent from taking unfair advantage of the other, not to prevent fatalities. European nations were so richly endowed with aggressive potential that they could afford to squander more of their fighting males.

Disputes between nonhuman primates are settled by agonistic encounters which differ in no really fundamental respect from human duels. Whether or not the degree of intelligence displayed in a duel between two Frenchmen was greater than that in a threat display between two male baboons is a debatable point, but some degree of intelligent self-control is involved in all agonistic encounters between primates. Human agonistic encounters are not confined to duels with clubs or pistols. Parliamentary debates, diplomatic exchanges, electioneering, demonstrations of nuclear capacities, "peacetime" movements of ships and armies, the erection of walls through cities, and many other human activities are essentially agonistic encounters. As in the case of nonhuman primates, success in human agonistic interactions often led to reproductive success. High rank in human social hierarchies usually conferred unusual reproductive freedom. Medieval kings were noted for genetic generosity, and nobles sometimes exercised a *droit du seigneur*. Certain husbands looked the other way when a proficient duelist began to show an interest in their wives.

Nonhuman primates do not mobilize large armies in response to external threats, but young male baboons may form the vanguard of an advancing group. They are the first to encounter and engage leopards, and thus function as an embryonic army. Young primate males are expendable genetically—provided the survivors can deal with predators and keep the females pregnant. Humans living in small, independent social groups do not have large armies, but young males are trained as warriors and used against external threats. In the case of humans, other human groups pose more serious external threats than leopards do, but whatever the form of the external threat, the basic principle is similar.

Cortical activity is involved in all agonistic interactions between primates, and social rank is therefore influenced, at least to some degree, by intelligence. In nonhuman primates, and in humans living at primitive cultural levels, this influence is direct. It is less direct in more complex human societies containing large privileged classes and factions with the power to facilitate promotion on the grounds of class or party membership rather than purely on merit. But even with help from influential friends, some degree of intelligence is required for sustained success. There are many kinds and varieties of intelligence, and social success requires a form of "social" intelligence which differs from the kinds required for musical, literary, and other more detached intellectual endeavors. People who have achieved success in these latter fields sometimes fail to perceive high levels of intelligence in successful business men, politicians, and military leaders—but when dealing with such a complex phenomenon as human intelligence it is often difficult to prove that one class, race, nation, or profession is intellectually inferior to another. People with relatively modest rank in the actual power structure of a dominance hierarchy sometimes assume that powerful men, or even powerful baboons, "act without thinking." There is an element of truth in this assumption. Both high-ranking and low-ranking individuals behave with rash impulsiveness at times. The penalties, however, are often more severe in the case of individuals of high rank. Social pressures are intense near the apex of a social hierarchy. Social power is coveted by others, and the powerful are threatened most seriously by those with the greatest neurophysiological stamina and flexibility. Biographies of kings and other famous political and military leaders show this very clearly indeed. Crowned heads lie uneasily because very high levels of cortical activity are required for dealing with palace intrigues and potential rebellions. Success in these agonistic interactions has been (and often still is) a matter of life and death to the leaders concerned.

Available evidence does not support the view that powerful primate leaders are unintelligent brutes who rule "without thinking," by force alone. The leaders of primate social groups control priority of access to special foods and receptive females, prevent serious fights within the group, protect mothers with infants from interference by other members of the group, come forward when the group is threatened from the outside, maintain alertness to external danger, threaten and chase "alien" conspecifics, and generally take the initiative in leading the group (Hall, 1968b). The reproductive success of a primate group is strongly influenced by the intelligence and self-control of its most dominant individuals. Lower-ranking individuals have an influence on the social behavior of the leaders, and thereby tend to ensure that the leaders must do far more than gratify their own desires "without thinking." Unfortunately, our understanding of the intelligence of dominant primates may be clouded by our natural antipathies to tyrants.

COMMUNICATION

Threat, appeasement, and other postures and displays used in agonistic encounters function through communication. They convey information to sense organs and this information is then processed in brains. Particular displays tend to elicit particular responses. The display of one rival and the response of another are interdependent and both are influenced simultaneously by selection. Individuals do not evolve in isolation, and display patterns tend to become uniform within a species. Neural and endocrine systems which respond effectively are favored by selection, but this will not in itself lead inevitably to what we call higher intelligence. Effectiveness, in evolution, is determined by reproductive success— and if this is conferred by close conformity to a given pattern of behavioral interaction, selection will oppose deviations from that pattern. If one basic pattern continues to favor survival, evolving lines may be held at a certain general level of behavioral complexity for very long periods. The song-producing apparatus of field crickets, for example, has remained essentially unaltered since the Cretaceous. This is not because crickets lack the raw materials required for evolutionary change or because the evolutionary process tends to lose its momentum. It is because crickets have been successful as they were, and as they still are. Another paradox of evolution is that natural selection always tends to *resist* deviation from an optimal pattern of organization. Only when these optima are altered by environmental change does natural selection favor major genetic innovations. Under certain conditions, selection has clearly favored the evolution of higher intelligence. Mammals have evolved, and the human brain trebled in size during the Pleistocene. These conditions, however, are unusual. They have clearly not affected most evolving lines, and the peculiarly human conditions have even failed to affect other primate lines. In our attempts to understand the evolution of intelligence we must look for these peculiar and particular conditions.

Human language is unique in the sense that it conveys an impressive quantity and complexity of information (or misinformation) through combinations of a few simple, basic symbols. This is possible because human brains are able to associate such symbols with very complex patterns of past experience and can do so very rapidly—whether the symbols are conveyed in visual, auditory, or tactile forms. Apart from the complexity of the information patterns, however, and the speed with which they are transmitted, human language does not differ fundamentally from other forms of animal communication. In all cases, the information is transmitted through physical media such as light or sound waves, chemicals that stimulate olfactory nerves, or direct tactile pressures. In all cases, the physical stimuli are processed by neurophysiological systems in animal bodies.

The basic function of all nervous systems is communication. The manifold activities of billions of body cells are coordinated by coded signals transmitted along nerve fibers. Visual, auditory, olfactory, and tactile signals from sources external to the body are coordinated with internal signals in ways that lead to the discovery of food, the avoidance of danger, and effective reciprocal interactions between males and females. Animal communication is very largely a by-product of sex. Sex serves a vital evolutionary function, and communication often enhances the effectiveness of the genetic recombination achieved by sex. Changes due to natural selection would be slow and relatively ineffectual without a wide range of genetic variation from which to select. Mutation alone could not have produced the array of organic diversity and complexity which now surrounds us. Mutation merely supplies a variety of raw materials which must then be combined and recombined to produce a great variety of organic wholes. Those organic wholes which function most effectively are favored by selection, and in every generation a vast quantity of these "genetic experiments" fail to pass the tests of survival. Without this constant re-production of genetic variety, and without continual "wastage" and death, evolutionary change could not occur. And just as a great variety of buildings can be built from the same kind of bricks, just as 103 or more elements can be recombined to produce all the variety in the visible universe, just as only 5 of these elements can produce an astronomical variety of genes, so a relatively small variety of genes can be recombined to form an enormous variety of different individuals, even within a single species. Sex achieves such a re-creation of variety with every generation in every bisexual species. The primary function of sex is not reproduction, but genetic recombination.

Eggs and sperms must meet before their genes can "recombine," and evolution has produced some very ingenious ways of bringing them together. The colors and odors of flowers communicate with the nervous systems of insects, who then inadvertently promote sexual intercourse between plants. The sperms of male mosquitoes can interact to produce more mosquitoes only under certain very special conditions. These conditions exist only in female mosquitoes. The males must find these females, and elaborate communication systems have been evolved to help them do so. Genes of many species swirl unseen around us, and they do not swirl entirely at random. Millions of communication systems are in action. The din of katydids and crickets on a summer night or the clamor of a teeming jungle is very largely a medley of messages tending to direct the right sperms to the right eggs.

Copulation is also facilitated by the communication of signals, and these can also be very complex, even in relatively simple animals. Earthworms, for example, are hermaphroditic. When they copulate, each member of the pair both transmits and receives spermatozoa. A very precise and accurate alignment of one individual with another is required before this can be achieved, and special organs have evolved to facilitate the mutual alignments. Such organs include paired sperm receptacles, protrusible penes, prostate and adhesive glands, suckers, claspers, seminal grooves, bristles with hooks or special microscopic teeth, special muscles, and so on. Initially, the worms must find and "recognize" each other, but this is only a first step in their intercommunications.

Many animal communication systems are almost entirely "automatic." Both the signals transmitted and the responses of the neural receiving apparatus are built into the organisms concerned, just as the signals and responses within a given body are very largely programmed in advance by the interacting genes. No more learning is required for the copulations of earthworms or mosquitoes than for the genetic exchanges between insect-pollinated plants. But learning did become involved in the communications between certain higher organisms, and capacities for learning evolved gradually and biologically.

The earliest manifestations of learning capacities were probably only minor alterations of the old automatic communication systems. *Imprinting,* for example, is a form of learning. Newly hatched goslings will respond to any object which emits a certain easily imitated pattern of stimuli and will then continue to behave toward this object as though it was their mother. The propensity to respond in this way to some such pattern of stimuli is built into their nervous systems before they hatch—but their nervous systems then "zero in" on the first particular pattern of stimuli which meets the more general requirements. The propensity to recognize a certain *kind* of information is inherited, but the particular pattern learned depends on early experience.

There is an important similarity between imprinting and the learning of a human language. In both cases the required neural apparatus is developed in advance; in both cases it provides a propensity (or capacity) to segregate certain patterns of stimuli from others experienced during early life and then to respond in certain ways to the particular patterns of stimuli thus learned. The response depends in part upon the neural structures inherited, in part upon the actual stimuli experienced. Humans inherit a neural structure which provides them in advance with a capacity and a propensity to learn a language—but the particular language they learn depends on the experience of the individual. The complexity of the information patterns learned and the extent of the capacity to expand this information content is much greater in humans than in goslings, but the basic principle is fundamentally the same.

Learning capacities vary widely in accordance with the complexity and organization of the nervous systems inherited. Newly hatched goslings are unable to discriminate between a real goose and a very rough imitation of a goose. Once they have learned to respond to an "artifical" set of stimuli, their ability to correct this mistake is very limited. An English robin will mistake a tuft of red feathers for a rival male robin. His relatively simple nervous system is unable to incorporate other stimuli from other parts of a male robin's body into a more complex whole, and so his discriminatory capacities are limited. Human brains are able to deal with far greater quantities of information than can the brains of robins. The simple signal *mother*, for example, conveys a wealth of information to humans, and as we mature we associate more and more information with this same simple stimulus. The effects of the signal on our nervous systems grow in complexity as development and learning proceed. But as in the case of goslings and robins, there are limits to the quantities of information our brains can process. We forget irrelevant details of past experience and often fail to perceive the relevance of certain bits of information. And like goslings and robins, humans are born with neural equipment that renders some kinds of learning easier than others.

The particular nervous systems we inherit influence the general course of our subsequent learning, and in this sense achievements in music, mathematics, athletics or business are due to a combination of inherited capacities and cultural experience. Attempts to segregate human behavior, in an either-or sense, into presumably discrete learned and instinctive components are due to a failure to understand the vital significance of interactions between inherited structure and environmental stimuli. Attempts to explain human behavior in terms of the simple reactions of sticklebacks or English robins overlook the significance of human abilities to correlate and associate greater quantities of information. Both humans and other higher primates, for example, respond to far more complex patterns of signals than red genital lips and rounded buttocks.

No human activity is possible without a functioning biological body, and biological urges have a strong influence on human behavior—but such urges are themselves strongly influenced by cortical activity, and the human brain differs greatly from that of a robin. The canine cerebral cortex has a profound influence on the basic emotional responses of dogs; robinlike responses could hardly have escaped the influence of human cortical activity throughout the two or three million years during which the human brain trebled in average size. Human sexual responses are derived from those of nonhuman animals, but they have been altered in the course of evolution rather as cerebral responses to the signal *mother* are altered during the lifetime of an individual.

Primates respond to very complex patterns of signals during their social interactions. Some components of these signal patterns may have an especially strong influence on the response elicited, but they are nevertheless associated with other components. The patterns of response are graded and controlled in accordance with the entire pattern of the composite signal received. The effect of a threat display varies with the combination of components in the compound signal as a whole, rather as the effect of a human verbal threat may be altered by a smile.

Vocal, visual, and tactile signals of nonhuman primates have been studied by Hinde and Rowell (1962), Hall and DeVore (1965), Marler (1965), Altmann (1965), Struhsaker (1967), Van Lawick–Goodall (1968), and others—in baboons, rhesus monkeys, macaques, langurs, vervet monkeys, chimpanzees, gorillas, and other species. Although nonhuman primate communication systems are not language in the human sense, they probably resemble the foundation from which human language evolved. Nonhuman primate signals correspond with the smiles, frowns, laughter, sneers, grunts, and moans which still underlie and enhance human linguistic communication.

Most of the compound signals transmitted by nonhuman primates convey motivational information which helps the individuals adjust to an ever changing dominance hierarchy. Their major function seems to be control and regulation of aggressiveness and maintenance of social order and peace within the group. The signals usually result in pacificatory exchanges, even when they convey threats (Marler, 1965). Maintenance of internal cohesion is the sine qua non for protection of the young against external threats. Monkeys and apes have relatively few signals which convey information about events outside their social group. They seem to have an "isolationist" mentality and show relatively little interest in "foreign affairs." Similar tendencies, at a somewhat higher level, are apparent in the space devoted to local events in human newspapers. But newspapers usually have at least one page devoted to foreign affairs, and similarly, nonhuman primates have signals which convey information about events external to their group. Barks and howls keep separate groups informed of one another's whereabouts and thereby help them to avoid direct confrontations. Vervet monkeys have distinctive sounds for snakes, big cats, and raptorial birds. Other vervet monkeys respond to these sounds by taking appropriate cover. They do not climb to the topmost branches of trees in response to the sound which means *raptorial bird*, as they often do when they hear the sound for *large predator* (Struhsaker, 1967). Basic structural foundations from which more elaborate communication systems could evolve are clearly present in these primates.

A young chimpanzee who is learning sign language applied the sign for *flower* to *all* flowers, including pictures of flowers in books. She also learned, without prompting, to use the same sign in response to strong cooking odors in a kitchen. And she has learned to combine signals into simple sentences (Gardner & Gardner, 1969). Chimpanzees may be unable to discuss philosophy, but they have at least some ability to symbolize. Signs and symbols may be no more mutually exclusive than are instincts and intelligence, or animals and man.

Monkeys and apes can obviously survive without a large "vocabulary" of signals about events outside their own social groups. Provided internal social cohesion is maintained, through frequent interchanges of complicated motivational information, they can help one another to deal with lions and snakes. Other members of their own species are not the greatest threats to their survival. In the case of humans, however, other human groups have been the most serious threats to survival since the dawn of history, and possibly since the thrust of natural selection first became distinctively human. The advent of this state of affairs greatly increased the importance of signals which convey information on "foreign affairs." In early humans, failure to maximize existing mental potentials for communicating information about external events tended to become fatal, and the resulting natural selection began to favor extensions and improvements of the physical source of the basic potential itself—that is, of the brain.

Adequate eyes and ears and sound-producing apparatus would already have been present. Living monkeys can emit a wide range of sounds in rapid succession. The number of different sounds required for linguistic communication need not be very great, provided they can be combined and recombined in many different ways. Nearly infinite varieties of genetic information are transmitted by recombinations of only four base-pair "letters" into long genetic "words." The English alphabet of only 26 letters suffices for the enormous variety of books in English now available. The basic vowel and consonant sounds of human languages vary from a few dozen to as many as 70 or 80. Monkeys can emit a sufficient variety of sound signals, but they lack the brains to formulate or to interpret concepts at the human level of complexity. The spoken English word *God*, for example, is a simple sound—but its interpretation taxes even human brains. Many other sounds can stimulate the same sort of mental effort (*Dieu, Yahweh, Jehovah*, etc.). With human brains and monkey vocal apparatus, the same conceptions could be conveyed by any one of a vast variety of chutters, barks, whoops, squeals, or grunts. Concepts are not contained within the sound signals used to convey them, for if they were, humans would now speak one language rather than thousands of quite different ones. Conversation is possible between two individuals who are transmitting different patterns of sound signals. A man can speak German to a woman who replies in French, and the two can exchange a lot of information if they understand each other's language. If we could learn to interpret the vocalizations of chimpanzees and speak slowly and simply enough to them, we could "converse" with them without vocalizing their sounds or expecting them to vocalize ours. Dogs respond intelligently to verbal commands from humans, who in turn respond to the whines, barks, and growls of dogs.

Physical anthropology can tell us little about the evolution of human language. We cannot arrange fossil skulls into those who could, or could not, talk. All we can do when we look at a fossil skull is ponder about the linguistic capacities of the brain it once contained. The problem is stated rather well by Howells (1963):

> There must have been a time when language was different, more limited or simpler, just as we know there was a time when men had smaller brains. We cannot dig up languages like skeletons, and we can never do anything but guess about beginnings. It seems only logical that very primitive men—hominids of the man-ape variety—made a good deal of constant expressive noise, just as chimpanzees do, and that, little by little, more symbolic content entered into this noise as the animals making it became mentally more capable of symbolizing. We cannot tell when this happened. We do not know what kind of brain would have been necessary, and so we cannot look at a fossil skull and say, "He talked." (Obviously the jaw will not tell us.)

We cannot resurrect the languages of *Homo erectus* or study the vocalizations of australopithecines, but in a general sense we can improve our understanding of the evolution of the basic capacity for human language. We can also consider the possible role of language in human evolution. Many of our responses and the signals that elicit them are built into the very structure and organization of our neural and endocrine systems. Babies smile a few weeks after birth, and smiles are common to all races, societies, and language groups. Smiles, frowns, and many other expressions reflecting mood and motivation are common to all humans. We all seem to have inherited the basic structural organization for such signals from common ancestors. They form a background foundation directly comparable to the motivational signals of nonhuman primates. We have not, however, inherited these "instinctive" gestures and expressions in unaltered form. We add frills and nuances to the basic expressions we observe and imitate in fellow members of our own groups. Many particular forms of smiling, handshaking, bowing, etc. are ritualized into more or less specific sign languages which can be misunderstood by foreigners who have not learned the specific sign language of a particular group.

In nonhuman primates there seem to be fewer frills, fewer ritualized nuances with somewhat different meanings in different social groups. There may be more of these than we now suspect, but they are probably fewer and less diverse than in humans. Interpretation of subtle differences in meaning requires more complex and more efficient brains. Other animals can interpret complex signals indicating rage, submission, etc. and can recognize subtle gradations in intensities of emotion indicating degrees of likelihood of future action—but they probably lack the neural equipment required for interpreting the more subtle nuances of those already very complex signal patterns. Consequently, many of their behavioral displays are common to the species as a whole. They all tend to "speak the same language."

In the case of human evolution a paradoxical situation began to appear as brains became more complex. As humans acquired a greater capacity to interpret the special meanings of particular variations in behavior, they began to subdivide into groups which could communicate only at the most basic levels. The capacity for greater understanding between members of the same group led to greater misunderstanding between members of separate groups. As they became more intimately integrated into their own groups, they became more sharply segregated from foreign groups. Such segregation was probably very marked during prehistoric times. There are more than 700 mutually unintelligible languages in New Guinea today, and American Indians spoke several thousand different languages a few centuries ago. When we try to visualize several million years of global prehistoric peace, we should also try to visualize peaceful interactions between people who could not converse with one another. The wide dissemination of today's major languages was due originally to conquest and political domination, not to a "natural" tendency for people everywhere to speak the same language.

It seems unlikely, therefore, that the evolution of human linguistic capacities brought a marked increase in global brotherly love and mutual understanding. It is far more likely to have brought an increase in the frequency and intensity of intergroup competition. Misunderstandings can arise even when people do speak the same language, as the annals of history (and today's newspapers) clearly show. When they cannot understand one another beyond the level of smiles and grunts and blatant gestures, people rarely achieve deep cultural bonds and common loyalties. It is therefore most unlikely that a sense of belonging and of mutual concern could have been extended through the whole of mankind during prehistoric times or that it could have persisted for several million years.

Unless communication between people who speak the same language is actively maintained, dialects begin to appear. Such dialects diverge until they become mutually unintelligible. Local dialects are still pronounced in modern Britain, despite television and other very widespread and active media of communication. There was no television during prehistoric times, and no transportation facilities with greater speed and endurance than human legs and feet, or primitive boats in some areas. Even if certain languages were widely diffused by conquest from time to time, they would have disintegrated rapidly into arrays of mutually unintelligible dialects. There is virtually no limit to the variety of human languages which could have been devised and redevised. Human languages are as unstable and dynamic as the evolutionary process which gave rise to them.

The evolution of linguistic capacities, therefore, would have served to reinforce territorial and other segregating forces during prehistoric times. And greater linguistic abilities would have simultaneously increased the social cohesion *within* each separate group. Conceptual and emotional differences between "us" and "them" would have been accentuated. The effects of this on intergroup competition, and hence on the intensity of natural selection and the rate of evolution, are not really hard to understand. We resist these very obvious possibilities not because we find them implausible, but because we find them disturbing. And as pointed out previously, we find them disturbing because we misunderstand the word innate.

THE EVOLUTION OF FUTURE-PREDICTION

Viewed from the heart of our own self-centered goals and wishes, evolution conveys the impression of a vast cosmic Plan unfolding toward some preconceived cosmic Purpose. If evolution should indeed be so motivated it is unlikely that we can understand the Plan and Purpose with the primitive brains and limited experience we now possess. We can, however, be reasonably confident that evolution was not conceived by a *human* cosmic "mind" and is not powered by a *human* cosmic "will." Since we do not understand our own goals and foresight, even in the narrow context of our own lives, it is unwise to project them too deeply into the universe surrounding us. Our understanding of evolution is more likely to grow into correspondence with reality if we avoid anthropomorphic, teleological "explanations" which merely extend the mystery of our own behavior without explaining it in terms that we can really understand.

There is, however, an unmistakable continuity in the flow of evolution, a profound relationship between past, present, and future events. We can recognize this relationship, and can at least begin to understand it without invoking the supernatural. Sperms and eggs, for example, are future oriented. They do little or nothing to maintain the bodies that produce them, and may even contribute toward the destruction of those bodies. Were it not for the possibility that, at some time in the future, certain sperms and eggs will combine, they would not be produced. Gametogenesis is oriented toward future fertilization, which is oriented toward the future birth of a complete organism, which is oriented toward future gametogenesis, and so on. This is not a cycle, turning ever back upon itself to produce a static repetition of the same old things. It is a thrust into the future, a profoundly creative process. The eggs and sperms produced are never quite the same, and their recombinations produce genetic innovations which have never before existed on the earth. We can begin to understand such future-oriented processes without invoking any form of conscious foresight. Physical systems that are organized in certain ways will tend to produce certain results in the future. Under certain conditions stars will explode, and new stars will coagulate from the scattered dust. Animals who produce no gametes will not become the parents of animals who, in turn, produce no gametes—and consequently most animals will continue to produce gametes as the generations flow onward into the unknown future. Future-oriented gametogenesis is related to the future-oriented communication systems which tend to bring gametes together. And many other future-oriented animal activities are equally related to this fundamental flow of genetic recombination. Animals tend to behave in ways that enhance their own chances of surviving long enough to produce and rear offspring—which requires some capacity to "predict" the future. Living things show a marvelous variety of such capacities.

Certain rhythmic events recur with great regularity for very long spans of time. The earth has been rotating for several thousand million years, and the sun has been "rising" and "setting" accordingly. The moon swings in a regular orbit around the earth, and the combined gravitational pulls of sun and moon produce high and low tides in the earth's oceans. Seasons correspond with the current position of the earth with relation to the sun. Because of this regularity in the motions of earth, moon, and sun, the future occurrence of sunrise and sunset, high and low tides, winter and summer can be predicted with great accuracy—and were being predicted long before the publication of the first almanac.

Forms of animal behavior that enhance survival during the daytime, at high tide, or in the summer may bring destruction if continued at night, at low tide, or in the winter. Animals who failed to alter their behavior in response to these rhythms of environmental change have left no offspring—and the surviving species of today show a great variety of alternating patterns of behavior which are switched on and off as the tides, days, and seasons come and go. They do this in response to clues which invariably precede the rise of sun or tide, or the onset of winter. The appearance of light in the eastern sky, spray from the approaching sea, the phase of the moon, relative lengths of day and night, and many other physical events regularly precede the coming changes in environment. Such clues make it possible to predict certain features of the immediate future very accurately. Consciousness is not required for such predictions. Networks of wires and other nonliving materials can automatically switch the streetlights of a city on at sunset and switch them off again at sunrise. And networks of nerves have been evolved which switch alternative patterns of animal behavior on and off unconsciously. (In some such animals we have not yet found the extrinsic clues which switch the nervous systems on and off—but this does not necessarily mean such clues do not exist.)

When a barnacle opens its opercular lids in response to clues that herald the incoming tide, it is predicting a future change in the environment that will permit feeding and prevent desiccation. The barnacle can make this prediction without being any more aware of the future than a gamete-producing gonad is aware of the evolutionary significance of genetic recombination. When a bird begins to migrate southward in response to new relationships between the relative lengths of day and night it is predicting the onset of winter conditions although it has never experienced such conditions and never will. Rhythmic regularity in the motions of earth, moon, and sun has persisted long enough to permit the evolutionary construction of complex neural "thermostats." These neural mechanisms "work" because they are adjusted to relatively invariable relationships between past, present, and future conditions. At some time in the future our solar system will disintegrate, but in the meantime thousands of animal species will continue to predict future conditions without knowing they are doing so.

Many of the conditions which influence animal survival are far less predictable than day and night, winter and summer. The process of evolution contains an element of unpredictability. Genetic innovations are produced with every generation, and some of these behave in novel ways. As noted previously, the creation of novelty is an inherent feature of the evolutionary process. In order to deal with novelty, neural systems must be more flexible and more complex than the relatively simple thermostats required for predicting tides or seasons. Such neural systems must mediate, "on the spur of the moment," behavior which tends to enhance survival. Some of these more flexible systems can still be relatively automatic. Not every shadow indicates the presence of a predator, but some animals respond to *all* shadows by taking evasive action. During the course of evolution, the association between shadows and predators has, in the case of these evolving lines, been frequent enough to favor the evolution of neural systems that mediate automatic evasive action in response to shadows. In other evolving lines such responses to shadows did not enhance survival. Caterpillars feeding on the swaying foliage of trees are continually exposed to alternating light and shadow, and under such conditions evasive action in response to every shadow could lead to starvation. Under these conditions, the neural systems must respond to *other* stimuli which tend to be associated with predators (for example, vibrations produced by an alighting bird). Lions are not always hungry, but the probability that the sight or smell of a lion will lead to an attack in the near future is high enough to favor the evolution of neural systems which mediate avoidance of *all* "lion-clues." After very long-continued associations, such neural systems can be constructed in ways that produce evasive response whether or not an individual animal has previously experienced the "trigger-clues." But the evolution of such automatic systems requires many generations of strong association between the clues and the future conditions they are likely to herald.

Neural systems complex enough to provide some capacity to learn from experience confer certain obvious advantages. When a young rabbit is driven from its home range into a new and strange territory, its survival may depend very largely on its ability to learn the salient features of this new territory. These features will differ from those of the old home range. Past evolution could not have provided the rabbit with built-in neural mechanisms able to predict the peculiarities of each and every region of the future earth or to recognize each of these future territories on first sight. The built-in mechanisms are related to more general associations which have, in general, persisted for many millennia. The *details* of each new territory must be learned by each rabbit individually— and they must be learned quickly if the rabbit is to survive. When he enters a strange territory, a rabbit may encounter a fox, and if he runs to the base of a cliff he may be cornered, caught, and eaten. If he is fortunate enough to have discovered the cliff *before* he meets the fox, he will be able to predict that flight in that direction may lead to disaster in the very near future. Whether or not he is conscious of this, his evasive behavior will be more effective when he has learned the whereabouts of burrows, briar patches, ponds, swamps, fox dens, clover patches, and other unique peculiarities of his own particular territory. It is probably because of this relationship between learning capacities and survival that animals are so often reluctant to leave their home territories—and many young animals come to grief before they can learn the lay of the land in a territory that is new and strange to them. Abilities to learn, and to learn quickly, are therefore strongly favored in some evolving lines. Evolution can provide neural mechanisms which render certain general kinds of learning easier than others, but the actual details learned must be left to the individual animal. And all forms of learning are to some extent related to prediction of the future.

In social species, abilities to learn how to predict the future behavior of other animals have been favored by selection. In the case of primates, capacities for this kind of learning have evolved to high levels of efficiency. It was this form of "social intelligence" that was favored strongly enough to treble the size of the human brain during the Pleistocene. Early humans did not compete with one another in literary composition, higher mathematics, or musical appreciation, sterilizing those who failed. They did, however, engage one another in agonistic social interactions, both within and between social groups, and the failure of the losers is reflected in the rapid extinction of smaller-brained humans during the Pleistocene. The prediction of human behavior is very difficult, but some humans can do it with almost uncanny efficiency. We refer to "woman's intuition" and "animal cunning" as though they were due to supernatural agencies or "animal instincts" rather than to human intelligence. But accurate predictions of the behavior of a particular human must be based on past experience of the behavior of that particular human. This requires learning, which in turn requires high intelligence. We inherit nervous systems which make this general kind of learning easy, just as rabbits inherit nervous systems which make it easy for them to learn the locations of burrows and hollow logs. But just as the individual rabbit must learn the particular details of its own unique territory, so each human must learn the particular idiosyncracies of each unique fellow human or of each cultural group of humans. Biological evolution has provided us with the right kind of brains, but we must then use those brains if we wish to predict one another's behavior. And some human brains are more efficient than others at learning to predict, and even to direct, the future course of human behavior. For some four thousand years, survival on the steppes of central Asia was determined very largely by capacities to predict the whereabouts and intentions of roving bands of mounted nomads. Many of the leaders were well acquainted with the leaders of other bands, and their predictions were based on learning and experience. Those who survived were particularly talented at judging other humans. They were illiterate but far from unintelligent. Wave after wave of mounted nomads conquered Europe, India, and China—where their immediate descendants displayed high levels of literary as well as social intelligence. Given the capacity to predict human behavior, other less difficult mental endeavors will naturally appear as a by-product—just as cultural evolution appeared as a by-product of biological evolution.

The mental and endocrine foundations of social intelligence were laid in the very remote past, long before our ancestors became human. We should not, however, attribute human social intelligence to a lower, "animal" level of mental activity. Although the foundations were laid a long time ago they have not been handed down to us unaltered. The cerebral cortex was a vital component in the brains of our nonhuman ancestors, and it was intimately linked with other neural and endocrine systems. The human brain was greatly elaborated during the Pleistocene, and it evolved as a whole. The links between the cerebral cortex, hypothalamus, cerebellum, and other parts of the nervous system were not gradually broken while the structure as a whole became more complex and efficient. The influence of cortical activity on other neural systems did not decrease; it was, on the contrary, greatly increased. And the other neural and endocrine systems were themselves elaborated and correlated with the gradually increasing levels of cortical complexity. As the human brain evolved, more complex patterns of sensual clues could be correlated and interpreted, more complex endocrine influences could be more intelligently influenced and controlled by cortical activity. As neural circuitry throughout the brain became more elaborate and more intimately integrated, more and more subtle variations in the expressions of eyes, face, and bodily movement could be incorporated into larger, more inclusive, and increasingly meaningful patterns. As brains grew in size and complexity they acquired not only a greater capacity for processing and correlating greater quantities of information at each present moment, but also greater capacities for correlating this information with past experience and for relating past and present information to future probabilities. The fact that we cannot, even yet, understand how our brains do this does not alter the fact that they can do it, and do it with far greater speed and efficiency than we have observed in any other animal species. Human social intelligence is therefore distinctively human and cannot, with reason, be degraded to a presumably low level of "animal cunning."

Success in human social interactions requires very rapid mental correlation of large quantities of past and present information. It requires a capacity to deal with disturbing uncertainties of the future by blending confidence in past experience with a frank recognition of those uncertainties. It requires great mental flexibility and very rapid learning during actual social encounters. And it requires an ability to prevent emotions from disturbing the efficiency of cortical activity. One of the most effective tactics during human agonistic confrontations is to rile the opponent and thereby cloud his better judgment by arousing his emotions. Those who are more adept at social confrontations are often more adept at holding their emotions under intelligent cortical self-control—or at keeping their cool, as the saying goes. When we are in action socially we rarely have time to consider each subsequent move in advance, to weigh and compare the possible future consequences of a variety of possible responses. The very rapid flow of events forces us to think fast and to respond on the spur of the moment. Because these responses are not preceded by fully conscious thought we think of ourselves as behaving instinctively. But we are not then behaving as "lower animals." Our brains, and the cerebral cortex in particular, are very active at such times. Our responses are strongly conditioned by what we have learned from past experience, and what we have learned is related to our intelligence. High levels of social intelligence resemble higher forms of what we call scientific intelligence, but high social intelligence is far more dynamic and flexible, and less vulnerable to the illusion of certainty.

Like many other biological phenomena, social intelligence operates at various levels of complexity. Women try to predict and manipulate the behavior of their children, their husbands, and those who influence their husbands' chances of promotion. Statesmen try to predict and manipulate the behavior of entire nations, including that of foreign nations. Success in all these levels of future-oriented social behavior is determined very largely by the biological efficiency of the brains involved. A large element of pure luck is also involved, but without intelligence we cannot take full advantage of good luck. As the complexity of the problems increases, the accuracy of predictions tends to decrease. Both our experience and the biological potential of our brains at any given stage of evolution are limited. Attempts to predict the future of our entire species are therefore particularly likely to be inaccurate. We can interpret the past with far more confidence than we can predict the future.

We must, however, try to predict the future of our species. The influence of our own activities is becoming so powerful that unless we can learn to control and direct these activities intelligently our entire species might become extinct. Awareness of this need is growing rapidly and is being manifested in a wide variety of books, articles, and conferences. No one of these attempts to solve the problem of our future has provided us with a simple panacea that can be used with confidence to cure our rapidly proliferating ills. And no simple panacea will ever be discovered. The books and conferences, however, considered as an interacting whole, as components of a dynamic, flowing, ever changing process, are one of the most encouraging of all the many aspects of human evolution. The brains that evolved biologically during the Pleistocene are becoming aware of this biological evolution. Their interactions are increasing, improving, correcting this awareness—and are beginning to use it in attempts to reduce the disturbing uncertainties of the future.

THE HUMAN FUTURE

The past and future are never identical, but certain broad and general features of the past can be used as guides on our journey into the unexplored future. We can, for example, be confident that peace within primate groups, human or nonhuman, will continue to depend on dominance hierarchies. The hierarchies of the future will differ from those of today, but future peace will still require social cohesion. We can improve our dominance hierarchies, but we must retain them as we change them. Though it is not uncontrollable, there is an unmistakable propensity for violence in all higher primates, and nonviolent behavior must be learned. We are still learning, and until we have learned to live in peace with one another on a global scale we will have to be restrained—by force, if necessary. A future without police or armies is a desirable goal which our species may some day attain, but we have not yet arrived at that goal.

We cannot return permanently to a "state of nature." We could revert temporarily to a state of social chaos, only too easily. Societies are more easily segregated than integrated. We could destroy our dominance hierarchies rather than improve them and thereby plunge our species into another Dark Age. This has happened in the past and could happen again. But another Dark Age would neither check the thrust nor alter the general direction of human evolution. New generations of humans would emerge from the chaos, and if we can judge from the rhythms of history some new generation would organize socially on a scale beyond anything ever achieved before.

It is widely believed that the conditions of human life are growing worse instead of better, and there are grounds for this belief. We must, however, refrain from basing our pessimism on illusions—and we do this when we look back with nostalgia to imaginary golden ages of the past. For example, V. S. Pritchett, in an introduction to a Collins edition of Jane Austen's *Pride and Prejudice*, said this in 1952:

> Our revolutions and our wars make us turn with relief to a novelist who wrote at the centre of the last small enclave of civilization in the history of our island: the eighteenth century before romanticism and the industrial revolution between them had poisoned the sources of our life. In her voice we hear again the classical inflection, the accent of irony or order, of grace and certainty. One hundred and fifty years of guilt separate us from her mind. Isolated,

unimitated, the only artist in the English novel, she is the last voice of a happier age.

Such beliefs ignore a host of relevant evidence. The French Revolution and the Napoleonic wars took place during Jane Austen's lifetime. A considerable part of the wealth which made graceful living possible for a small minority in early nineteenth-century England was derived from the transport and sale of Africans as slaves. Some 200 offenses were punishable by death in late eighteenth-century England. For millions, Jane Austen's lifetime was not a "happier age."

If we define progress in terms of social peace, then *Homo sapiens* has made impressive progress since the dawn of history. There has been an unmistakable growth in the size of those "we-groups" within which murder is regarded as a crime. There have been relapses, but on the whole the "we-groups" have grown enormously, not only in size but also in the quality of cooperation and the degree of voluntary acceptance of the rule of law. At the dawn of history a crude form of social cohesion had been imposed (by force) along the Nile, and small city-states were waging war in Mesopotamia. Throughout the remainder of the earth, mankind was subdivided into a multitude of very small, "independent," and probably interhostile social groups. Judging from early historical records and from the great mass of available information on societies living at primitive cultural levels during recent centuries, the relationships between this fragmented multitude of social groups were far from peaceful. Personal loyalties and a sense of belonging were probably confined to a few hundred people in the vast majority of cases. Even today, people who live beyond the reach of modern law-enforcement agencies often see death and violence during their early childhood. Casualties from intervillage feuds and other forms of intergroup violence are often very high in such societies; estimates range from 14 to more than 24 % of adult males, as compared to 6% during the brief 4-year period of the American Civil War (Livingstone, 1967).

Despite today's wars, riots, and rising crime rates, most citizens of large nations live out their lives without ever seeing two men in mortal combat (except on television and movie screens). Hundreds of millions of people now live together in relative peace and travel alone and unarmed for thousands of miles without fear of being killed and eaten or enslaved by hostile foreigners. How long this precarious peace can be maintained we do not know. If current crime rates continue to increase, the majority of tomorrow's children may see men in mortal combat before they reach their teens. But it may be true, nevertheless, that more people have spent more time living at peace with one another during the twentieth century than during any previous period of comparable length. This is a recent achievement. We only vaguely understand how it came about, and are only beginning to learn how peace on such a scale can be maintained. It is not surprising that we are often frightened and confused—and that there have been outbursts of shocking violence. The wonder is that these outbursts have failed to destroy civilization altogether and that despite them we have achieved so much.

Nazi gas ovens are still fresh in living memory, but we recoil from such memories with strong revulsion. This is also a recent development. During the biblical conquest of Canaan, genocidal slaughter was not regarded as immoral—provided it was applied to "them" rather than to "us." The Lord of the ancient Israelites was very blatantly a god of war, and his commands were executed, with the sword, as a high moral duty. Those who doubt this should reread the Book of Joshua and several other early books of the Old Testament. Mankind has progressed since the second millennium B.C., and has progressed toward more widespread peace.

Such progress might continue. We have not inherited an uncontrollable instinct for warfare. We have inherited brains three times the size of those in our australopithecine ancestors. And if our brains were indeed fashioned by the selective force of warfare, we may now be in a position to conquer war. We may not be doomed to fight insanely until some Armageddon finally exterminates our species. Evolution is change, and the future is not a repetition of the past. We are descended from reptiles, but we are not reptiles now, and our descendants never will be. We are also descended from fish. The basic foundations of our bodies were laid by the selective forces of underwater life—but those forces no longer affect us. If we can use our relatively primitive but very remarkable brains effectively *now*, our descendants may some day be as free from war as we ourselves are free from underwater life. Our descendants will have disturbing and perplexing problems, but war in the primeval sense may not be one of them.

REFERENCES

Alexander, R. D. The search for an evolutionary philosophy of man. *Proceedings of the Royal Society of Victoria*, 1971, **84** (Part 1), 99–120.

Altmann, S. A. Sociobiology of rhesus monkeys. II. Stochastics of social communication. *Journal of Theoretical Biology*, 1965, **8**, 490–522.

Ardrey, R. *The territorial imperative: A personal inquiry into the animal origins of property and nations.* New York: Atheneum, 1966; London: Collins, 1967.

Ardrey, R. Accomplices to violence. *New York Times Book Review*, July 14, 1968.

Berkowitz, L. Simple views of aggression: An essay review. *American Scientist*, 1969, **57**, 372–383.

Bigelow, R. *The dawn warriors: Man's evolution toward peace.* Boston: Little, Brown, 1969; London: Hutchinson, 1970.

Bigelow, R. The relevance of ethology to human aggressiveness. *International Social Sciences Journal*, 1971, **23**, 18–26.

Bigelow, R. "Genetic drift" and human evolution. *Bolletino di Zoologia*, 1972, in press.

Burnet, M. Biology and the appreciation of life. In *Boyer Lectures of 1966*, Australian Broadcasting Commission. Sydney: Ambassador Press, 1966.

Cavalli-Sforza, L. L. "Genetic drift" in an Italian population. *Scientific American*, 1969, **221**, 30–37.

Chagnon, N. A. Yanomamo—the fierce people. *Natural History*, 1967, **76**, 22–31. (a)

Chagnon, N. A. Yanomamo social organization and warfare. *Natural History*, 1967, **76**, 44–48. (b)

Crook, J. H. The nature and function of territorial aggression. In M. F. A. Montagu (Ed.), *Man and Aggression.* New York: Oxford University Press, 1968. Pp. 141–175.

Dart, R. A. The Kisoro pattern of mountain gorilla preservation. *Current Anthropology*, 1961, **2**, 510–511.

Dethier, V. G., & Stellar, E. *Animal behavior.* (3d ed.) Englewood Cliffs, N. J.: Prentice-Hall, 1970.

Dobzhansky, T. *Mankind evolving: The evolution of the human species.* New Haven, Conn.: Yale University Press, 1962.

Eibl-Eibesfeldt, I. *Ethology: The biology of behavior.* Translated from the German by Erich Klinghammer. New York: Holt, Rinehart & Winston, 1970.

Freeman, D. Aggression: Instinct or symptom? *Australia and New Zealand Journal of Psychiatry*, 1971, **5**, 66–73.

Gardner, R. A., & Gardner, B. T. Teaching sign language to a chimpanzee. *Science*, 1969, **165**, 664–672.

Hall, K. R. L. Field studies of primates. *Science Journal*, 1967, **3**, 71.

Hall, K. R. L. Aggression in monkey and ape societies. In P. C. Jay (Ed.), *Primates: Studies in adaptation and variability.* New York: Holt, Rinehart & Winston, 1968. Pp. 149–161. (a)

Hall, K. R. L. Social organization of the old-world monkeys and apes. In P. C. Jay (Ed.), *Primates: Studies in adaptation and variability.* New York: Holt, Rinehart & Winston, 1968. Pp. 7–31. (b)

Hall, K. R. L., & DeVore, I. Baboon social behavior. In I. DeVore (Ed.), *Primate behavior: Field studies of monkeys and apes.* New York: Holt, Rinehart & Winston, 1965. Pp. 53–110.

Hamburg, D. A. An evolutionary perspective on human aggressiveness. In D. Offer & D. Freedman (Eds.), *Modern psychiatry and clinical research: Essays in honor of Roy R. Grinker, Sr.* New York: Basic Books, 1972. Pp. 30–43.

Hinde, R. A. Energy models of motivation. *Symposia of the Society for Experimental Biology*, 1960, **14**, 199–213.

Hinde, R. A. *Animal behavior: A synthesis of ethology and comparative psychology.* (2d ed.) New York: McGraw-Hill, 1970.

Hinde, R. A., & Rowell, T. E. Communication by postures and facial expressions in the rhesus monkey (*Macaca mulatta*). *Proceedings of the Zoological Society of London*, 1962, **138**, 1–21.

Howells, W. *Back of History.* Garden City, N.Y.: Doubleday, Anchor Books, 1963.

Howells, W. *Mankind in the making: The story of human evolution.* Baltimore: Penguin, 1967.

Jay, P. C. Field studies. In A. M. Schrier, H. F. Harlow, & F. Stollnitz (Eds.), *Behavior of nonhuman primates.* Vol. 2. New York: Academic Press, 1965. Pp. 525–591.

Kummer, H. *Social organization of hamadryas baboons: A field study.* Chicago: University of Chicago Press, 1968.

Livingstone, F. B. The effects of warfare on the biology of the human species. *Natural History*, 1967, **76**, 61–65.

Lorenz, K. *On aggression.* Translated from the German by Marjorie Latzke. London: Methuen, 1966; New York: Harcourt, Brace & World, 1967.

Manning, A. *An introduction to animal behaviour.* London: Edward Arnold, 1967.

Marler, P. Communication in monkeys and apes. In I. DeVore (Ed.), *Primate behavior: Field studies of monkeys and apes.* New York: Holt, Rinehart & Winston, 1965. Pp. 544–584.

Montagu, M. F. A. The new litany of "innate depravity," or original sin revisited. In M. F. A. Montagu (Ed.), *Man and aggression.* New York: Oxford University Press, 1968. Pp. 3–16.

Morgan, C. T. *Physiological psychology.* (3d ed.) New York: McGraw-Hill, 1965.

Morris, D. *The naked ape: A zoologist's study of the human animal.* London: Jonathan Cape, 1967; New York: McGraw-Hill, 1968.

Muller, H. J. What genetic course will man steer? In *Proceedings of the Third International Congress of Human Genetics.* Baltimore: Johns Hopkins Press, 1957. P. 253.

Neel, J. V. Lessons from a "primitive" people. *Science*, 1970, **170**, 815–822.

Pritchett, V. S. Introduction to Collins edition of Jane Austen's *Pride and Prejudice*. London: Collins, 1952.

Ripley, S. Intertroop encounters among Ceylon gray langurs (*Presbytis entellus*). In S. A. Altmann (Ed.), *Social communication among primates*. Chicago: University of Chicago Press, 1967. Pp. 237–253.

Roper, M. K. A survey of the evidence for intrahuman killing in the Pleistocene. *Current Anthropology*, 1969, **10**, 427–459.

Schenkel, R. Play, exploration, and territoriality in the wild lion. *Symposium of the Zoological Society of London*, 1966, No. 18, 11–22.

Scott, J. P., & Fredericson, E. The causes of fighting in mice and rats. *Physiological Zoology*, 1951, **24**, 273–309.

Southwick, C. H., Beg, M. A., & Siddiqi, M. R. Rhesus monkeys in north India. In I. DeVore (Ed.), *Primate behavior: Field studies of monkeys and apes*. New York: Holt, Rinehart & Winston, 1965. Pp. 111–159.

Storr, A. *Human aggression*. New York: Atheneum, 1968.

Struhsaker, T. T. Auditory communication among vervet monkeys (*Cercopithecus aethiops*). In S. A. Altmann (Ed.), *Social communication among primates*. Chicago: University of Chicago Press, 1967. Pp. 281–324.

Sugiyama, Y. Social organization of Hanuman langurs. In S. A. Altmann (Ed.), *Social communication among primates*. Chicago: University of Chicago Press, 1967. Pp. 221–236.

Van Lawick–Goodall, J. A preliminary report on expressive movements and communication in the Gombe Stream chimpanzees. In P. C. Jay (Ed.), *Primates: Studies in adaption and variability*. New York: Holt, Rinehart & Winston, 1968. Pp. 313–374.

Washburn, S. L., & Hamburg, D. A. The implications of primate research. In I. DeVore (Ed.), *Primate behavior: Field studies of monkeys and apes*. New York: Holt, Rinehart & Winston. 1965. Pp. 607–622.

Washburn, S. L., & Hamburg, D. A. Aggressive behavior in Old World monkeys and apes. In P. C. Jay (Ed.), *Primates: Studies in adaptation and variability*. New York: Holt, Rinehart & Winston, 1968. Pp. 458–486.

Wright, S. Evolution in Mendelian populations. *Genetics*, 1931, **16**, 97–159.

Wright, S. The role of mutation, inbreeding, crossbreeding, and selection in evolution. *Proceedings of the Sixth International Congress of Genetics*, 1932, **1**, 356–366.

Wright, S. Random drift and the shifting balance theory of evolution. In K. Kojima (Ed.), *Mathematical topics in population genetics*. Berlin: Springer-Verlag, 1970.

Yoshiba, K. Local and intertroop variability in ecology and social behavior of common Indian langurs. In P. C. Jay (Ed.), *Primates: Studies in adaptation and variability*. New York: Holt, Rinehart & Winston, 1968. Pp. 217–242.

Zuckerman, S. *The social life of monkeys and apes*. London: Kegan Paul, 1932.

Fighting and Punishment from a Developmental Perspective[1]

ROBERT B. CAIRNS

Indiana University

Analyses of injury-producing and punitive behaviors in young humans and nonhumans have proceeded along separate, virtually independent, pathways. Investigations involving children have been dominated by the problem of how specific learning experiences contribute to the behavior and its control. Animal studies of fighting, conversely, have been predominantly concerned with the evolutionary functions of the behavior and the physiological mechanisms by which such functions may be mediated. The problem of how to achieve an integration of these emphases (human-nonhuman; learning-physiological; evolutionary-individual) has proved to be formidable. Attempts to reduce behavioral concepts to presumably more fundamental evolutionary and physiological ones typically give short shrift to the effects of individual experience and vice versa (see reviews of the problems in Montagu, 1968, and in Eleftheriou and Scott, 1971).

My aim in this paper is to explore an ontogenetic resolution to the issues of comparative integration. In this, I will follow Schneirla's lead when he held that "behavioral ontogenesis is the backbone of comparative psychology" (1966, p. 284). Accordingly, we will be concerned with the specific ways in which social learning and ontogenetic events are synthesized in the establishment of injury-

1. I am indebted to several persons who, as graduate students, contributed greatly to the research reported here: Joseph S. Nakelski, Susan D. Scholz, Albert A. Einsiedel, Jr., Judith T. Milakovich, Jane Midlam, Scott G. Paris, and Stephen Brown. It is my pleasure also to thank Professors Conrad Mueller and Donald D. Jensen for their perceptive comments on an earlier version of this paper. The research connected with this report was supported by the National Institute of Child Health and Human Development (PHS HD 5693).

producing and punitive behaviors. The goal itself is scarcely newsworthy, since virtually all behavioral statements from Watson on carry some general recognition of the importance of ontogenetic events. Then, save in a few instances,[2] they are ignored. From the present perspective, mere acknowledgment of the existence of ontogenetic contributions is not sufficient. What is called for is a revision of social-learning explanations of fighting and punishment so that the changing conditions of the individual form an integral feature of the account.

A second matter concerns the appropriate level of analysis for fighting and punishment. In order to trace the longitudinal history of a response pattern across development, it becomes necessary to focus upon the actual behaviors, activities, and events relevant to the pattern. In the present view, fighting and punishment are essentially relational terms, referring to noxious and pain-producing behaviors that occur in a dyadic interchange. Their description at any developmental stage requires that explicit attention be given to the reciprocal acts that elicit them and to the exact behaviors that they provoke. A focus on the dyadic controls of behavior, as Sears (1951) envisioned, has the potential of forcing a revolutionary shift in social-learning strategies and theoretical organization.

The first part of this paper will involve some further comments on the concept of aggression and the ontogenetic perspective. In the second section, I will review some recent observations and experiments on the establishment of fighting and punishment from that perspective. The final part of the chapter will be addressed to the issues of comparative generalization as seen by a developmentalist.

Aggression: Towards a Revision

The view that all acts that produce harm or injury belong to a unitary response class is traditional. William McDougall, for example,

---

2. Including J. B. Watson. In *Psychologies of 1925*, he asserted what he considered to be the "fundamental point of view of the behaviorist—viz. that in order to understand man you have to understand the life history of his activities" (1926, p. 34). This assertion came at the conclusion of an account of the unlearned behavior repertoire of the infant. Basic as this message may have been for Watson, it was muted by other contradictory, more extravagant claims. In the same lecture, he guaranteed to shape any healthy infant into a "doctor, lawyer, . . . yes even into beggar-man and thief."

proposed that social-behavior phenomena could be partitioned into several separable neurophysical dispositions in terms of their functions, such as pugnacity and gregariousness. Although the motivational basis for the several behavior systems has shifted over the past 70 years, the essential functional criteria for classification and analysis have remained remarkably stable (compare, for instance, McDougall's, 1908, discussion of pugnacity with contemporary descriptions of aggression). The assumption that different social response systems can be accounted for and explained relatively independently of the rest has also remained unchanged. For example, to account for the development of social preferences or sexual responses it has not seemed necessary to consider the problem of aggression, and vice versa. These are viewed as representative of relatively independent motivational systems.

Paradoxically, the problems raised by social-motivation constructs follow from what appear to have been their fundamental strengths. Two of these may be mentioned: one has to do with descriptive economy; the other with matters of methodological analyses. First, aggression has seemed attractive because of its economy. It permits diverse behaviors (across contexts, developmental stages, and species) to be considered as representative of a unitary response system or process. However, a major criticism of aggression is that it is altogether *too* economical, lumping together behaviors that are best considered separately. In their insightful discussion of the ills of child-rearing research, Yarrow, Campbell, and Burton (1968) note that once a behavior interchange or observation has been categorized as aggression, it serves to blur distinctions among the behaviors so assigned. The net effect is to obscure the analysis of what are the different antecedents for quite different behaviors. What is true of child-rearing analyses seems to hold in comparative and animal-behavior treatments as well, where a single term has been applied to injury-producing behaviors, regardless of basic differences in their functions for the individual and the species.

Another apparent attraction is methodological. The research task has been made more manageable because such constructs permit one to parcel out significant and salient acts from the stream of social activity. Once identified, the behaviors and correlated emotional states of the individual can be examined more or less independently of the context in which they occur. And this is where the second and possibly the most important problem arises. As R. R. Sears (1951) pointed out, the contributions of social and contextual events as determinants of behavior are lost by such a "monadic" strategy. This would be a minor issue for the analysis of pain-producing acts if the primary determinants of such responses were in fact internal and endogenous. But, should the behaviors be significantly controlled by the reciprocal activities of the other individual or by events in the situation or the context in which the interaction occurs, then serious problems arise. Abstraction of the behavior from the more general dyadic interchange would then serve to inhibit rather than facilitate the identification of the principal determinants of the phenomenon.

Such considerations are consistent with the view that fighting and punishment are essentially interactional concepts, referring to pain-producing acts that occur in social interchanges. It follows from a dyadic analysis that research on fighting and punishment should be concerned with the entire interaction sequence in which the behaviors occur, and not with just the most salient stimulus and response elements of the sequence. Accordingly, it has been proposed that configurations of events serve to elicit social interchanges and provide for their maintenance and synchronization, once elicited (Cairns, 1966, 1972). In this view, the behaviors of other individuals are integrated with other stimulus events in the immediate control of the interaction sequence.

Since we will later consider in some detail how the behavior of others contributes to the control of pain-producing interactions, comments are in order at this juncture on the potential relations of other major controlling events (self-produced, internal, and contextual) to fighting and punishment.

Self-produced events. In the performance of well-organized response patterns, self-generated proprioceptive and perceptual events appear to take on increasing significance. Although their contribution is necessarily modified in social responses, where the synchronization of behavior is as dependent upon events provided by others as by oneself, it would be hazardous to ignore self-produced contributions. For some social behaviors, including the stereotyped attack and defense patterns of nonhuman species, the responses are inherently organized, and species-typical in form. Such behavior sequences appear to be virtually self-maintaining once they have been initiated. Nonetheless, even for these behaviors, self-produced events obviously do not carry the entire burden of behavior integration. Stereotyped social activities, including attacks, can be facilitated or disrupted by changes in the context or in the responses of the other individual. For instance, vigorous attack sequences can be immediately suppressed in rats by high-intensity shock (Myer, 1968). And conversely, attack behavior can be facilitated by a counterreaction of lesser intensity. A weak defensive bite may lead simply to a more vigorous reciprocal attack.

Intraorganismic states. At any given point in an integrated behavior sequence, it may be assumed that the internal state of the individual is normally synchronized with the overt behavior that is performed. For some social responses, such as those involved in reproduction, the correlation is obvious. The dyadic response of intromission require preparatory states that permit erection and lordosis. It also seems reasonable to expect that the vigorous actions involved in fighting, defense, and punishment are also normally supported by particular states of arousal. Once attacks have been initiated, we can speculate that the vigorous acts themselves can serve to recruit supporting internal states and thus provide the conditions for the persistence or inhibition of the activity.

A question concerns whether such states serve to *initiate* attacks as well as reflect their presence (see Scott, 1966, 1971; Moyer, 1971). The problem seems to be how these states can be involved in behavior instigation. As Moyer has observed, the results of a wide range of manipulations of organismic states (through drugs, brain stimulation and ablation, or hormonal changes) implicate them in assertive-attack initiation. The twofold problem for a dyadic analysis of fighting and punishment will be to specify how these states may be translated into behavioral acts, and how the acts, when they occur in a social interchange, modify the responses of the other individual.

Contextual events. The context in which an interaction occurs has been repeatedly shown to be associated with the recurrence or inhibition of organized behavior patterns. One of the more important lessons that ethological research teaches us is that social responding is related to the setting in which interaction occurs. The notion of territoriality, for instance, reflects the general observation that the behavior of the animal in one geographic location differs markedly from his behavior in another. Kuo (1967), in an experimental analysis of the situational supports of fighting, makes the point dramatically. In a case of what he called Dr. Jekyl and Mr. Hyde in the dog, he showed that chows will attack cats in one setting and interact with them in an entirely peaceful and harmonious fashion in another, for example, eating and sleeping together. These apparently inconsistent behaviors are demonstrated in one and the same animal.

In overview, patterns of stimuli, as opposed to single events, appear required to support organized social responding. It seems necessary to conceptualize the controlling events as stimulus patterns because of the interactions that occur among the component events. For instance, dyadic feedback cues that occur in a reciprocal interchange elicit not only particular response sequences in the subject, but the supporting internal (i.e., "emotional") states as well. Also, changes in the context promote changes in the nature of the responses evoked in the subject and, simultaneously, alter the stimulus properties of the behavior of the other individual.

Furthermore, social activities are more than discrete units of behavior somehow glued together by equally disparate stimulus configurations. While only preliminary steps have been taken to analyze formally the organization of response patterns qua patterns (but see Restle, 1970, and Mandler, 1964), there can be no question but that social behaviors occur in definable clumps, sequences, and patterns. One of the problems of a molecular analysis of social behavior is that higher-order behavioral consistencies can be overlooked. Whatever gains are made by a precise analysis of behavior to be explained can be compromised by a failure to recognize the coherence, organization, and species-typical adaptiveness of the activity.

In brief, although an analysis of stimulus controls is essential for a developmental account, it is not sufficient. Stimulus analyses, taken alone, cannot tell us much about the initial establishment and inherent organization of the responses themselves (Bindra, 1961). For that information, it is necessary to pay attention to the developing organism: its capabilities, limitations, and species-typical characteristics. The obviousness of maturational events has perhaps belied their importance for response establishment. In a direct way, ontogenetic changes determine the physical-morphological capabilities of the young to produce noxious stimuli and to respond to them. Less direct but of potentially greater significance are maturational changes in hormonal organization, neural structure, and sensory and cognitive capabilities.

According to the developmental models of Z. Y. Kuo (1967) and T. C. Schneirla (1966), the development of response capabilities and social behavior should be viewed as "bidirectional." The bidirectionality comes about because the course of biophysical development is presumed to be determined in part by the social conditions in which the young are maintained. And the maturational and biophysical status of the young are seen as significant determinants of the behavior that it performs and evokes in social interchanges. Compare, for example, the benign outcomes of licking and gnawing by a 7-day-old puppy with the painful outcomes produced by a similar behavior when he is 70 days of age. Such "unlearned" modifications of behavior can be responsible for changing the character of the relationship from a nonpunitive to a punitive one. Stimultaneously, the hormonal states of the mother undergo modification as do the response capabilities of the other members of the litter. According to the bidirectionality hypothesis, the rate and type of biophysical changes in each member of the relationship is partly determined by the nature of the interactions that take place, and the physical changes feed back to alter the character of the relationship.

From a developmental perspective, then, the processes of social-response establishment are broader than implicated by the learning mechanisms that have been assigned the task, such as modeling, selective reinforcement, and response shaping. At the heart of the analysis should be the changing capabilities of the young themselves. If the Kuo-Schneirla proposals are correct, then response establishment and its initial organization will not likely be reduced to a single learning or biophysical mechanism. On the contrary, it should reflect the operation of multiple, semiautonomous processes. The exact contribution, say, of modeling or tactile-reactivity thresholds or adrenocortical levels to response acquisition would depend upon the specific behavior established, the age of the individual, and the species in which it is established.

To summarize, the term that has been used traditionally to characterize social-interaction sequences has been unfortunately biased. Aggression as a construct has been useful in pointing to problems but not very helpful in yielding solutions. A basic difficulty has been that the experimental procedures that it supports have not facilitated attention to the details of the relevant interactions or to the ways that the behaviors of each individual in a sequence serve to elicit, maintain, or inhibit noxious and painful actions of the other individual.

An essential concern of a developmental analysis is the identification of the particular ways in which maturational changes are bidirectionally interlaced with experiential events. Hardly any contemporary behavioral theory would deny that a synthesis must occur. A nontrivial difference is that the developmental orientation is necessarily committed to the task of unraveling how the integration takes place. In the light of that commitment, we will turn now to some recent attempts to trace the establishment of fighting and punishment.

THE DEVELOPMENT OF VIOLENT MICE

The experimental analysis of fighting is a relatively recent pursuit for psychologists. Nonetheless, the work that has been completed implicates a broad range of biophysical and situational factors. The variables that have been shown to be relevant range from genetic (King, 1957a; Lagerspetz, Tirri, & Lagerspetz, 1968) and biochemical (Edwards, 1968; Fox & Snyder, 1969; Welch, 1967; Welch & Welch, 1971) to contextual (Archer, 1968; Cairns & Nakelski, 1970) and experiential (Banerjee, 1970; Denenberg, 1971; Kahn, 1951; Scott, 1958).

Due to the pioneering work and catalytic influence of J. P. Scott and his co-workers at the Jackson Laboratory, a reasonably standard set of procedures has been developed for the study of fighting and related phenomena in mice (see Scott, 1958, 1966). Because of the prior information and procedures, and since fighting is a prepotent behavior for this species, it appeared to be a good candidate for a detailed ontogenetic analysis. A programmatic study of the development of relevant interactions in at least one species should serve to clarify some of the basic ways in which biophysical events and experience interact.

Is Training Necessary?

Our research on fighting in mice had an inauspicious beginning. Despite their reputation for fighting, animals in our laboratory appeared to get on rather well with each other. More accurately, they virtually ignored each other in the test setting. This outcome was puzzling, since we had followed training procedures described by previous workers (Scott, 1958). The actual training is an approximations procedure, where the "trainee" is given controlled doses of fighting experience. The recruits or trainees in this case were male C57BL/10 mice (a pigmented inbred strain of the common house mouse, *Mus musculus*). In the first stage, a docile, defenseless male conspecific was literally "dangled" by the tail in front of the mouse-in-training. When the trainee approached, the dangled one was dragged along and pulled away or, in some instances, bumped against the training subject. The exploratory behavior of the subject is supposed to become increasingly more vigorous, erupting into actual biting or attacking within the first 2 or 3 days of training. From there the recruit is graduated to unrestricted interactions with a submissive sparring partner. Following a few days of this experience, where the interaction is terminated at the beginning of an attack, the subject is ready to be tested against other untrained or trained mice.

The problem was that the mice that we attempted to train were dropouts in the first stage. They showed little inclination to approach the dangled animal, much less attack him. After considerable trial and error, it became clear that we had omitted an important preliminary step: we had failed to isolate the animals prior to the training proper. The animals had been kept together in small groups prior to the introduction of the training procedures and reintroduced to their normal living group following the manipulation. When this oversight was corrected, a marked change in behavior was observed. If the subject was isolated 4 or 5 weeks before the onset of training, the training proceeded rapidly and successfully.

To what extent is training or specific experience in fighting necessary for the establishment of fighting? Since the mice were readily trained following isolation and not trainable without it, the question arises as to what role isolation per se plays in the process. It was unclear whether there is a significant interaction between rearing conditions and training procedures, as Kuo (1960) found in the grey quail, or whether training is necessary at all. The matter seemed to be appropriate for ontogenetic analysis, since animals could be separated from each other as weanlings, before fighting or attack experiences.

Two essentially parallel experimental-rearing studies were completed (Cairns & Milakovich, 1972; Milakovich, 1970). Since neither study has yet been published, some description of the procedure will be given. All animals were male. In each study, half of the 60 subjects were assigned shortly after weaning to a condition of relative isolation and the remainder were maintained in small groups of 5 animals per group. Isolation in this case means only that the subjects were kept in separate compartments and were not permitted to interact or see each other. They were, however, maintained in the same colony room, and they thus shared the same general odors, illumination, feeding practices, and noises as the total colony.

After 25 additional days, the isolation-reared and group-reared conditions were each subdivided into three training conditions, yielding a 2 × 3 factorial design. The three training conditions were as follows: (a) One set of groups was given explicit fighting training, (b) another set was permitted to interact with another mouse each day, but given no explicit training, and (c) a final set of groups was given neither training nor interaction experience. The actual training followed the outline described above: 3 days of exposure to a submissive and dangled target animal followed by 7 days of controlled attack experience. Following a 2-day respite, all subjects were then tested for 2 days in a standard test series. Mice in the other conditions were given no explicit training. Those mice in the interaction conditions were permitted to interact with another animal for 3 minutes each of the 10 "training" days, and those in the no-training, no-interaction condition were simply placed alone into the test apparatus for 3 minutes a day over that period.

The test condition was the same as we described earlier (Cairns & Nakelski, 1971). Briefly, it involved placing the subject into a compartment identical to the home compartment, except that it was covered with a Plexiglas top and divided into two sections by a guillotine door. After 5 minutes in the one side of the apparatus, the door was removed and the subject was exposed to another animal. In all conditions, the "other" animal was a previously untested male mouse maintained in a group-rearing circumstance until the time of testing. The tests were repeated the next day. On each occasion, the subject was permitted to interact with a group-reared animal for 5 minutes.

The results of the first study, in which C57BL/10 animals were used, were clear-cut. We were here concerned with simply whether or not fighting occurred, and how soon and how frequently. The data indicate a primary effect of rearing condition and virtually no effect of training. Shown in Figure 1 are the results of the latency measure analysis. When the other traditional measures are used (duration of fighting, attack frequency), the same results are obtained.

Further analysis of what happened during the training period indicates that to-be-trained group-reared subjects simply failed to approach and vigorously groom the dangled animal. Isolated animals, whether trained or not, pursued and vigorously explored their partners. In this regard, it should be noted that in all of the comparisons in the initial study, the only one which differentiated between the isolated groups was "latency to attack" on the first of the 2 days of testing. The trained and previously exposed mice tended to attack sooner than did the nontrained, nonexposed isolates. This difference was not stable, however, and it disappeared by the second day of testing. One 5-minute exposure was sufficient to equate all isolated groups, regardless of their training condition.

In view of the diverse results that have been obtained when different mouse strains are used (e.g., Denenberg, 1971), we thought it prudent to carry out parallel replication experiments to see if the same results held up for a different strain. The males of the strain selected (ICR, an albino mouse) are somewhat larger and tend to

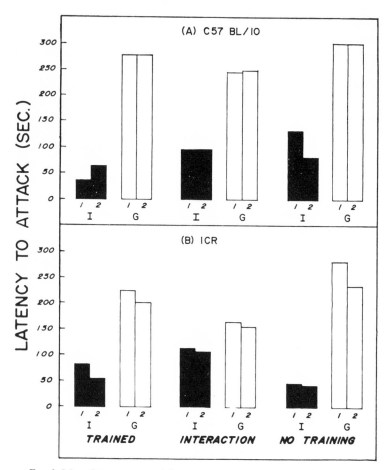

Fig. 1. Mean latency to attack in two test sessions as a function of rearing condition (isolation = shaded; group rearing = unshaded) and training condition. The "target" animal in each instance was a naive animal taken from a group-rearing compartment. Each test was terminated at 300 seconds regardless of whether the animals had begun to attack. The results of the C57BL/10 experiment and the ICR experiments are plotted separately (n = 10 in each subcondition). Statistical analyses indicate a strong effect of rearing (F = 18.92, $p < .001$) in both groups. (From Cairns & Milakovich, 1972.)

fight more vigorously and frequently than do the C57BL/10 animals. They also consistently defeated the C57BL/10 in individual cross-specific pairings. However, the method of rearing was again found to be the primary main effect (Figure 1). The untrained, nonexposed isolated ICR males attacked their test partner as rapidly as did trained isolates, even on the first day of testing. In addition, there was apparently an effect of training-exposure for group-maintained animals. This effect is possibly due to the fact that the animals against which the training was given (other group-reared ICR) sometimes initiated attacks against the subject-in-training. This behavior, in turn, elicited reciprocal fighting and a subsequent tendency to inhibit attacks among some isolates.

To the question, Is training necessary for the establishment of fighting in mice? the answer must be clearly negative. No interaction or training whatsoever is required if the animals had been previously maintained alone (see also Banerjee, 1970; Welch, 1967; Welch & Welch, 1971).

If the findings are simply viewed in terms of a learning-instinctive dichotomy, the social-learning interpretation of fighting establishment obviously loses ground. But a question can be raised as to how much progress is made by merely labeling the behavior as "unlearned," "species-typical," or "instinctive." As Hinde (1970) has observed, an inherent weakness of a dichotomous categorization is that it is not addressed to the actual processes by which the behavior comes about. An assignment of a given behavior pattern to nature or nurture does not substitute for precise information about the effective mechanisms underlying it, especially when they necessarily involve the interlacing of biophysical and experiential factors. Accordingly, it is necessary to identify the specific differences between isolated and nonisolated animals and to find how these differences develop under different conditions of rearing.

Dyadic Contributions to Fighting

In keeping with the proposal that fighting is only one salient aspect of the ongoing interaction, the next task was to determine precisely how isolation rearing biased the dyadic interchange. For this purpose, a system of making continuous observations of interaction sequences was developed (Cairns & Nakelski, 1970, 1971). Using a letter coding scheme, the first dyadic response is recorded, along with the reaction by the other animal. Only interactional events are recorded. Each 5 seconds the system is reset and a new observation period begins. The behavioral record permits the plotting of reciprocal interaction sequences, including information about the initiating agent, the outcome of the interaction, and the response probabilities for any given unit of behavior. Although the coding scheme is initially demanding for the observer, the inter-rater reliabilities of the individual categories are sufficiently high (median $r = .92$) to permit between-category and sequential analyses. In the course of the work, direct observations have been supplemented by high-speed 16-mm movie films (45 to 64 frames per sec.), stop-action photography ($\frac{1}{500}$ to $\frac{1}{2000}$ sec. exposure), and video-tape visual and sound recording.

Given the refined analysis that the dyadic coding system permits, certain basic differences in response dispositions and interaction are observed between isolation-reared and nonisolated mice. Since this study was reported recently (Cairns & Nakelski, 1971, Exp. 1), only a brief account of the procedures and findings is required. The comparisons were made between 30 isolated and 30 nonisolated C57BL/10 male mice, tested in the above situation for 10 minutes, but without the preceding "training" or "control" exposures to the apparatus. For the present purposes, it is of considerable interest to observe that the animals assigned to the two different conditions differed markedly in their nonfighting behavior toward the test animal.

Two major differences in dyadic orientation between isolated and nonisolated animals are obtained:

1. The isolated animals are more likely to initiate interactions than are the group-reared animals. This includes interactions of all sorts, such as sniffing, nosing the anogenital region, grooming, climbing upon, and the like (Figure 2). When only the more vigorous interactions are considered, such as rough grooming of the other animal, there is little overlap between the two groups of animals.

2. The animals differ in their reactions to the dyadic initiations of the other. Isolation-reared animals are extremely reactive. Even the mildest stimulation by the test partner, such as species-typical investigatory sniffing, can elicit an immediate startle or freezing

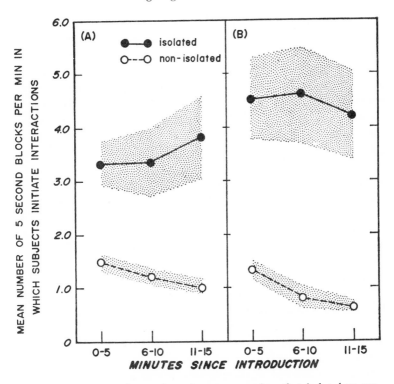

Fig. 2. The above figures show the mean occasions that isolated or non-isolated subjects initiated dyadic interactions in the test circumstance. (A) shows the results of the first test series (after 5 weeks in isolation or group rearing) and (B) shows the results of the second test series (after 10 weeks in isolation). (From Cairns & Nakelski, 1971.)

response in isolation-reared animals. The startle response is characterized by a sharp withdrawal, and jerking away. In other instances, the behavior is a freezing in a catatoniclike state, with eye-closing. In either case, there is a marked effect in that ongoing response patterns are disrupted, and the previously isolated animal is highly responsive to stimulation of the other individual. Group-maintained C57 mice, on the other hand, typically show little or no change in ongoing activity when sniffed or otherwise mildly stimulated by the other animal.

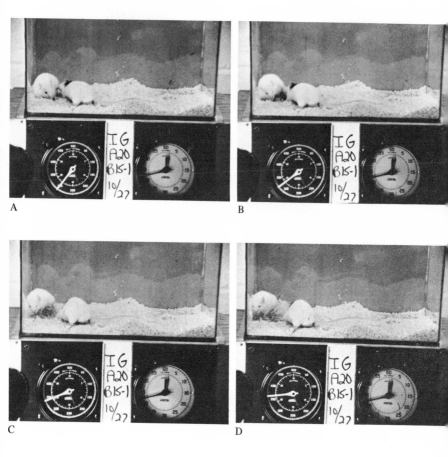

PLATE 1. Series of photographs showing the startle response of previously isolated ICR male following 5 weeks of isolation (beginning at 25 days of age). The isolated mouse is unmarked; the group-reared animal is marked with black dye. Time between frames shown is 18 to 22 milliseconds (millisecond clock in lower left). Species-typical sniffing by group-reared animal (A), followed by reflexive withdrawal by the isolate (B to D), and counterwithdrawal by the group-reared subject (C and D).

Evidence for this "hyperreactivity" effect was first obtained from the behavior coding scheme, where the number of *W*, or withdrawal-startle, responses in the first 60 seconds of interaction was markedly higher for the previously isolated animals than for the group-maintained ones. The hyperreactivity was quite pronounced and can be readily detected by naive observers in classroom demonstrations. A more precise picture of the response is provided by high-speed films, as shown in Plate 1.[3]

Since the differences in reactivity were so pronounced, it should be possible to study the phenomenon in a nonsocial setting as well. The most promising technique has involved testing the animal on a small stabilimeter, then introducing a light tap on the hind quarters with a cotton swab or air puff. The procedure was originally intended to mimic the force and tactile characteristics of conspecific social stimulation. In the standard Reactivity to Tactile Stimulus procedure (RTS), the stimulus is introduced on six occasions, with an interstimulus interval of 15 to 60 seconds. The stabilimeter floor is large enough (20 × 20 cm.) to permit an assessment of open-field activity prior to the initial stimulation and between stimuli. The stabilimeter floor itself is floated on four sensitive springs. The transducer is an electrical magnet located beneath the base of the apparatus and is responsive to minute changes in floor positions in three dimensions. Resultant variations in electrical current are amplified through a recording oscilloscope, then graphed.

The differences in reactivity to nonsocial tactile stimuli were in line with expectation: there was virtually no overlap between group-maintained and isolated mice (Figure 3). In addition, the differences were in terms of *reactivity*, not *activity*. That is, open-field measures of locomotion show only modest, if any, differences in activity, a finding supported by an analysis of pre- and poststimulus activity patterns in the test apparatus.

Dyadic Escalation and Reciprocal Feedback Stimulation

On the basis of these observations, we speculated that the initial establishment of fighting or mutual attack in isolated animals

3. The advice and assistance of Richard Bundy, Director of Athletic Photography at Indiana University, is gratefully acknowledged in the filming and processing of the films.

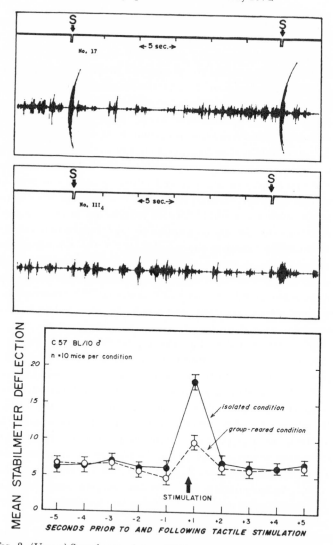

Fig. 3. (Upper) Sample records from RTS measures, with animal No. 17 from an isolation condition, and animal No. III₄ from a group-rearing condition. "S" indicates delivery of tactile stimulus.

(Lower) Second-by-second summary of activity prior to and following tactile stimulation. The only reliable difference between points occurred in the interval immediately following stimulation ($t = 4.11$; $df = 18$; $p < .001$).

was the outcome of an escalating dyadic interchange. The orienting and approach behavior of the isolated animal ensures that he will maintain a close proximity to the test partner, and his hyper-reactivity predisposes him to overrespond to any reciprocal advance by the other animal. Given these two response propensities in a dyadic interchange, the previously isolated animal becomes entrapped in an increasingly more vigorous interchange. Observations of the C57BL/10 animals supported this interpretation. First, attacks do not usually occur immediately. The fighting itself appeared to be typically preceded by increasingly vigorous activity, including pulling at the fur of the other, intense sniffing, and climbing upon and sometimes mounting the other. Second, the outbreak of fighting was associated typically with other indications of heightened arousal, including piloerection, jumpiness, eye-squinting, and heightened reactivity. It was unclear whether the stimulation of the subject evoked a counterresponse of biting in the grouped animal and went from there to full-fledged combat or, alternatively, whether the rough-grooming-associated arousal states provided the occasion for increasingly more vigorous initiations by the isolated animals themselves.

What seemed called for was a procedure to disentangle the effects of the feedback stimuli of the "other" from self-produced events. If the escalation account is correct, then it should be possible to reduce the probability of the isolate-object interaction evolving into attacks by reducing the reactivity or activity of one of the two participants. One direct way to accomplish this trick would be to drug the isolated animal. As several studies indicate, such a manipulation does indeed reduce the probability of fighting (see Moyer, 1971; Valzelli, Giacalone, & Garrattini, 1967). The interpretation of many pharmacological studies is unclear, however. The problem is that the drugged animal may simply be too sedated or otherwise impaired to execute a successful attack. A more interesting, and more demanding, test of the hypothesis would involve changing the reactive characteristics of the "target" or "victim." Presumably a diminished feedback from the vigorous stimulation would provide fewer of the cues that operate to support continued exploration and increased arousal levels.

In the relevant experiment (Cairns & Scholz, 1972a), target

animals were given a control saline injection, or 4, 8, or 16 mg/kg injections of chlorpromazine. Another group of target animals was given a lethal injection of Nembutal. The isolated animal itself was not drugged. A sequential dyadic plot was made of the interactions that occurred between the two animals in the test setting. To be consistent with the dyadic escalation account, the target animals that were least reactive to the behaviors initiated by the isolated animals should also be the least likely to evoke an attack.

The results provided reasonable support for the feedback-stimulation idea (Figure 4). There was a very close relationship between the probability of attack and the activity-reactivity level of the target animal. All subjects in the saline condition attacked their partners at least once, and none of the animals tested against a completely inactive animal (the lethal-dose group) attacked. There were no differences in the initial tendency of the isolated animals to explore their test partners, in that all objects regardless of activity level were initially explored. What did differentiate the conditions was the tendency for the exploration to escalate to the point of vigorously grooming, biting, or attacking the target animal.

Observations of the responses of isolated subjects to the virtually immobilized target animal in the 16 mg/kg condition suggest why so few attacks occurred in that condition. The grooming and exploration activity of the previously isolated animal did indeed involve deeper and deeper penetration, but not to the point of breaking the skin or of resembling an attack in terms of the sheer vigor and intensity of the behavior. Nonetheless, had the target animal been capable of responding, such exploration would have been sufficient to provoke sharp withdrawal, escape, or counter-stimulation. In any case, the test animal would have likely become involved in even more vigorous and damaging exploration.

As far as these observations go, they are consistent with the dyadic escalation account. There was a direct and immediate relationship between the extent to which the target animals recip-rocated or responded actively to the dyadic stimulation. Even though they had not been trained or given prior experience in fighting, attacks evolved in the short (10 min.) session in all instances where the target animal had not been drugged. Events internal to

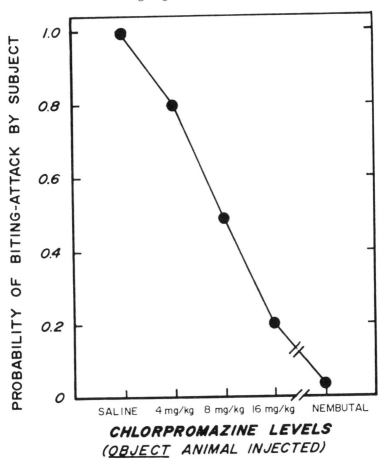

FIG. 4. Probability of attacking target animal as a function of the activity-reactivity of the target animal, n = 10 per condition $F = 13.49$, $df. = 4/45$, $p < .001$. (From Cairns & Scholz, 1972a.)

the interaction sequence itself appear to be sufficient to elicit and support attack behavior. "Aggression" was reduced by a kind of milieu therapy: changing not the "aggressor," but the ones with whom he interacts.

A follow-up of the last study indicates that the dyadic reactions of the other individual are less critical for the recurrence of attacks

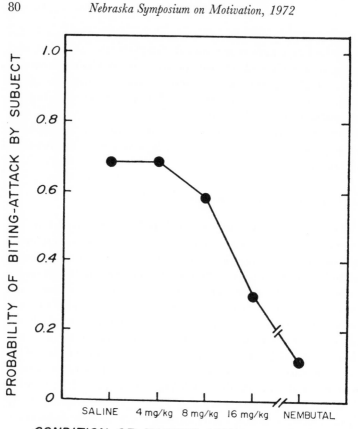

Fig. 5. Probability of attacking inactive target animal in second test as a function of the activity-reactivity of target animal in the first test, n = 10 per condition $F = 3.19$, $df = 4/45$, $p < .05$. (From Cairns & Scholz, 1972a.)

than they are for its initial establishment. After the test series, all subjects of the preceding experiment were returned to their original isolation conditions. One week later they were retested under similar conditions, except on the second test all of the target animals were totally nonresponsive (i.e., dead). Even though the dyadic reactivity of the other was in most cases drastically changed, the behavior of the subjects in the second test closely paralleled their behavior in the first (Figure 5). Subjects that had been induced to attack initially tended to viciously and repeatedly attack the entirely nonresponsive target animal. Similarly, those subjects that had not attacked initially tended not to initiate attacks in the second series. A single exposure was sufficient to produce carry-over effects of both sorts. Attack behaviors, once elicited, appear to be rapidly conditioned to the social-contextual configurations in which they have occurred. In brief, the dyadic events that were originally necessary for the establishment of the behavior were not required for its recurrence and generalization.

The Development of Interspecific Attacks

The fact that previously isolated ICR males reacted to the movement and behavior initiation of the normally responsive group-maintained conspecific males with an increase in the intensity of stimulation raised the question of whether the same effect would be obtained with other stimulus objects. This is essentially the question of the effect of the nature of the stimulus. From the perspective of a dyadic analysis, the type of object with which the subject is paired will inevitably influence the nature of the interaction that develops and the ones that recur. Presumably one of the basic differences between intraspecific and interspecific attacks would be in the events that each participant provides the other individual. However, there are also factors that make for similarity of behavior, regardless of object animal. These include the species-typical organization of attack and defense behaviors. Moreover, in the case of isolation rearing, it seems likely that even minimal reactions of the other organism would be sufficient to produce heightened states in the isolation animal and intensification of the interchange.

To determine whether object animals other than unfamiliar conspecific males would be sufficient to escalate to an attack, isolated ICR males were tested in an interspecific condition (Cairns & Scholz, 1972b). In this case, the "other" was an adult Sprague-Dawley rat, raised from weaning with an ICR cohabitant. Because of its own prior exposure and interaction with mice, the rat responded initially in a reasonably amiable fashion, sniffing and approaching the previously isolated ICR male. The isolated animals, on the

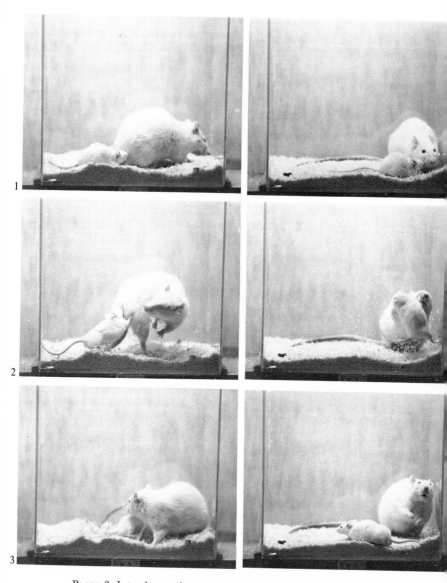

PLATE 2. Interchanges between mice kept in isolation and Sprague-Dawley rats reared from weaning with mice. The interval between each set of three frames is approximately 510 milliseconds.

other hand, responded to the investigative acts of the rat in a typically hyperreactive fashion (Plate 2). The ICR isolate males initiated attacks in 56% ($\frac{9}{16}$) of the cases, where animals reared with other mice initiated attacks in 19% of the pairings ($\frac{3}{16}$), and mice from a rat-mouse rearing initiated attacks in only 6% of the tests ($\frac{1}{16}$) (Cairns & Scholz, 1972b; see also Lagerspetz & Heino, 1970).

Apart from the curious "mighty-mouse" effect produced by isolation rearing, the data are of interest because of their relevance to the question of whether *interspecific* "aggression" is different from the *intraspecific* form. In this instance, using animals that had both experienced atypical rearing, it appears that at least some common elements were involved in supporting attacks toward same-species and alien-species targets. Observations suggest, moreover, that the particular forms of the attacks were adapted to the stimulus configuration provided by the target animal. The commonalities and differences between prey killing, intraspecific fighting, and interspecific attacks can possibly be illuminated by more detailed accounts of the differential contribution of the "other."

Circadian Rhythm and Interaction Initiation

Another test of the dyadic proposal being discussed here deserves comment, partly because of its methodological implications (Cairns, Scholz, & Einsiedel, 1972). We reasoned that if it was possible to change the character of the dyadic interchange by pharmacological manipulations, then it may be possible to modify the relationship by capitalizing on endogenous variations in activity. For this analysis, 40 ICR mice were tested at different stages of their day-night cycle. Half of the animals in all conditions were kept on a day-night circadian cycle, and the remainder were on a night-day cycle. Counterbalancing for the room in which the animals were maintained, a 2×2 factorial test series was conducted, where isolated ICR males in their active (night) phase were tested against group-reared animals in their active phase; active isolated versus inactive group-reared; inactive isolated versus active group-reared; and inactive isolated versus inactive group-reared.

When both animals were in the active phase, the probability of dyadic initiation, likelihood of attack, and attack speed was the greatest. Conversely, when they were both in the inactive phase, they were less likely to initiate interactions and attack. The differences were statistically reliable only in comparisons between the two extreme groups (i.e., active-active versus inactive-inactive). Nonetheless, the methodological lesson seems obvious. The differences were attenuated at the time most behavioral experiments are performed, that is, the experimenter's daytime. Oversights in the control of this ubiquitous and accessible variable can obscure the analysis of nonsocial as well as social processes. In the present case, the circadian influence on dyadic activity and reactivity was about as expected: direct and reliable but not overwhelming.

Contextual Determinants of Dyadic Initiation

The setting in which the interaction takes place is also a significant determinant of its course and outcome. In some contexts, isolation is *not* a necessary precondition for the initiation and establishment of fighting. The likelihood of initiating vigorous dyadic stimulation appears to be a direct function of the salience of the other animal relative to the setting in which the interaction occurs. The relevant phenomena include:

1. *Home compartment behavior* (*"territoriality"*). If an unfamiliar animal is introduced into the home compartment of group animals, the residents vigorously sniff, investigate (e.g., climb upon, groom, mount) the new animal. Not infrequently, the dyadic intragroup stimulation escalates to fighting, with attacks initiated by the group-reared residents (Cairns & Nakelski, 1970).

2. *Relative novelty of the other individual.* Vigorous exploration and stimulation is not confined to unfamiliar conspecifics. When a member of the resident group itself is removed, then replaced 5 minutes later, the animal is treated as if he were a stranger. In one study, the dyadic intragroup stimulation produced by the removal-replacement operation led to fighting in over 50% of the observations (Cairns & Nakelski, 1970, Exp. 1, Figure 6).

3. *Context disruption.* Manipulations that serve to enhance the probability of mutual stimulation within the group—such as changing

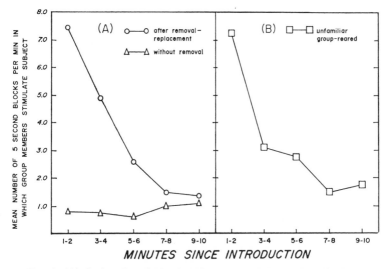

FIG. 6. (A) depicts the relationships between time since reintroduction of a resident animal and the number of social behaviors initiated by other residents of the group. In the removal-replacement manipulation, the animal had been removed for a 5-minute period. (B) shows the relationship between time since introduction and the number of social behaviors initiated by group members toward an unfamiliar group-reared animal. (From Cairns & Nakelski, 1970.)

the bedding material or transferring animals to a new setting—reliably serve to trigger heightened intragroup stimulation and fighting (unpublished observations in our laboratory; Archer, 1968).

4. *Adaptation.* A standard procedure adopted in studies of aggression in mice has been to introduce subjects to the test compartment for a brief (e.g., 5-min.) period for 1 to 3 days preceding the test in the neutral compartment. The actual test is normally preceded by 3-to-5-min. "adaptation." Omission of this prior exposure serves to diminish the probability of interaction initiation and escalation.

Such observations are consistent with the empirical generalization that the probability of an attack is increased by manipulations that elicit an increase in the frequency and amplitude of dyadic activity among male mice, isolated or not. Included in such manipulations is the presentation of a relatively novel "other": an animal that is distinctive by virtue of its odor, activity, or appearance. Events that diminish the unfamiliarity of the other animal relative to other events in the environment, or reduce the capabilities of the subject to discriminate whether or not he is unfamiliar, also diminish intense exploratory behavior and consequent attacks (e.g., Ropartz, 1968). In a "neutral" compartment, group-reared animals do not explore the stranger, but investigate the new surroundings instead. For isolation-reared mice, however, virtually any other male conspecific is highly salient, regardless of context. Even when placed in the home compartment of the "other," the isolate will vigorously investigate the resident on his own "territory." The heightened exploratory behavior and spiraling levels of mutual arousal follow.

Sequential analyses leave little doubt but that chronic irritability and hyperreactivity are significant factors in the kinds of interchanges that develop, even though they are not necessary preconditions for the occurrence of attacks. The hyperreactivity of the subject apparently can influence the interchange in three different ways: (a) through lowering the threshold of the subject for initiating an intense counterresponse toward the other animal, (b) through eliciting heightened exploration and more intense dyadic activity by the other animal, and (c) through decreasing the probability of mutual interchange because the subject consistently withdraws from the other individual, or is frozen or immobilized by stimulation. The last outcome occurs when the subject is so highly reactive that approach behavior is inhibited, and the latency of attack is paradoxically increased by extended isolation (see King, 1957b; King & Gurney, 1954). Whether the hyperreactivity will be translated into mutual attacks and fighting in the test setting seems dependent upon the level of chronic reactivity produced and upon the events that occur in the test circumstances. In short, hyperreactivity is an organismic state; fighting is a dyadic one. The relationship between the two is not invariant: it depends upon both the responsivity of the other and the context in which the interchange occurs.

Why Does Isolation Increase the Probability of Fighting?

Male mice, when maintained alone, tend to become involved in interactions that eventuate in fighting. The analysis of dyadic sequences indicates, further, that the isolate differs in two major respects: (a) the tendency to initiate interactions, especially vigorous ones, and (b) its reactivity to stimulation. We will turn now to the events that occur during the period of isolation or group rearing to determine how these differences were produced.

Our principal focus was upon the interactions of animals in the group-rearing compartments. With Schneirla (1966), we felt that it was necessary to establish precisely what the animals were exposed to during ontogeny in order to have an adequate basis for understanding the "deprivation" condition. In this case, "normal" group rearing can be viewed as an experimental condition. Such information is necessary in order to establish precisely what the "deprived" animal is deprived of. We were initially interested in evaluating the hypothesis that specific encounters in the group compartment served to inhibit subsequent fighting. Two types of response-inhibition hypotheses seemed relevant. For one, animals kept in groups could learn to avoid behaviors that elicited attacks from others. The mechanism could be an avoidance-conditioning process, whereby the young animal learns to avoid performing responses which elicit noxious responses from the other. A second possibility that has been proposed is learning-not-to-fight by the development of competing responses. Group-maintained animals may develop a range of competing responses, such as sniffing, grooming, and the like, that compete with attack-oriented behaviors. An interpretation cast in terms of such specific learning experiences can be contrasted with a more general sensory-habituation hypothesis. In the latter view, one of the principal effects of group maintenance would be to habituate the young animal to the characteristics (tactile, olfactory, auditory, and visual) of others of its kind.

A preliminary evaluation of these possibilities requires an account of what in fact happens in group rearing. In a representative study (Cairns & Nakelski, 1971, Exp. 2), groups of C57BL/10 male mice were observed twice daily, 30 minutes per observation, one of which was in the active and the other in the inactive period. They were kept in transparent cages so as to permit observations while they remained on the laboratory shelf. All instances of fighting-biting were recorded in rapid scans.

At the time, and in subsequent replications, we were surprised to find the low incidence of fighting in the home compartment of the C57BL/10 mice. The incidence of fighting in this strain was .06 attacks per daily half-hour observation period.[4] Nor did they, in contrast with immature rats, spend much time in play-fighting and mutual grooming. Such observations were something of a disappointment for either specific social-learning hypothesis, in that an uncomplicated interpretation of the competing-response proposal would seem to require the establishment of explicit attack-competing behaviors, and the avoidance-conditioning hypothesis a greater incidence of fighting than was observed. But the observations can scarcely be viewed a critical test of either hypothesis, especially in the light of the disparity between the incidence of fighting (and play-fighting) in ICR and C57BL/10 groups.

What was of more interest was the interactive behaviors that did occur. Observation of the animals, both C57BL/10 and ICR groups, indicated that they spend a great deal of time in close body contact. It was very close indeed, for the animals characteristically were heaped together in one corner of the compartment. The arrangement was an orderly linear alignment during the very early stages of life, and less orderly heaps later on. The behavior is not unfamiliar to those who have watched mammalian young, especially species that give birth to multiple offspring. The animals characteristically crawl over, and through, the heap, but typically maintain close contact with each other (Plate 3). The effect held regardless of the size of the compartments, which ranged from 494 cm² to 2,581 cm².

Why do the young clump? Insofar as explanations have been offered, (e.g., Barnett, 1963; Soulairac, 1952; Welker, 1959) the phenomenon has been variously linked to the poikilothermia of infant mammals, to the inherent need for physical contact, or to the carry-over effects of prenatal maintenance conditions. Our observations of mice and Welker's work with neonatal puppies indicate

4. In subsequent observations, it was found that the incidence of such home-compartment fighting among ICR male groups observed under similar conditions was much higher (in one study, 1.04 attacks per daily half-hour observation period). Also in contrast with the C57BL/10, there was considerable play-fighting from weaning to maturity in the ICR groups. Some implications of this higher base-rate of group fighting are commented upon later in this paper.

PLATE 3. Typical "clumping" observed in groups of five ICR male mice of approximately weaning age (24 days). Floor dimensions of compartments were 17.7 × 27.9 cm.

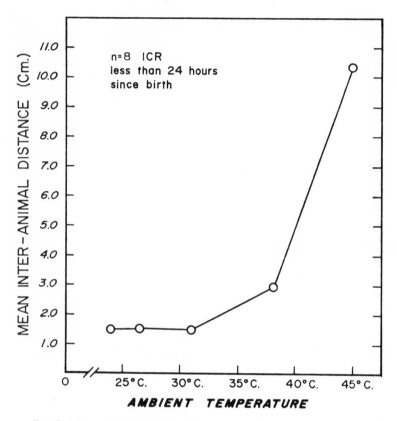

Fɪɢ. 7. Mean distance between ICR neonates (less than 24 hours of age) as a function of ambient temperature.

that ambient temperature is one determinant of clumping and dispersion. Even when the animals were less than 24 hours of age, dispersion from others was produced by gradually raising the ambient temperature from 24°C to 35°C (Figure 7, Plate 4). Placement in a progressively cooler environment produced heightened activity, but no dispersion. The movement was toward the center of the heap, not away from it, as in the case of heat induction. Of course, remaining in, or on, the heap is not exclusively under the control of the young animal. Maternal retrieval and nest-building behavior, which is determined in part by the mother's

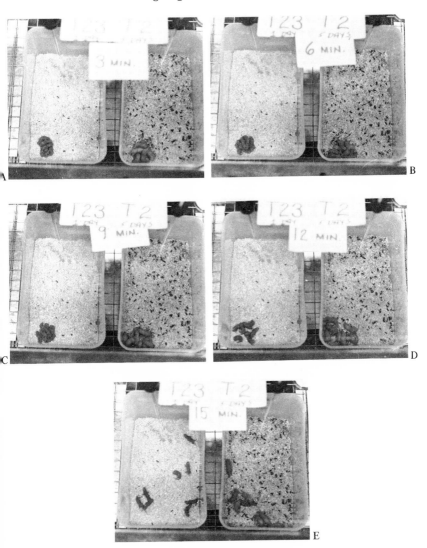

PLATE 4. Series of photographs showing the effects of gradual increases in temperature upon the mean interanimal distance of ICR neonates (less than 24 hours and 5 days of age). The ambient temperature in centigrade for each compartment, T23 and T2, respectively: (A) 24.0, 24.0; (B) 26.5, 26.0; (C) 31.0, 29.0; (D) 38.0, 33.5; (E) 45.0, 39.0.

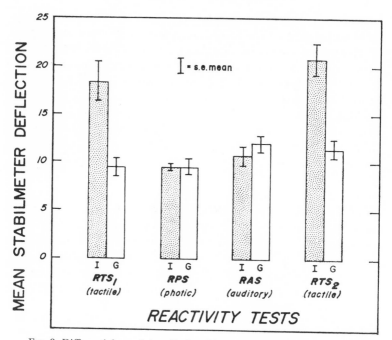

Fig. 8. Differential reactivity of isolated (I) and group-reared (G) C57BL/10 animals as a function of sensory modality. Only the reaction to tactile stimuli (RTS$_1$ and RTS$_2$) proved to be statistically reliable.

own propensities to conserve bodily warmth, indicate that the heaping is not supported solely by the activity of the young.

Whatever the effective mechanism in maintaining the close physical proximity and contact, the observations indicate that both C57 and ICR mice maintain the behavior up to and through maturity, if provided the opportunity. It seems entirely plausible, then, to expect that the diminished reactivity to tactile stimuli reflects this recurrent exposure to the cutaneous stimulation from cohabitants. The animals may have, in effect, been "tamed," or habituated each other to tactile stimulation. Hence when they are later exposed to such events, either from another animal or from the experimenter, the event is neither novel nor unique. For the previously isolated animal, it is both.

A question arises as to whether the effects were general—across sensory modalities and response systems—or relatively specific to the stimulus events from which the animals were deprived. Since all mice were housed in the same large colony room—hence exposed to the same patterns of auditory and photic stimulation—it seems reasonable to expect that the heightened reactivity would be restricted to the somatosensory modality. This possibility was tested by exposing isolated and group-reared animals in weekly tests to the tactile stimulus, a flashing stroboscope, an electronically simulated pistol shot of 100 dB, and a second tactile stimulation. The tests were conducted on the stabilimeter described earlier, with animals that had been isolated or group-reared for 8 months. The data indicate that the differential reactivity is most easily detected in the cutaneous modality, at least in the C57BL/10 (Figure 8). A replication of this experiment for ICR males yielded the same results (i.e., differentiation only in somatosensory reactivity). The specificity of the isolation effects should be a signal for caution for nonspecific biochemical explanations of the phenomenon (e.g., Welch, 1967; Welch & Welch, 1971; see Anton, Schwartz, & Kramer, 1968).

How Soon and How Long: A Critical Period for Isolation?

The question of whether there is a critical period for early social experience and fighting has been frequently raised. The matter has proved to be as difficult to evaluate empirically as it has seemed attractive theoretically. The problems arise because of the limitations inherent in using age as a principal independent variable. One type of design that should be useful in plotting the interaction between age of isolation and duration of isolation would be a factorial which manipulates these two variables simultaneously. In one such parametric analysis, independent groups of ICR males (10 per group) were isolated at one of five ages (21, 28, 35, 56, and 84 days) and kept in isolation for different periods (0, 1, 4, 16, and 64 days) prior to being tested in the usual dyadic setting (Cairns, Midlam, & Scholz, 1972).

The results of the interaction analysis and attack measures are shown in the next figure (Figure 9). Regardless of age of isolation, the animals became increasingly more reactive to conspecific partners as a direct function of the length of isolation, and the

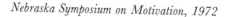

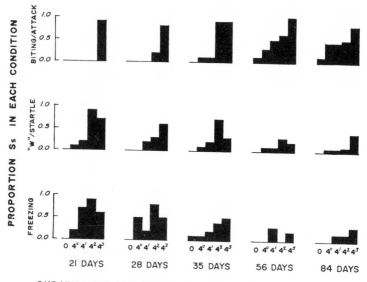

Fig. 9. Attacking, hyperreactivity, and freezing shown by subjects in the dyadic test circumstance as a function of the duration of isolation and age at which the animal was first isolated. Duration is indicated in days (0, 1, 4, 16, and 64), as is the age at which the animal was first isolated (21, 28, 35, 56, and 84). Each subgraph in the figure represents the data from 50 ICR male mice (10 per bar), except for the graphs of the 84-day conditions, which summarize the data from 80 different animals (20 animals each at 4^0, 4^1, and 4^2). Note that scores of 0 are shown as a line.

reactivity, in turn, was roughly correlated with an increased probability of attack. Nonetheless, the age of initial isolation had an effect upon the magnitude of the effects produced. Those ICR males isolated at the weaning stage for 64 days tended to be more hyperreactive than those initially isolated following sexual maturity (i.e., at 56 and 84 days of age). In addition, a shorter period of isolation was required at maturity to heighten the probability of attack than was necessary early. Even a brief (i.e., 1-to-4-day) isolation for mature animals was sufficient to produce animals that would attack others in the neutral test setting. In the case of the older ICR males —who had fought in the home compartments prior to isolation—the effects of isolation were confounded with the effects of earlier fighting. Further, at least part of the age-isolation interaction in attack initiation seemed due to the incapability of the younger animals to initiate attacks or vigorous interchanges during the early stages of isolation. Precisely what other response or structural components are necessary in the younger animals were not ascertained. It seems plausible that the reactivity will not be translated into attacks and biting until certain hormonal or morphological conditions are met. In this regard, it should be observed that even the youngest animals studied (i.e., 21 days old) were significantly more reactive after 4 to 16 days of isolation than their group-maintained peers.

The Plasticity of Isolation Effects

Once the dyadic behaviors associated with attacking-biting (i.e., high probability of initiation, hyperreactivity) have become established, they by no means become an unmodifiable characteristic of the individual. The plasticity of the behavior can be readily demonstrated by reversing the conditions in which the animals are maintained, from isolation to group maintenance. Within a relatively short period—how short depending upon the strain observed and the conditions of interchange—the animals moved from isolation to group cohabitation become indistinguishable from those that had been maintained continuously with conspecifics since birth.

Observations of what happens when the isolated animal is first introduced to the group-rearing situation are of interest. As might be expected, the previously isolated animal is at first vigorously investigated by the residents of the compartment. But rather than docilely reacting, the previously isolated one ordinarily responds vigorously and initiates attacks against the residents in their own compartment. Typically a battle royal ensues, involving most or all of the animals in the compartment. Fights occur with the isolate and each other. Once the mayhem begins, the pairs appear to fight at random, with animals rebounding from one encounter to another. Attacks initiated against one animal become transferred to another in midcourse. Animals that do not actively enter the mutual combat are drawn into it by the indiscriminate

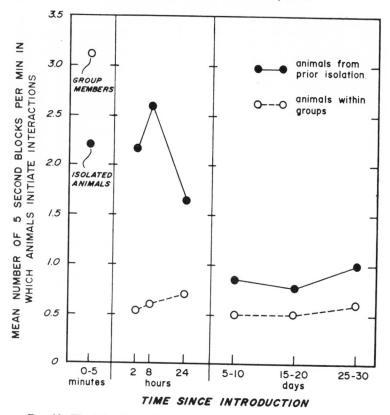

FIG. 10. The left column shows the mean number of occasions that the previously isolated or group-reared subjects initiated dyadic contact in the first 5 minutes after introduction of the previously isolated animal. The middle and right columns summarize similar observations taken after longer intervals of cohabitation (n = 8 groups of C57BL/10 animals). (From Cairns & Nakelski, 1971.)

biting of the rest. The most extravagant phase of the massive attack runs its course during the initial 30 minutes or the initial hours of observation. In the C57 observations, the return to a more stable circumstance is accompanied by the previously isolated animal emerging dominant in the living compartment. The remainder of the group (i.e., the original residents) react to the previously isolated animal by freezing against the walls of the compartment or

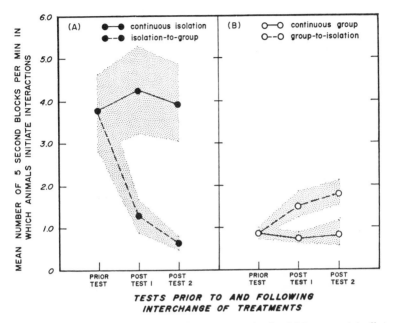

FIG. 11. (A) summarizes the test behavior of animals which were originally isolated, then either kept in isolation or interchanged to the group-rearing condition. Posttest 1 occurred 5 weeks after the interchange, and Posttest 2 occurred 10 weeks after interchange. (B) summarizes comparable results for animals that had been originally maintained in groups, then shifted to isolation (n = 8 C57BL/10 in each subcondition.) (From Cairns & Nakelski, 1971.)

otherwise avoiding behaviors that elicit further attack and fighting. Direct observations of the living compartment indicate that the probability of further attacks initiated by the previously isolated C57BL/10 diminish sharply over the first 5 days of cohabitation and become infrequent thereafter (Figures 10 & 11).

Among the ICR, a similar picture of total disruption is obtained. However, the previously isolated ICR male emerges dominant in the new group with no greater frequency than might be expected by chance. This difference is doubtless related to the generally lower threshold for the elicitation of attack behavior in group-maintained ICR and the higher incidence of fighting within ICR groups (1.04 per half-hour observation vs. .06 per half-hour observation for C57).

In any case, the previously isolated ICR is often quickly and thoroughly defeated by the group. Thereupon the previously isolated animal permits investigatory sniffing—by remaining immobilized—and allows others to huddle about him. Again, intragroup stimulation and fighting rapidly returns to normal or preintegration levels over the next 5 to 10 days. Regardless of whether or not the isolated ICR or C57 male is defeated or is dominant, he eventually begins to huddle with the rest of the animals in the compartment (see also Uhrich, 1938).

In summary, when there is an interchange of living conditions for previously isolated male mice, a new social organization rapidly develops. Observations indicate that all animals, both group-maintained and isolated ones, rapidly adapt to the punishment contingencies in the new setting. On the part of animals that were severely defeated, those behaviors that serve to elicit a continuation of attacks appear to be suppressed. The suppression, in turn, permits the assimilation of previously isolated animals into the resident group and huddling with them. Such integration is associated with a rapid diminution of hyperresponsivity. A parallel assimilation occurs in the case of isolated animals that emerge dominant, but over a slower time course. In both instances, what is learned in terms of response suppression seems to provide the occasion for changes in behavior and thereby modifications in the basic reactivity of the individual.

The plasticity is not completely symmetrical, however. Animals that have been shifted in the opposite direction at maturity—from living in small groups to isolation—do not show as great a change from their previous interaction patterns (Figure 11). Again, the rate and magnitude of the effect is species-typical. ICR males seem more influenced by isolation at maturity than C57BL/10 males. In both strains, the group-to-isolation animals do tend toward greater exploration of the test partners, heightened reactivity to stimulation, and an increased probability of attack initiation.

Conditioning and Generalization of Attack Behavior

Learning processes are involved not only in the suppression of attack behavior, but in its elicitation and generalization as well.

Once attacks occur in a dyadic interchange and are not inhibited by the counterresponses of the other, the attack behavior itself becomes conditioned to the events that are present at the time. The basic *training school for aggression* of J. P. Scott (1958) reflects the pervasiveness of the conditioning to contextual stimuli. Scott indicates that events (e.g., scratching of the guillotine door) associated with the experience of attacking another animal in themselves have the capability of eliciting the precursors of attacks. More generally, the systematic decrease in latency to attack as a function of prior fighting tests appears to reflect the acquired control properties of dyadic and contextual events in the setting. The diminished latency has been repeatedly confirmed (e.g., King, 1957b), and it seems consistent with what might be expected from a contiguity interpretation of the process. The standard procedure is to terminate the test shortly after the fight is initiated, so that neither animal has been defeated. In such procedures, the last activity to be performed in the context was likely to be an attack. Hence prior exposure to the same context presumably would reinstate the events that serve to elicit vigorous behavior and correlated internal states.

Equally compelling are the effects of a single 10-minute interaction for the cue properties of others when attacks were *not* elicited (pp. 79–81). It seems reasonable to expect that the isolation operations that followed the sessions helped to "preserve" the modification in stimulus properties of conspecifics, in that no opportunities were provided for the acquisition of alternative responses.

In general, there appears to be an organization or consolidation of behavior with respect to the other animal by virtue of a brief initial exposure. The recent work of Lagerspetz and Hautojärvi (1967) suggest that "carry over" effects are not limited simply to those interchanges that involve fighting-biting behaviors. Using previously isolated males, Lagerspetz and Hautojärvi first exposed one of their groups to another male. However, in a second group, the previously isolated male was exposed to an estrous female. Fighting typically occurred in the male-male pairs, as expected, and intromission-copulation in the male-female pairs, also as might be expected. What was especially interesting was what happened in a later test, where different test partners were used. Those animals that had been first tested with a male were then tested with a female, and vice versa. The original behaviors tended to persist, regardless of the actual sexual status of the test partner. That is, the subjects in the later series tended to bite the females and mount the males. Such findings, while still preliminary, are in accord with the general proposition that the stimulus properties of conspecifics can be markedly altered for previously isolated animals following a very brief interaction.

Recapitulation: On Fighting in Mice

A bidirectional view of behavior development underscores that an ontogenetic analysis is necessarily a complex business. In the tracing of social behavior patterns, one must contend with a continuing synthesis of biological and experiential processes. Nonetheless, the contributions of some of the basic processes are semiautonomous and appear to be susceptible to experimental manipulation. The ontogenetic strategy provides a procedure to disentangle influences that are inseparably fused in the adult animal. The results fit a preliminary but coherent outline of the development of the behavior:

1. In the analysis of fighting in mice, the distinction between the processes required for the establishment of the behavior and those relevant to its maintenance and suppression has been useful as a starting point. Considering the issue of establishment, it is clear that the capacity to produce harm and injury is paced primarily by the maturation of the necessary sensory and motor structures. Specific attack-related experience is not required: attack-biting interchanges are established in mice in the apparent absence of imitation, reinforcement, play-fighting, tuition, or any other specific criterion-related training experience.

2. Variations in rearing experience are, however, clearly related to the phenomenon of attack-fighting establishment. Paradoxically for a social-learning viewpoint, rearing conditions that preclude exposure to fighting and punishment facilitate the establishment of the behavior.

3. The paradox is partially resolved by an analysis of the dynamics of the interchanges that are associated with the initial

occurrence of biting and attack behaviors in isolated animals. Attacks and vigorous biting appear initially as the outcome of a spiraling interchange, where the behavior of at least one member of the pair becomes increasingly more intense and provocative. Diminishing the reactivity of the other, or its activity with respect to the subject, serves also to reduce the probability of escalation of the interchange to severe attacks. Feedback events that are produced in the course of the interchange itself seem of basic significance in determining its direction and termination.

4. Species-typical social stimulation in group-maintained mice serves to diminish somatosensory reactivity of the young animal, as well as his tendency to vigorously explore other males in a new setting. Observations of the development of these animals suggests that the conspecific "taming" is linked to the ubiquitous clumping and huddling behavior of the species.

5. Isolation rearing increases the reactivity of the individual to the physical stimulation of the other and his tendency to orient toward and vigorously explore the other. Such behaviors predispose the isolated animal to entrap himself in escalating sequences that terminate the attacks and counterattacks. What seemed significant for the bidirectional hypothesis was that the chronic states of the individual are drastically modified by social interactions (or their absence) in ontogeny, and that these states in turn biased subsequent social interchanges.

6. Although fighting and associated behaviors are not established through specific learning experiences, they are clearly learnable. Dyadic injury appears to share many, if not all, of the properties of pain or injury produced by nonsocial means. Noxious events, social or nonsocial, can provide the occasion for behavior suppression or facilitation, depending upon the intensity of the event, its timing, and the ongoing behavior of the other individual (see Church, 1963; Solomon, 1964). Similarly, attack behaviors are like other vigorous, integrated response patterns in that they become conditioned to the contexts, behaviors, and circumstances in which they were last performed without disruption or inhibition.

By virtue of our interest in the ontogeny of the behavior and its initial establishment, we have focussed on the distinctive contributions of rearing experience. There are ample empirical data (see

Clemente & Lindsley, 1967; and Eleftheriou & Scott, 1971) to indicate that interchanges can be directly influenced by a wide range of manipulations, including pharmacological, genetic, and physiological (brain stimulation, ablation). It would be of considerable interest to determine whether such disparate operations are mediated through alterations in the capabilities of the individual to habituate to conspecific stimulation or through directly increasing the activity and irritability of the subject. Although the manipulations by which the behavior dispositions are brought about may differ, the dyadic mechanisms by which the dispositions are translated into particular social interchanges may share a common basis. In any case, it seems worthwhile to make a detailed sequential account of the *initial* interchanges involving animals where fighting has been linked to various physiological or endocrinological manipulations.

Even though chronic hyperreactivity of the subject can influence the course of an interchange terminating in fighting, it is not a prerequisite for the phenomenon. Feedback events internal to the interchange are themselves sufficient to produce acute (i.e., temporary) levels of hyperreaction and invigoration of dyadic stimulation. Although we have not discussed the various kinds of events that are sufficient to produce such acute states, an attack by another animal is apparently one of the most reliable means (Scott, 1971). Both chronic and acute procedures can be seen as serving to magnify or distort critical features of the interaction and thereby altering the threshold for mutual reaction and response intensification. And once fighting-attack behavior is established, it tends to preempt alternative responses.

In short, specific social-learning experiences do not appear to be necessary for the initial establishment of fighting and attack behavior in mice. Such experiences, however, appear to be of primary significance for its generalization, control, and suppression.

FURTHER OBSERVATIONS OF FIGHTING AND PUNISHMENT IN MAMMALIAN DEVELOPMENT

Whatever gains are made by a detailed analysis of behavior development in one species can be cancelled out by a failure to respect its limitations. The study of fighting and punishment in mice is no exception. One way to appreciate the limits and the breadth of the preceding outline would be to consider, in overview, the development of the behavior in other mammals. Of special interest are the questions of what are the various ways that the young of other mammals experience and deliver noxious stimulation in social relationships, and how changes in the psychobiological status of the young influence its behaviors and reactions to them. First, we will consider the more general relations between isolation and fighting.

Isolation and Fighting in Mammals

The profound differences between isolated and group-reared mice in terms of fighting-attack propensities raise the question of whether parallel differences have been identified in other species. In such comparisons, one had best proceed cautiously. Even when an experimental manipulation has been labeled "isolation," there is little assurance that the procedures are in fact paralleled to those followed in the analysis of mice. In studies of primate development, distinctions are commonly offered between partial isolation (not interacting, but seeing, smelling, and hearing others of their own kind), complete isolation (rearing in a different setting than others of their own kind), and total isolation (rearing without interactions with any other animal, including the experimenter).

Despite the range of procedures adopted and the diversity of the species-typical behaviors and social organizations of the animals studied, there are, nonetheless, basic consistencies across isolation studies (see reviews by Johnson, 1972; Kuo, 1967; Prescott, 1971). For most species considered, the individual is more likely to attack or bite conspecific partners if it has been reared away from others of its own kind than if it has been reared with them. The effects have demonstrated over a broad range of isolation procedures, tests, and species. Monkeys, for instance, that are maintained in partial isolation are more likely to bite others than are nonisolated animals (Mason, 1960; Sackett, 1967). Similar outcomes have been observed in such diverse types as chow dogs (Kuo, 1967), female sheep (my observations), female mice if test objects are appropriate (Edwards,

1968), rats (Galef, 1970), and Japanese grey quail (Kuo, 1960). The generalization must be qualified, however. Not all breeds of dogs that are isolated show a strong tendency to attack (Scott & Fuller, 1965). It must also be emphasized that not all animals that are members of susceptible breeds show the effects of isolation equally.

To determine whether the isolation-attack correlation is mediated by the same factors as found to be effective in mice, we must ask whether isolation is also associated with differences in reactivity. In most cases, it is. Prescott (1971), for instance, implicates a heightened somatosensory reactivity in accounting for the differences in irritability and fighting of isolated monkeys. In a similar vein, Fuller (Fuller, 1967; Fuller & Clark, 1966a, 1966b) proposes that one of the principal effects of isolation rearing is to produce a heightened reactivity to stimuli to which the dog is exposed. This effect could serve, in turn, to bias the kinds of social interactions in which the animal becomes involved.

There is less consistency among studies in whether or not isolation also produces a heightened tendency to explore and otherwise investigate the characteristics of others, including conspecific partners. In at least some breeds, such as beagles, the effect of isolation is to produce a traumatization and freezing, which in turn is translated into an apparent docility of the animal following isolation. Whether or not a change in reactivity will also produce heightened locomotor activity or lessened activity seems directly dependent upon the genetic background of the individual. As Fuller and Clark (1966b) have shown, isolation leads to heightened activity in wirehaired terriers and diminished activity in beagles. In both, however, isolation leads to a heightened reactivity to environmental events. If so great a difference in the translation to social behavior can be found among breeds in a single species, it should be hardly surprising to find a similar set of differences across species.

In addition to the isolation manipulation, comparative ontogenetic data are available in three primary types of interaction situations relevant to fighting and punishment. These include (a) dyadic interchanges between the young and adult members of the species, (b) those among young animals interacting with each other, and (c) those involving the young interacting with members of other species. A peculiar virtue of a microanalysis of fighting and punishment is that it promotes the precise identification of the behavior ongoing at the time of the noxious stimulus delivery, and the immediate antecedents and consequences of the noxious event. Such detail seems required in order to offer parallels between experimental studies of "punishment" and the injuries that occur in the context of social interchanges. In this regard, Solomon (1964) observed that "a punishment is not just a punishment. It is an event in a temporal and spatial flow of stimulation and behavior, and its effects will be produced by its temporal and spatial point of insertion in that flow" (p. 242). The behavioral flow, in the dyadic case, is determined by two or more individuals acting together.

Pain and Punishment in Filial Interactions

The introduction of a noxious event appears to be one of the more reliable techniques that the individual has available to produce an immediate shift in the behavior of the other. Whatever other properties it might have, a painful event is a compelling stimulus. When this stimulus occurs in a child-rearing or maternal-infant relationship, and the older individual provides the noxious event, it is ordinarily called punishment. But when the offspring is the initiator, it is called aggression. A common feature of the response sequences subsumed by the two labels is that they both involve the occurrence of noxious actions.

Newborn mammals typically enjoy an immunity from noxious stimulation directed at them by conspecific adults. The rule is not inviolable, however. Mothers, especially primiparous ones, sometimes ignore, bite, or mutilate and cannibalize their young. Furthermore, attacks and rebuffs can be readily elicited in some females by seemingly modest experimenter interventions. In sheep or goats, for instance, removal of the offspring for even a few hours beginning immediately at parturition reliably produces maternal rejection of her own lamb. Maternal sheep in general are quite discriminative in their acceptance of offspring in that they ordinarily rebuff and butt away unfamiliar young (Hafez, Cairns, Hulet, & Scott, 1969). Other species are more tolerant. Maternal rats promiscuously nurture not only unfamiliar rat pups, but mice as well. Nonetheless, under some conditions of disruption, primiparous rats will attack and cannibalize their own offspring. Partial disruption of the rat litter, involving removal of only some of the offspring for 5 to 10 minutes and then returning them, serves to reliably elicit attacks by the primiparous mother toward the returnees (Scholz, 1973).

But these are exceptions. Left to themselves, and given a reasonably benign and undisturbed environment, mammalian mothers typically behave in a fashion consistent with the survival requirements of the offspring. Rosenblatt and Lehrman (1963) described how the hormonal states and behavioral reactivity of the mother are neatly synchronized with the behavioral propensities and survival needs of the offspring. Ingestion of the afterbirth and maternal licking and stimulation of the offspring appear to heighten the probability of appropriate orienting, rooting, and sucking in the young (e.g., Alexander & Williams, 1964). In turn, the sucking of the young is instrumental in eliciting the prolactin and oxytocin secretions that maintain the female in a "maternal" condition. The overt actions of the offspring at this stage seem scarcely capable of achieving a sufficient intensity to elicit punishment.

Whatever the reasons for the neonatal immunity from adult attack, it is ordinarily lost as the young animal matures. From his observations of hamadryas baboons, Kummer (1968) finds that the loss of special status is associated with the changing of the infant's coat color from black to brown at about 6 months of age. Maternal dogs commonly nip or rebuff their pups in the second and third month. Discussions of the phenomenon of neonatal immunity suggest that some distinctive features of the young (its odor, coloration, and vocalizations) serve as species-typical events for attack inhibition (Barnett, 1963).

A dyadic analysis suggests that the behavior of the young—as opposed to its nonspecific qualities—may also contribute significantly to punishment elicitation and inhibition. In early postnatal development, even the most intensive response of precocial young are scarcely capable of inflicting injury or pain. Since the behavior of the young animal is also synchronized with the activity of the mother, there would appear to be few occasions for the direct elicitation of pain or behavioral interferences. However, with the changes in size and the musculature of the young, the persistence of earlier "appropriate" behaviors can be both disruptive and capable of producing noxious byproducts. Even species-typical action patterns of the infant, when performed by the postinfancy young, are likely to be behaviorally disruptive for the mother and possibly physically hurtful. In the course of development, mammalian infants typically must undergo drastic changes in feeding and locomotion patterns, becoming progressively less dependent upon the mother or other adults. When the infantile behaviors persist beyond their time, they are likely to elicit vigorous counterresponses by the affected adults. These actions can serve, in turn, to suppress the offending behavior and to promote in the young animal the development of alternative forms of responding.

A behavior in point would be the universal one of weaning. The extent to which maternal rebuff and punishment contribute to the cessation of sucking and the development of other forms of ingestion has been a matter of debate. The shift in ingestive behavior is also linked to changes in morphology and dentation which makes the sucking response increasingly less efficient and more difficult to perform, on the one hand, and changes in the physiological status of the mother that diminish lactation, on the other. What has confounded the comparative analysis of the role of punishment further is the fact that punishment appears to be reliably correlated with weaning in some species and not in others. Even within a single species, there are consistent and marked variations among different subtypes. Maternal pigtail macaque monkeys, for instance, are considerably more punitive with respect to their offspring than are bonnet macaques. As Rosenblum and Kaufman (1968) observe, "punitive deterrence" or maternal restraint of the offspring is more common in pigtail filial interactions than bonnet interactions, including those concerned with the termination of sucking.

While the efficacy and the long-term effects of such punishment has been debated, there can be no question but that one of its immediate effects is to disrupt the ongoing behavior of the young. In the hamadryas baboon, 1-year-old infants who try to suck are sometimes preemptively bitten by their mothers (Kummer, 1968). Maternal elk butt older offspring away (Altmann, 1963). However, the behavior sequence of sucking can be disrupted in other ways.

Rat mothers, for instance, simply make the act more difficult by lying on their stomachs and otherwise eluding their offspring. Some primates, such as the bonnet, gently remove the offspring from themselves. Whatever the maternal action by which the behavior is disrupted, it serves to promote the development of alternative, and uninterrupted, modes of ingestion in the offspring.

From a dyadic perspective, then, punishment would appear to be only one of the several ways that the mother has to react to the disruptive intruding or noxious behaviors of the young. Precisely why one species or one individual reacts by reciprocal noxious stimulation more frequently than other species or other individuals remains a question of basic importance. The occurrence of this alternative as opposed to more gentle ones is probably linked to intensity or noxiousness of the behavior of the offspring, the history of the mother, and the social organization of the species. In any case, punishment is a prominent means by which some animals redirect the dyadic actions of their young, and this appears to be correlated with the species-typical usage of punishment as a means of social control.

Ontogeny of Fighting and Attacks in Peer Interactions

Any discussion of the precursors of adult attack behavior must attend to the occurrence of "play-fighting" among littermates and peers in development. Whatever may be the functional properties of the behavior, and whatever its relation to adult fighting, there should be no question about its prominence in several mammalian species.

The ontogeny of the behavior has been carefully plotted in dogs (Rheingold, 1963; Scott & Fuller, 1965). Play-fighting begins virtually as soon as the animals are physically capable. Puppies do not open their eyes until approximately 13 days after birth, and standing alone is not observed until about 21 days (Fuller & Fox, 1969). It is all more noteworthy that play-fighting with other puppies begins at about Day 15, virtually as soon as the young animal can move around in a reasonably coordinated fashion. At first this involves chewing on the ears or licking the face of one pup by another. Such activity frequently elicits reciprocal licking and chewing. At about the third week, the mouthing and biting increases rapidly. The targets are their own and each other's bodies and various parts of the mother's anatomy (e.g., her ears, tail, leg feathers, and back fur).

Soon the activities become less like play and more like fighting. In the second month of life, the tussling is marked on occasion by growling, snarling, biting, and painful yelps by one of the animals. The fights become increasingly more severe with the eruption of teeth and the development of the large muscle systems. By the seventh week after birth, puppies that are left together in litters begin to attack each other in groups. The target animal is usually the smallest of the litter, but not always. In most breeds, the "gang-ups" are episodic and ephemeral. But for certain breeds, such as the fox terrier, the victim can be seriously and permanently maimed. Fuller (1953) reports a case where the smallest member of a litter of six terriers was a female. After the other five began to terrorize the dog, she was removed. At that point, the others began to attack the next smallest female, until she was taken out. Then the three males left in the litter directed their attacks at the sole remaining female. These attacks certainly were not of the playful variety. In the larger groups, "one puppy would get hold of the ears and another the tail, stretching their victim between them, while the third animal attacked in the middle" (Scott & Fuller, 1965, p. 106). For the animal suspended in the center, the behavior would hardly seem like "play."

This general picture of play-fighting merging into more serious attacks is replicated in several mammalian species, including rhesus monkeys, baboons, and rats. Among those species in which the behavior is prominent, observations indicate the following:

1. Males are more likely to become involved in rough-and-tumble play (monkeys), play-fighting (dogs), or wrestling and tumbling (baboons) than are females. Pseudohermaphroditic females are more likely to become involved in play-fighting and attacks than normal females, as shown in rhesus monkeys (Phoenix, Goy, & Resko, 1968).

2. Play-fighting increases in intensity and decreases in frequency following its initial onset. Adults are less likely to become involved in the activity. But when they do, it is less likely to be described as play than as a mutual attack sequence.

3. As the animals develop, the behaviors that were previously labeled "playful" become capable of producing bodily damage and serious injury. The point of developmental crossover from play-fighting to fighting is often difficult to establish.

Given these observations, it is tempting to speculate that the play-fighting experience is a *necessary* step in the developmental progression towards adult forms of attack behavior. At this point, there are good reasons to resist the temptation. The most compelling one is that the capability to attack develops among animals that have been reared in total or partial isolation. In addition, the behavior reliably develops in at least one species (i.e., C57BL/10 mice) that is distinguished both by the violence of its adult attack behavior and the relative absence of such developmental precursors.

Other interpretations of the functions of play-fighting have emphasized the inevitability of the adult forms of fighting-attack behavior (Eibl-Eibesfeldt, 1967; Lorenz, 1966), the innate and compelling features of play (Gerall, Ward, & Gerall, 1967), and the role of play-fighting in the generalization and suppression of attack behavior as opposed to its establishment. The proposal on the compelling features of play itself is of some interest. Noting that appropriate sexual activity is disrupted by the intrusion of "playful" responses, Gerall et al. speculate that if an isolated animal is not permitted to become involved in playful interactions in ontogeny, the tendency will persist inappropriately into adulthood. The final possibility—one which would be consistent with the findings for species that play-fight as well as those that do not—is that the activity is relevant to the conditioning and control of fighting and attack behaviors. According to this view, a byproduct of the play-fighting would be its suppression in some contexts and settings, and its generalization in others. Play-fighting experiences would provide the occasion for intense behaviors to become conditioned to different features of the individual's self-produced responses as well as to the responses of others. Although the playful activity would not be required for the establishment of the attack behavior, it would be instrumental in its direction and control. Which of these interpretations—or which combination of them—is most appropriate remains to be determined.

Cross-Species Rearing

Cross-species rearing studies are of special interest for ontogenetic treatments because they provide a picture of how punitive dyadic interchanges develop in the absence of species-typical supports for the behavior. Although the cross-species rearing design was one of the first experimental procedures to be used in ontogenetic study of behavioral plasticity, it remains one of the least understood with respect to advantages and limitations. George Romanes, Darwin's protege and sometimes recognized as the father of comparative psychology, relied heavily upon interspecific rearing experiments to identify the limits of behavioral plasticity. In his discussions of the modifiability of behavior, Romanes cites such observations as those of Dudgeon (1879) on young suckling rats that were reared in an entirely maternal fashion by an adult cat. Over the intervening 93 years the method had been used with varying degrees of success by a handful of investigators, including Romanes (1884), Rogers (1928), Kuo (1930), Denenberg, Hudgens, & Zarrow (1964) and Johnson, DeSisto, & Koenig (1972). Unfortunately, most secondary accounts of the procedure have focused upon the curious Disney-like outcomes that can be achieved and less attention has been given to the mechanisms by which the effects come about and are maintained.

Used in combination with other rearing procedures, the interspecific method can yield useful information on the effective dyadic contributors to social development. Basically a conspecific isolation procedure, it focuses attention upon the distinctive contribution of the "other" to social development and change. The limits of behavioral plasticity can be explored by selecting others which differ progressively in terms of the species-typical stimulation normally provided the young animal. It is for such reasons that Kuo (1967) considers the cross-specific rearing technique to be a method of choice for the development of "behavioral neophenotypes," or unique patterns of social behavior. From a dyadic perspective, then, the cross-specific method is useful because it permits the identification of the distinctive contributions of variations in dyadic responsiveness to the development of behaviors in the young animal. But the procedure is not without problems. A basic difficulty is that the reactions of the "other" are not invariant and are likely to be changed systematically by virtue of interaction with the young animal. Hence the effective dyadic events must be traced in individual pairs, because the behavior of the alien-species partner is likely to undergo progressive modifications in the course of the cross-specific rearing experiment.

The dynamic nature of the interchanges that occur in cross-specific rearing experiments can best be appreciated by examining one in detail. In this case, young puppies were reared either from 2 to 3 days after birth or from 4 weeks after birth away from other dogs and with an adult rabbit (Cairns & Werboff, 1967). When initially placed together in a 4 × 8-foot enclosure, the 4-week-old puppy and adult rabbit typically showed a mutual avoidance. But typically, by the 24th hour of cohabitation, and invariably by the 96th hour, they were in physical contact with each other. Shortly after making the initial contact, the puppies would perform species-typical responses with respect to their cohabitant in that they would climb on her, lick her fur, tug at her ears, burrow beneath her mid-section, and so on. In short, the pups performed with respect to the cohabitant those activities that occur in the litter context.

With changes in musculature and size the behaviors that were once innocuous became increasingly capable of inflicting damage. The reciprocal behaviors in the repertoire of the adult rabbit, however, were not sufficient to disrupt the injury-producing behavior. On the contrary, the escape attempts only intensified the vigor of the pursuit and the intensity of the interaction. Impressive shifts in the form and function of interaction patterns were apparently determined by maturation-paced changes in the structure and behavior organization of the dog. In the absence of reciprocal responses that serve to inhibit the behavior and elicit alternative interaction patterns, the injurious behavior escalated to more damaging levels and the study was terminated.

However sublime the myth that early togetherness automatically makes for peaceful coexistence, the data indicate that such an outcome is not inevitable (Cairns & Johnson, 1965; Johnson, 1972; Kuo, 1967). On the contrary, cross-specific social behavior is not so different from conspecific behavior in that both require a continuing realignment of the relationship. The need for the realignment is magnified when there is a marked disparity between two animals in size or activity at maturity. The capabilities for mutual response inhibition are less necessary when the pairing involves animals where the species-typical interaction behaviors are not likely to be pain producing. Although the behavior of interspecific pairs may become synchronized and mutually dependent in time, the synchronization does not necessarily produce outcomes that are beneficial for both members of the pair. Independent tests of preference indicated that some young animals preferred to be with their cohabitants, even though the interactions were in fact destroying themselves or their cohabitants (Cairns & Johnson, 1965; Cairns & Werboff, 1967).

In summary, the cross-specific rearing procedure provides the occasion for the development of mutual dependencies in the behavior of animals that do not normally interact. The interaction sequences depend—as in normal development—upon the conditions of the organisms involved and their species-typical response characteristics. In unevenly matched pairs, the persistence of the young animal's infantile modes of stimulation can become increasingly more noxious as he matures. The relationship not infrequently escalates to a series of attack-defense sequences. Peaceful cohabitation in such cases can be facilitated by inhibiting the noxious response patterns or by the elicitation of alternative and competing behavior sequences. The former outcome has been sometimes achieved with the help of the experimenter who acts as an equalizer by inhibiting noxious behaviors with shock (Myer, 1968), acid (Kuo, 1967), or restraint (Cairns and Johnson, 1965). Whatever the means, the capacity to control, disrupt, or shape the pain-producing behavior of the young animal through reciprocal action is central to the problem of mutual adaptation. In the species-typical rearing circumstance, the "other" (either the littermates or the mother) ordinarily has the capabilities to modify or suppress the noxious behavior of the young. However it may be achieved, a balance of power throughout ontogeny provides the occasion for the development of alternative, nonnoxious modes of dyadic organization.

Returning to the original question that inspired this comparative inquiry: In what ways must the preceding outline (pp. 100–102) be revised by information from other mammalian young? Despite

differences in response propensities, including species-typical exposure to play-fighting and punishment, the basic outline appears to
hold up surprisingly well. Both cross-specific and isolation procedures
indicate that attack-biting *can be* (but not necessarily *are*) established
in the absence of specific training experiences. The nature of the
noxious behaviors that develop, and when they develop, seems dependent upon the genetic background of the individual as well as
the behavioral capabilities of the "other."

Since little attention has been given to the immediate precursors
of attacks in mammalian interchanges, we cannot determine whether
or how relationships are typically biased toward fighting and punishment. While the escalation account seems to be a plausible way to
view the mediation of some isolation-produced behavior changes,
relevant information on other ways that relationships are biased is
presently incomplete.

CONCLUDING REMARKS

Why Not Aggression?

Generalizations on aggression, from fish to man, have been
invited by a recognition of the evolutionary adaptiveness of the
behavior. In particular, it has been proposed that aggression serves
such survival functions as the control of population density, the
selection of mates, and the protection of the brood (Lorenz, 1966;
Etkin, 1964). Whatever the merits of these specific propositions, the
emphasis on the potential importance of such functions of aggression *for the species* seems well taken. Nonetheless, it is unfortunate
that the interpersonal functions of the behavior *for the individual* have
received so little theoretical attention.

The two levels of analysis—evolutionary and interpersonal—
need not be viewed as mutually exclusive. If both proposals are in
fact valid, then evolutionary and interpersonal analyses should
prove to be supplementary. By way of example, consider the proposal that aggression is a significant determinant of population
dispersion. Ethological observations indicate, in addition, that
aggression (i.e., extreme attacks and severe biting) sometimes leads
to group *cohesion*. In the hamadryas baboon, the unit leader ensures

togetherness in his harem by attacking the females that stray, not the males that attract them (Kummer, 1968). In this instance, it is the temporal relationship between the ongoing behavior and the injurious act that is important. Similarly, the noxious rejection of unfamiliar lambs by maternal ewes serves indirectly to preserve the exclusiveness of the maternal-infant attachment in sheep. One and the same aggressive act can serve to maintain a group or disperse it, according to the timing of the injury relative to the ongoing behavior of the other individual.

Examination of the interactions that occur during ontogeny suggest that the punishment or attacks upon another animal serve a wide range of immediate dyadic functions for the young. In general, the infliction of pain and/or injury appears to be one of the primary means that the young or the mother has available to disrupt the ongoing activity of the other individual. And notwithstanding psychological legends to the contrary, punishment (i.e., injury) is a most effective procedure for suppressing or redirecting behavior (Solomon, 1964). When attacks or injury occur, the behavior of the other organism is drastically modified, either by behavioral redirection or intensification.

In the light of its dyadic control properties, possibly the question should be, *Why not aggression?* instead of, Why aggression? The establishment of injury-producing behavior in development appears highly probable, if not inevitable. At least some noxious consequences may initially occur as a byproduct of the performance of other species-typical maintenance behaviors, such as ingestion or locomotion. The additional fact that most species are amply endowed with the structural prerequisites for the production of pain would appear to guarantee the emergence of such acts in ontogeny for those species. Once the noxious behavior of the young is established, its utility can then be confirmed or disconfirmed, in its several relationships.

The problem of why there is not more aggression remains to be systematically investigated across species. One answer may be found in an examination of the reciprocal behaviors that are provoked when noxious acts occur in an interchange. Moreover, it seems likely that self-produced events inherent in the performance of the act itself are relevant to its subsequent control.

Of Mice and Men

Another matter of general concern is the question of how relevant are the principles identified in the development of fighting in mice to the essential problems of aggressive development in children. The answer depends on what principles and what problems. Certainly it would seem unwise to abstract specific substantive generalizations that pertain to fighting in mice and apply them to "homologous" behaviors in children. One problem is that it would be difficult to judge a priori, on polythetic grounds, what would be homologous in these species (Jensen, 1967). In the light of the vast differences in cognitive capabilities, structures, and social organization, direct substantive generalizations on social interchanges would be hazardous. Consider the isolation-fighting relationship. It may be the case that socially alienated or functionally "isolated" children are more likely to behave in an aberrant fashion in a doll-play test or in small-group settings. But the social alienation in such instances may be a consequence of the child's aberrant social behavior as much as it is an antecedent for it.

On the other hand, it seems a mistake to conclude that the developmental processes in two mammalian forms—even those so different as mice and men—are nonoverlapping. There is likely considerable commonality in at least some of the basic processes. Chronic and long-term deprivation of somatosensory stimulation, for instance, is likely to produce hyperresponsiveness in both children and nonhumans. But whether such responsiveness and irritability would be translated into a heightened tendency to attack or injure others in children requires further information about response organization. Physiological or behavioral reactivity must be mediated in the social context in which the behavior is elicited, as well as in the kinds of reactions evoked in others with whom the child interacts. Reactivity and irritability are individual states; aggressive behaviors are dyadic events. The last point seems especially important for the analysis of relations between behavior and physiological events in humans, where the child and those with whom he interacts have the capabilities for interpreting a given behavior in a number of different ways and responding differentially in accordance with those interpretations.

Perhaps it will be at the level of method that the most immediate comparative payoffs may lie. The dyadic procedure, in particular, appears to offer a powerful technique for the analysis of ontogenetic contributions to fighting and punishment in children. It may also help to resolve some of the problems that have arisen in child-rearing analyses of the behavior. Consider, for instance, the contradictory relations that have been reported between punishment and aggression in children. Although there is considerable ambiguity in the evidence (Yarrow et al., 1968), it has been generally accepted that the punishment of children begets aggression (Feshbach, 1970). Laboratory studies, on the other hand, indicate that punitive consequences serve to suppress or inhibit the behavior (Duer & Parke, 1970). It remains to be established from child-rearing studies what are the exact functions of the parental events for the ongoing behaviors of the child, and how these outcomes influence subsequent dyadic interchanges. A sequential analysis over at least a short-term period is required to determine precisely what behaviors are inhibited or elicited by the punishment. Such information seems a prerequisite to determining whether the positive punishment-aggression correlations should be attributed to frustration, to modeling, or to the child's control of the parent rather than vice versa.

The notion of escalation in interchange has been repeatedly invoked in discussions of international conflict and experimental economics (e.g., Boulding, 1965). Toch (1969), in the provocative volume *Violent Men*, applies a similar idea to the interchanges between police and offender. But surprisingly little information is available on sequential analyses of aggressive interchanges in children. Insofar as experimental studies of aggression in children have been developed, aggression has usually been treated as a behavior to be imitated, reinforced, or inhibited as an entity unto itself. Unfortunately—for the purposes of a dyadic analysis—Bo Bo dolls do not fight back. In an important exception to unidirectional procedures, Patterson, Littman, and Bricker (1967) have shown that assertive behaviors can profitably be studied in children in the context of the interchanges in which they occur.[5]

5. This work by Patterson and his colleagues has now been extended in a series of papers that came to my attention after the presentation of this paper (Patterson & Cobb, 1971). These papers constitute a significant contribution to the dyadic analysis of fighting and punishment in humans.

Summary

The principal thesis of this paper has been that a developmental analysis would be useful—perhaps essential—in disentangling the semiautonomous processes that determine the establishment and control of pain-producing behaviors. The concept of aggression, because of its methodological limitations and unitary motivational connotations, was seen as providing an inadequate basis for an ontogenetic analysis. Instead, the focus has been upon a molecular account of dyadic events that occur in a relationship and their immediate and long-terms determinants. It was argued, from the perspective of interpersonal control, that pain-producing responses could be functional (i.e., adaptive) for the individual as well as for the species. When noxious acts occur in an interchange, they can serve as compelling stimuli to disrupt or intensify the ongoing behavior of others.

In an application of the ontogenetic strategy to fighting and punishment in mice, it was found that neither specific attack-related experience nor direct training is required to establish attack behavior. Variations in rearing experience, however, determine the ease with which the behavior can be established. Isolation rearing increases both the somatosensory reactivity of the individual as well as his tendency to orient toward other animals and vigorously explore them. Such experience-produced propensities predispose the isolated animal to become entrapped in an escalating interchange that often terminates in attacks and counterattacks. Once established, the injury-producing behaviors are clearly learnable. What seems significant for the bidirectional developmental hypothesis is that chronic states of the individual are drastically modified by social interactions in ontogeny, and such states in turn bias subsequent social interchanges.

Perhaps the major lesson that a comparative overview of social development teaches us is that social behaviors, including pain-producing sequences, must be viewed in the context of the behavioral organization of the individuals in which they occur. Such a relativistic framework points up that the effects of "experience" upon painful social interchanges are multileveled and can differ according to the developmental stage of the individuals involved and the species to which they belong. "Experience" and "learning" thus encompass not only response-specific contingencies designated as conditioning but also such phenomena as habituation (in all mammalian young) and the development of higher-order expectancies (in children and adults). The inescapable conclusion is that there can be no substitute for the detailed analysis of painful interchanges in those forms to which the explanation is addressed. Moreover, since the "problems of aggression" are in fact the problems of social interaction, it seems unlikely that they will yield to a single biochemical or behavioral solution.

REFERENCES

Alexander, G., & Williams, D. Maternal facilitation of sucking drive in newborn lambs. *Science*, 1964, **146**, 665–666.

Altmann, M. Naturalistic studies of maternal care in moose and elk. In H. L. Rheingold (Ed.), *Maternal behavior in mammals*. New York: Wiley, 1963. Pp. 233–253.

Anton, A. H., Schwartz, R. P., & Kramer, S. Catecholamines and behavior in isolated and grouped mice. *Journal of Psychiatric Research*, 1968, **6**, 211–220.

Archer, J. The effect of strange male odor on aggressive behavior in male mice. *Journal of Mammology*, 1968, **49**, 572–575.

Bandura, A. Social learning through imitation. In M. R. Jones (Ed.), *Nebraska symposium on motivation, 1962*. Lincoln: University of Nebraska Press, 1962. Pp. 211–269.

Banerjee, U. An inquiry into the genesis of aggression in mice induced by isolation. *Behavior*, 1970, **12**, 86–99.

Barnett, S. A. *The rat: A study in behaviour*. Chicago: Aldine, 1963.

Bindra, D. B. Components of general activity and the analysis of behavior. *Psychological Review*, 1961, **68**, 205–215.

Boulding, K. E. The economics of human conflict. In E. B. McNeil (Ed.), *The nature of human conflict*. Englewood Cliffs, N.J.: Prentice-Hall, 1965. Pp. 172–194.

Cairns, R. B. Attachment behavior of mammals. *Psychological Review*, 1966, **73**, 409–426.

Cairns, R. B. Attachment and dependency: A psychobiological and social learning synthesis. In J. L. Gewritz (Ed.), *Attachment and dependency*. Washington, D.C.: V. H. Winston, 1972, in press. Pp. 29–80.

Cairns, R. B., & Johnson, D. L. The development of interspecies social preferences. *Psychonomic Science*, 1965, **2**, 337–338.

Cairns, R. B., Midlam, J., & Scholz, S. D. The joint effects of age of isolation and length of isolation on fighting in mice. Unpublished manuscript, Indiana University, 1972.

Cairns, R. B., & Milakovich, J. F. On fighting in mice: Is training necessary? Unpublished manuscript, Indiana University, 1972.

Cairns, R. B., & Nakelski, J. S. On fighting in mice: Situational determinants of intragroup dyadic stimulation. *Psychonomic Science*, 1970, **18**, 16–17.

Cairns, R. B., & Nakelski, J. S. On fighting in mice: Ontogenetic and experiential determinants. *Journal of Comparative and Physiological Psychology*, 1971, **71**, 354–364.

Cairns, R. B., & Scholz, S. D. On fighting in mice: Dyadic escalation and what is learned. *Journal of Comparative and Physiological Psychology*, in press. (a)

Cairns, R. B., & Scholz, S. D. The effects of cross-species rearing on fighting in mice. Unpublished manuscript, Indiana University, 1972. (b)

Cairns, R. B., Scholz, S. D., & Einsiedel, A. Variations in social interchanges as a function of circadian cycle in mice. Unpublished manuscript, Indiana University, 1972.

Cairns, R. B., & Werboff, J. Behavior development in the dog: An interspecific analysis. *Science*, 1967, **158**, 1070–1072.

Church, R. M. The varied effects of punishment on behavior. *Psychological Review*, 1963, **70**, 369–402.

Clemente, C. D., & Lindsley, D. B. (Eds.). *Aggression and defense: Neural mechanisms and social patterns*. Vol. 5. Brain function. Los Angeles: University of California Press, 1967.

Denenberg, V. H. The mother as a motivator. In W. Arnold (Ed.), *Nebraska symposium on motivation, 1970*. Lincoln: University of Nebraska Press, 1971. Pp. 69–93.

Denenberg, V. H., Hudgens, G. A., & Zarrow, M. X. Mice reared with rats: Modification of behavior by early experience with another species. *Science*, 1964, **143**, 380–381.

Dudgeon, P. Intellect in Brutes. *Nature*, 1879, **20**, 77.

Duer, J. L., & Parke, R. D. Effects of inconsistent punishment on aggression in children. *Developmental Psychology*, 1970, **2**, 403–411.

Edwards, D. A. The organization and activation of aggression in male and female mice. Unpublished doctoral dissertation, University of California, Irvine, 1968.

Eibl-Eibesfeldt, I. Ontogenetic and maturational studies of aggressive behavior. In C. D. Clemente and D. B. Lindsley (Eds.), *Aggression and defense: Neural mechanisms and social patterns*. Vol. 5. Brain function. Los Angeles: University of California Press, 1967. Pp. 57–71.

Eleftheriou, B. E., & Scott, J. P. (Eds.). *The physiology of aggression and defeat*. New York: Plenum Press, 1971.

Etkin, W. *Social behavior and organization among vertebrates*. Chicago: University of Chicago Press, 1964.

Feshbach, S. Aggression. In P. H. Mussen (Ed.), *Carmichael's manual of psychology*. Vol. 2. (3d ed.). New York: Wiley, 1970. Pp. 159–260.

Fox, K. A., & Snyder, R. L. Effect of sustained low doses of diazepam on aggression and mortality in grouped male mice. *Journal of Comparative and Physiological Psychology*, 1969, **69**, 663–666.

Fuller, J. L. Cross-sectional and longitudinal studies of adjustive behavior in dogs. *Annals of New York Academy of Sciences*, 1953, **56**, 214–224.

Fuller, J. L. Experiential deprivation and later behavior. *Science*, 1967, **158**, 1645–1652.

Fuller, J. L., & Clark, L. D. Effects of rearing with specific stimuli upon postisolation behavior in dogs. *Journal of Comparative and Physiological Psychology*, 1966, **61**, 258–263. (a)

Fuller, J. L., & Clark, L. D. Genetic and treatment factors modifying the postisolation syndrome in dogs. *Journal of Comparative and Physiological Psychology*, 1966, **61**, 251–257. (b)

Fuller, J. L., & Fox, M. W. The behavior of dogs. In E. S. E. Hafez (Ed.), *The behavior of domestic animals*. (2d ed.) Baltimore: Williams & Wilkins, 1969. Pp. 438–481.

Galef, B. G., Jr. Aggression and timidity: Responses to novelty in feral Norway rats. *Journal of Comparative and Physiological Psychology*, 1970, **70**, 370–381.

Gerall, H. D., Ward, I. L., & Gerall, A. A. Disruption of the male rat's sexual behaviour induced by social isolation. *Animal Behavior*, 1967, **15**, 54–58.

Hafez, E. S. E., Cairns, R. B., Hulet, C. V., & Scott, J. P. The behavior of sheep and goats. In E. S. E. Hafez (Ed.), *Behavior of domestic animals*. (2d ed.) Baltimore: Williams & Wilkins, 1969. Pp. 296–348.

Hinde, R. A. *Animal behaviour: A synthesis of ethology and comparative psychology*. (2d ed.) New York: McGraw-Hill, 1970.

Jensen, D. D. Polythetic operationism and the phylogeny of learning. In W. C. Corning and S. C. Ratner (Eds.), *Chemistry of learning: Invertebrate research*. New York: Plenum Press, 1967. Pp. 43–55.

Johnson, R. N. *Aggression in men and animals*. Philadelphia: Saunders, 1972.

Johnson, R. N., DeSisto, M. J., and Koenig, A. B. Social and developmental experience and interspecific aggression in rats. *Journal of Comparative and Physiological Psychology*, 1972, **79**, 237–242.

Kahn, M. W. The effect of severe defeat at various age levels on the aggressive behavior of mice. *Journal of Genetic Psychology*, 1951, **79**, 117–130.

King, J. A. Intra- and interspecific conflict of *Mus* and *Peromyscus*. *Ecology*, 1957, **38**, 355–357. (a)

King, J. A. Relationships between early social experience and adult aggressive behavior in inbred mice. *Journal of Genetic Psychology*, 1957, **90**, 151–166. (b)

King, J. A., & Gurney, N. L. Effect of early social experiences on the aggressive behavior in C57BL/10 mice. *Journal of Comparative and Physiological Psychology*, 1954, **47**, 326–330.

Kummer, H. *Social organization in hamadryas baboons: A field study*. Basel: Bibliothica Primat, 1968.

Kuo, Z. Y. The genesis of the cat's responses to the rat. *Journal of Comparative Psychology*, 1930, **11**, 1–35.

Kuo, Z. Y. Studies on the basic factors in animal fighting: VII. Interspecies co-existence in mammals. *Journal of Genetic Psychology*, 1960, **97**, 211–225.

Kuo, Z. Y. *The dynamics of behavior development: An epigenetic view.* New York: Random House, 1967.

Lagerspetz, K., & Hautojärvi, S. The effect of prior aggressive or sexual arousal on subsequent aggressive or sexual reactions in male mice. *Scandinavian Journal of Psychology*, 1967, **8**, 1–6.

Lagerspetz, K., & Heino, T. Changes in social reactions resulting from early experience with another species. *Psychological Reports*, 1970, **27**, 255–262.

Lagerspetz, K. Y. H., Tirri, R., & Lagerspetz, K. M. J. Neurochemical and endocrinological studies of mice selectively bred for aggressiveness. *Scandinavian Journal of Psychology*, 1968, **9**, 157–160.

Lorenz, K. *On aggression.* New York: Harcourt, Brace & World, 1966.

Mandler, G. The interruption of behavior. In D. Levine (Ed.), *Nebraska symposium on motivation, 1964.* Lincoln: University of Nebraska Press, 1964. Pp. 163–219.

Mason, W. A. The effects of social restriction on the behavior of rhesus monkeys: I. Free social behavior. *Journal of Comparative and Physiological Psychology*, 1960, **53**, 582–589.

McDougall, W. *An introduction to social psychology.* London: Methuen, 1908.

Milakovich, J. T. Factors influencing aggressive behavior in mice. Unpublished M.A. thesis, Indiana University, 1970.

Montagu, M. F. A. (Ed.). *Man and aggression.* London: Oxford University Press, 1968.

Moyer, K. E. A preliminary physiological model of aggressive behavior. In B. E. Eleftheriou and J. P. Scott (Eds.), *The physiology of aggression and defeat.* New York: Plenum Press, 1971. Pp. 223–264.

Myer, J. S. Associative and temporal determinants of facilitation and inhibition of attack by pain. *Journal of Comparative and Physiological Psychology*, 1968, **66**, 17–21.

Patterson, G. R., & Cobb, J. A. A dyadic analysis of "aggressive" behaviors. In J. P. Hill (Ed.), *Minnesota symposia on child psychology.* Vol. 5. Minneapolis: University of Minnesota Press, 1971. Pp. 72–129.

Patterson, G. R., Littman, R. A., & Bricker, W. Assertive behavior in children: A step toward a theory of aggression. *Monographs of the Society for Research in Child Development*, 1967, 32 (Whole No. 113).

Phoenix, C. H., Goy, R. W., & Resko, J. A. Psychosexual differentiation as a function of androgenic stimulation. In M. Diamond (Ed.), *Reproduction and sexual behavior.* Bloomington: Indiana University Press, 1968. Pp. 33–49.

Prescott, J. W. Early somatosensory deprivation as an ontogenetic process in the abnormal development of the brain and behavior. In I. E. Goldsmith and J. Moor-Janowski (Eds.), *Medical primatology, 1970.* Basel: Karger, 1971. Pp. 356–375.

Restle, F. Theory of serial pattern learning: Structural trees. *Psychological Review*, 1970, **77**, 481–495.

Rheingold, H. L. Maternal behavior in the dog. In H. L. Rheingold (Ed.), *Maternal behavior in mammals.* New York: Wiley, 1963. Pp. 169–202.

Rogers, W. W. An experimental study of the behavior of kittens toward white albino rats. *Psychological Bulletin*, 1928, **25**, 476–478.

Romanes, G. J. *Mental evolution in animals*. New York: D. Appleton & Co., 1884.

Ropartz, P. The relation between olfactory stimulation and aggressive behavior in mice. *Animal Behaviour*, 1968, **16**, 97–100.

Rosenblatt, J. S., & Lehrman, D. S. Maternal behavior of the laboratory rat. In H. L. Rheingold (Ed.), *Maternal behavior in mammals*. New York: Wiley, 1963. Pp. 8–57.

Rosenblum, L. A., & Kaufman, I. C. Variations in infant development and responses to maternal loss in monkeys. *American Journal of Orthopsychiatry*, 1968, **38**, 418–426.

Sackett, G. P. Some persistence effects of different rearing conditions, on pre-adult social behavior of monkeys. *Journal of Comparative and Physiological Psychology*, 1967, **64**, 363–365.

Schneirla, T. C. Behavioral development and comparative psychology. *Quarterly Review of Biology*, 1966, **41**, 283–302.

Scholz, S. D. The effects of brief separations upon maternal behavior and infant development. Unpublished doctoral dissertation, Indiana University, 1973.

Scott, J. P. *Aggression*. Chicago: University of Chicago Press, 1958.

Scott, J. P. Agonistic behavior of mice and rats: A review. *American Zoologist*, 1966, **6**, 683–70.

Scott, J. P. Theoretical issues concerning the origin and causes of fighting. In B. E. Eleftheriou and J. P. Scott (Eds.), *The physiology of aggression and defeat*. New York: Plenum Press, 1971. Pp. 11–41.

Scott, J. P., & Fuller, J. L. *Genetics and the social behavior of the dog*. Chicago: University of Chicago Press, 1965.

Sears, R. R. A theoretical framework for personality and social behavior. *American Psychologist*, 1951, **6**, 476–483.

Solomon, R. L. Punishment. *American Psychologist*, 1964, **12**, 239–253.

Soulairac, A. L'effet de groupe dans le compotement sexuel du rat male: Etude experimentale du comportement en groupe du rat blanc. In *Structure et physiologie des societes animales*. Paris: Centre National de la Recherche Scientifique, 1952.

Toch, H. *Violent Men: An inquiry into the psychology of violence*. Chicago: Aldine, 1969.

Uhrich, J. The social hierarchy in albino mice. *Journal of Comparative Psychology*, 1938, **25**, 373–413.

Valzelli, L., Giacalone, E., & Garattini, S. Pharmacological control of aggressive behavior in mice. *European Journal of Pharmacology*, 1967, **2**, 144–146.

Walters, R. H. On the high magnitude theory of aggression. *Child Development*, 1964, **35**, 303–304.

Watson, J. B. What the nursery has to say about instincts. In C. Murchison (Ed.), *Psychologies of 1925*. Worcester, Mass: Clark University Press, 1926. Pp. 1–36.

Welch, B. L. Discussion of "Aggression, defense, and neurohumors." In C. D. Clemente and D. B. Lindsley (Eds.), *Aggression and defense: Neural mechanisms and social patterns.* Vol. 5. *Brain function.* Los Angeles: University of California Press, 1967. Pp. 150–170.

Welch, A. S., & Welch, B. L. Isolation, reactivity and aggression: Evidence for an involvement of brain catecholamines and serotonin. In B. E. Eleftheriou and J. P. Scott (Eds.), *The physiology of aggression and defeat.* New York: Plenum Press, 1971. Pp. 91–142.

Welker, W. I. Factors affecting aggregation of neonatal puppies. *Journal of Comparative and Physiological Psychology,* 1959, **52,** 376–380.

Yarrow, M. R., Campbell, J. D., & Burton, R. V. *Child rearing: An inquiry into research and methods.* San Francisco: Jossey-Bass, 1968.

Patterning Mechanisms, Patterned Reflexes, and Attack Behavior in Cats

JOHN P. FLYNN

Yale University School of Medicine

A number of years ago Wasman and I (1962) wanted to study an emotional behavior that could be elicited from a cat regularly and did not require training the animal. The behavior we decided on was "rage," a classical object of study in physiology. At the time, there was still some uncertainty as to whether the rage elicited by stimulation of the brain was sham or not. The display seen consisted of actions such as retraction of the lips, exposure of the canine teeth, piloerection, and arching of the back. An inner emotional feeling is not a necessary condition for the appearance of this display, since these overt behaviors can occur in decerebrate cats (Woodworth & Sherrington, 1904), in which the entire forebrain has been removed, and even more easily in hypothalamic cats (Bard, 1928), in which much of the forebrain except for a posterior segment is eliminated, as well as in animals lacking neocortex (Bard & Rioch, 1937). Masserman (1941) claimed that the effect elicited in the otherwise normal animal was a purely motor response, much like that obtained when the nerve to a muscle is stimulated. On the other hand, Hess (1928) and his associates (Hess & Akert, 1955) asserted it was not. To see if it was sham, in the nature of a simple display, we placed a rat in the observation cage with the cat. The cats used in our experiments, if left unstimulated, did not attack rats. When the current was passed through an appropriate site in the brain, the cat chased and struck or bit the rat, killing it if the current was left on, demonstrating that the attack was directed. From a rat's point of view, it was definitely not sham. Two forms of attack were seen. One was accompanied by the classical rage display which Hess and Brugger (1943) called affective defense (Figure 1). In the other, which we called quiet biting attack, the cat moved swiftly about the cage with its nose low to the ground, back somewhat arched, and hair slightly on end, and usually went directly to the rat and bit it viciously (Figure 2). In the absence of an attack object, the cat moved around the cage, sometimes sniffing. If the intensity of the stimulus is increased, the display often approaches that of the affective form of attack.

We have studied attack elicited by stimulation rather than naturally occurring attack for a number of reasons. In comparison to spontaneously occurring behavior, elicited attack is less variable; the form of the behavior can be selected within limits by the experimenter's choosing proper sites for the electrodes, and the experimenter can regulate the ferocity of the attack by manipulating the parameters of stimulation. Finally, stimulation tends to exaggerate particular aspects of a behavior pattern, often giving rise to an effect associated primarily with one side of the body. Thus, the consistency and laterality of the responses elicited by stimulation make them more amenable to analysis and provide the experimenter with an opportunity to study particular aspects of attack behavior in detail. Nonetheless, the overt elicited behavior closely resembles that occurring naturally, and for this reason we think that the same kinds of changes observed during the stimulated behavior occur in the natural state, although this remains to be documented.

The question that my colleagues and I have attempted to answer is, What is the neural basis of attack behavior? I emphasize neural basis because there are many other ways in which to attempt to answer the general question of how the attack is brought about. One might wish to know if the behavior results from an affective state, i.e., from the cat's being made angry by the stimulation, or if the behavior is simply a response to pain. Both Hess (1957) and Masserman (1943) thought that the answer lay in the realm of the psyche, with Masserman ultimately on the basis of his experiments denying the presence of affect, and Hess asserting it. Certainly the question of affect arises naturally when noxious stimulation is applied either to the cat's skin or to central pathways that are known

Fig. 1. Affective attack.

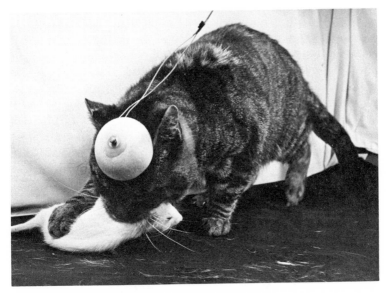

Fig. 2. Quiet biting attack.

to be associated with the transmission of noxious stimulation. Intact cats shocked through the paws attack rats (Ulrich, Wolf, & Azrin, 1967). Adams and Flynn (1966) showed that some forms of centrally elicited affective attack, namely, those accompanied by several types of vocalization, were associated with noxious stimulation. In this connection it should be noted that aversive stimulation is not always associated with attack (Nakao, 1958; Plotnik, Mir, & Delgado, 1971), and that attack can be dissociated from aversive stimulation (Flynn, Vanegas, Foote, & Edwards, 1970).

Another way of answering the general question of how the attack is brought about is to say that the behavior results from a drive or motive induced by stimulation. This answer by itself does not raise the issue of the cat's subjective state. One reason for invoking the concept of motivation is that at times an object in the environment may elicit an action, and at other times the same object may not. If, in accord with this, we regard motivation as an internal state which determines whether or not the behavior occurs, and which furthermore gives direction to the activity, then elicited attack can be regarded as motivated. Since our cats do not attack rats in the absence of stimulation, attack depends on an internal state which is electrically generated. The behavior is directed in the sense that the cat follows the fleeing rat and in the sense that the cat will go to a rat which is out of sight in the arm of a maze (Roberts & Kiess, 1964). So in a general way one can say that the behavior is motivated.

Before proceeding, however, there are several comments that I wish to make that are related to the statement that attack behavior is motivated. First of all, we have not investigated motivation for attack experimentally because even if we learned the similarities and differences between naturally occurring and centrally elicited attack in terms of motivation, we would still not know the neural mechanisms underlying the behavior, since we cannot as yet point to a common integrated core of neural mechanisms underlying motivated behaviors. My second comment is concerned with the dichotomy between motivated and reflexive behavior. This dichotomy is not as clear as it might seem at first glance. For example, reflexive behavior is akin to Pavlov's unconditioned reflexes, some of which embrace motivated states (Pavlov, 1928). Pavlov deprived his dogs of food and pointed out that the formation of conditioned reflexes was dependent on the activity of the food center which was set in operation by the deprivation. Similarly, Konorski's preparatory alimentary unconditioned reflex is a hunger reflex (Konorski, 1967). These reflexes are simply not of the same order as those investigated by Sherrington (1961). Moreover, it seems to me that behavior may both be motivated and embody reflexes that are an integral part of the motivated behavior. These patterned reflexes, as we call them, are very similar to those investigated by Sherrington. In this connection, it should be noted that a major portion of elicited attack is ordinarily dependent on the presence of a rat, which serves as a stimulus for the actual reflexes. This behavior once started is not an automatic motor sequence, since the sequence of opening the mouth and biting repeatedly is blocked by sectioning sensory branches of the trigeminal nerve (MacDonnell & Flynn, 1966a). The concept of a fixed action pattern does not jibe with our experimental data in so far as the patterned reflexes, to be described later, do not require that they be elicited in sequence for them to appear.

As stated earlier, our primary interest has been in the neural basis of attack behavior, not in the neural basis of motivation. In saying that we are interested in the neural basis of behavior, rather than motivation, we do not regard this as in any way unique. Historically much of the work on the problem has proceeded along these lines. Nonetheless, there are several aspects to such an approach that are important and worth noting. The end point, namely attack, is more obvious than motivation to attack. This may have a bearing on the aspects of attack that are studied. With a focus on motivation, one is more likely to study the animal's behavior in the absence of an attack object, i.e., its performance in reaching a hidden object. With a focus on the attack behavior itself, one is more likely to look at the acts immediately involved in attack. Certainly that is what we have done. The problem of the neural mechanisms underlying the cat's locating a target, whether absent or present, seems at the moment a more difficult task than the study of the behaviors of striking, biting, or lunging. A study of these terminal behaviors may provide clues about the basis of the cat's performance when an attack object is available but hidden or when a learned act has to be interpolated before the cat reaches the rat. The second aspect of this approach is that experiments are designed somewhat differently, centering on obvious aspects of the behavior. A third advantage lies in the fact that once the segments of the behavior are understood, it is not difficult to hypothesize and test probable physiological mechanisms underlying them.

The behavior that we have been most concerned with is the behavior that ensues when a rat is present and is attacked. This includes the cat's approaching a rat, striking at it, placing a paw on it, lunging at it, and biting it. Thus far we have not studied in any detail the cat's behavior when an attack object is available but not present. In our view, when a cat is stimulated at an attack site, the stimulation brings about more than a central motive state. Stimulation sets up a pattern of excitation within the sensory and motor systems. In other words, the visual system is influenced by stimulation, as is the tactile system, and similarly, the motor pathways involved in striking and biting are influenced by stimulation. The influence often manifests itself more strongly on the side of the animal contralateral to the site stimulated than on the ipsilateral side. In order to emphasize the neural nature of the effects of stimulation we have referred to those areas from which attack is elicited as patterning mechanisms, since they are capable of imposing a pattern on the nervous system. Some of these facilitated sensory and motor systems constitute reflexes, and since they are found ordinarily only while the patterning mechanism is active, they have been called patterned reflexes. A combination of these reflexes make up important elements of the attack, but they are probably not the complete mechanism. These reflexes include the cat's striking at the rat, placing a paw on it, lunging at it, and moving its head to bite it, and finally, the opening and closing of the cat's mouth. These mechanisms are in addition to those producing the overt responses of the rage display, which involves not only autonomic effects but also facial expressions and vocalization. While this display is not as dependent on objects in the environment as is the previous category of activities, it can be modified by them.

First we will look at aspects of the patterning mechanism and then at a number of patterned reflexes. In order to find out how stimulation at a given site can affect different systems, we have

begun to look at the neuroanatomical structures which are presumably excited by stimulation. Carl Chi and I (Chi & Flynn,
1971a; 1971b) have been studying the degeneration that resulted
when sites in the hypothalamus from which attack was previously
elicited were destroyed. The lesions made were small (maximum
diameters varied from 0.5 to 1.0 mm), and attack could no longer
be elicited after the lesion, even at intensities of stimulation two to
three times greater than those previously effective. The degenerated

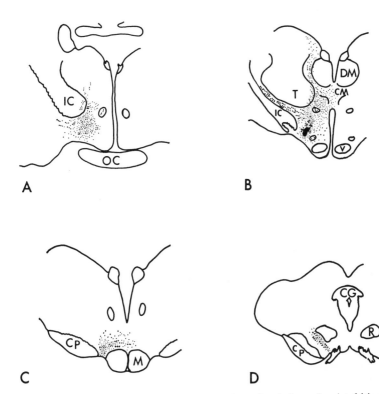

Fig. 3. Representative chart of degeneration after lesion of quiet biting
attack site, plotted on frontal sections, Cat Brain 01130. (A) Most rostral section;
(D) most caudal section. Abbreviations: *CG*, central gray; *CM*, nucleus centralis
medius; *CP*, cerebral peduncle; *DM*, dorsomedial nucleus; *IC*, internal capsule;
M, mammillary body; *OC*, optic chiasm; *R*, red nucleus; *T*, ventral nucleus of
thalamus; *V*, ventromedial nucleus of hypothalamus.

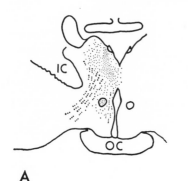

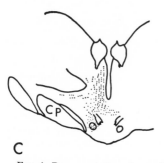

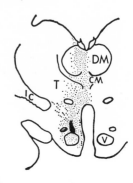

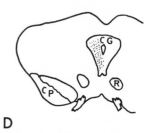

Fig. 4. Representative chart of degeneration after lesion of affective attack site, plotted in frontal sections, Cat Brain 03180. (A) Most rostral section; (D) most caudal section. See Fig. 3 caption for abbreviations.

fibers were stained with silver according to two recent modifications of the Nauta technique. Both degenerating fibers and axon terminals can be stained by these methods. In general, degeneration techniques reveal only one link in the chain of neurones that are presumably activated by stimulation. Successive links in the chain can be discovered by going to the site of termination of degenerating fibers and seeing if in fact stimulation there gives rise to attack (as in fact it does) or some component of it and then extending the degeneration studies.

The actual degeneration seen from lesions of the sort just described are shown in Figures 3, 4, and 5. The degeneration was in the medial forebrain bundle and in the periventricular system.

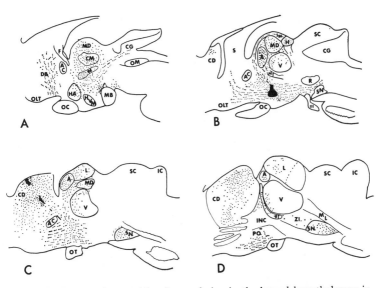

A   B

C   D

Fig. 5. Degeneration resulting from a lesion in the lateral hypothalamus in Cat 04030, plotted on charts of sagittal sections. (A) Most medial section; (D) most lateral section. Electrode track is indicated in section C. Abbreviations: *A*, anterior nucleus of thalamus; *AC*, anterior commissure; *DC*, caudate nucleus; *CM*, nucleus centralis medialis; *DB*, diagonal band; *F*, fornix; *H*, habenula; *HA*, anterior nucleus of hypothalamus; *HVM*, ventromedial nucleus of hypothalamus; *IC*, inferior colliculus; *INC*, internal capsule; *L*, lateral nucleus of thalamus; *MB*, mammillary body; *MD*, dorsomedial nucleus of thalamus; *ML*, medial lemniscus; *MT*, mammillothalamic tract; *OC*, optic chiasm; *OLT*, olfactory tubercle; *OM*, oculomotor nucleus; *OT*, optic tract; *PO*, preoptic area; *R*, red nucleus; *SC*, superior colliculus; *SM*, stria medullaris; *SN*, substantia nigra; *V*, ventral nucleus of thalamus; *ZI*, zona incerta.

In the course of our studies, two kinds of attack were seen, as was stated earlier. One was quiet biting attack, often marked by the cat's stalking; the other was affective attack, marked by a display and vocalization and striking the rat. Degeneration in the medial forebrain bundle was more marked in the case of quiet biting attack (Figure 3), while that in the periventricular system was more marked in the case of affective striking attack (Figure 4). However, both systems may be involved in both forms of attack, the involvement of the periventricular system in quiet attack being illustrated in Figure 5. Work extending these findings is under way.

Michael Sledjeski and I (Sledjeski & Flynn, 1972) have also attempted to look at the nature of the excitation which is produced by stimulation at sites from which attack is elicited. We wished to look at the nature of the internal changes brought about by electrical stimulation. Our approach has been somewhat indirect. We assessed the nature of the excitation by looking at the effects of prior stimulation on subsequent stimulation, in a fashion similar to that employed in looking at temporal and spatial facilitation. We stimulated the brain with a train of pulses and then after a short delay stimulated the brain at the same site with a second train of pulses, and compared the effects due to the second train with those elicited by a control train, which was not preceded by any stimulation. In that way one could see the effects of the initial train.

In this experiment 5 seconds of priming stimulation were followed at intervals of 2, 4, 8, 16, or 32 seconds by a stimulus train which was continued until attack occurred. The current was fixed at an intensity that was insufficient to elicit attack within 5 seconds, but sufficient to elicit attack after 5 seconds. Each experimental trial was preceded or followed in balanced order by a control trial without priming. Ten pairs of control and priming trials, two at each temporal interval, were carried out in each of five daily experimental sessions. Five minutes elapsed between trials. The primary measure was latency to attack, which was the time from the onset of stimulation until the cat bit the rat. This latency was timed with a stopwatch. The results for five individual animals and for the group are presented in Figure 6. At all but the longest interval, the latencies to attack were shorter when the test stimulus was preceded by a priming stimulus than when it was not. The results indicate an increased excitability after priming, but with the parameters employed, the excitation returns to control levels before some 32 seconds. The return to control levels is linear (by inspection) with respect to the logarithm of the time elapsed after priming.

We then looked at some geographical as well as temporal properties of the excitation. From a physiological point of view this is a meaningful question. If one stimulates two sites within the

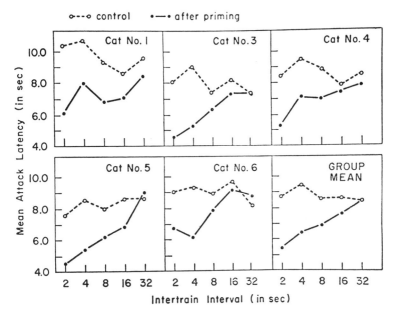

Fig. 6. The latencies to attack are reduced when a test pulse train is preceded by a priming train. The effect of the priming train decreases as the time from the end of the priming train to the beginning of the test train increases. Control values were obtained during trials without priming, which were paired with the priming trials. The abscissa is a logarithmic scale.

brain, does stimulation at one site influence the effects of stimulation at the second site? That is essentially the question of spatial facilitation or inhibition. We have employed this paradigm before in investigating the effects of concurrent stimulation of the amygdala and hypothalamus, hippocampus and hypothalamus, and midbrain and hypothalamus. In the present experiment the study of temporal and spatial facilitation was combined. This combination gives us a sensitive measure of the interaction, telling us something about the direction of conduction of the excitation.

If one looks at the experiment in terms of states such as arousal or drive, the question raised is harder to understand. Temporal facilitation can be translated without much difficulty. Does prior motivation alter later motivation? Does arousing an animal by stimulating its midbrain reticular formation increase the probability of its attacking? The question of summation of psychological entities originating from two spatially separated sites presents difficulties. One has difficulty in understanding a concept such as drive or arousal from an anterior as opposed to a posterior position. In the physiological terms, however, the question retains its meaning in terms of the interaction of two spatially separate groups of neurones.

Let us first look at the data just presented from a behavioral point of view. The priming may be effective because of its behavioral effects. With the initial or priming train the animal was alerted, moved about, and in some instances would attack if the stimulation was prolonged, whereas in the absence of priming the animal was not specifically alerted and was often in a resting state until stimulated. To see if these behaviors were the important elements, they were induced at sites in the brain other than the test sites. In Cats 1, 2, and 3, alerting and movement, but not attack, could be elicited at the alternate priming site. In Cats 4 and 5, alerting and movement were elicited by the priming stimulus. However, at both a and b sites, in Cats 4 and 5 attack could be elicited by longer stimulation than that used in the priming train. Priming at the alternate site and at the test site was equated by adjusting the intensities of the current to yield similar initial movement latencies, that is, the time from which the stimulation was begun until the animal made its first movement from the place of initial stimulation. If the behavior were the important variable, the site of priming should be secondary. The priming sites were all in the hypothalamus except for Cat 1, whose priming site was in the lower mesencephalic reticular formation. Some priming sites were posterior to the test site and others anterior. In each of the five cats the alternate priming site was ipsilateral to the test site. The priming trains lasted 5 seconds and the test trains were initiated 2 seconds later, and were terminated when the cat bit the rat. Priming at alternate sites was compared with no priming, and with priming at the test site. There were 10 trials under each condition, for a total of 30 trials.

The results are presented in Table 1. The elicited behavior does not account for the effectiveness of priming. At four priming sites other than the test site, even though priming alerted the cats and

TABLE 1
Reduction in Latency to Attack When Priming Occurred at Site Other Than Test Site and at Test Site

Cat (number) and Test Site (letter)	Priming at Other Site	Priming at Test Site
1	7%	36% *
2	10%	60% *
4a	3%	31% *
5a	−11%	30% *
3	25% *	66% **
4b	20% *	34% **
5b	25% *	35% **

Note: Priming always elicits alerting and movement. (Movement latencies at other site and test site were equated.)
* Indicates that priming significantly different from no priming (.001)
** Priming significantly different from priming at other site (.01).

produced locomotor activity these behavioral responses were not effective in shortening the latencies to the test stimuli. In three other instances the priming was effective in reducing the latencies, but the effect was significantly less than the effect of priming at the same site even though the latencies for movement were similar. In this case also a purely behavioral explanation is inadequate. Priming was most effective when it was at the same site as the test site. In all instances the reduction in latencies was greatest in that condition and significantly different from any other condition.

Now let us look at these data in terms of the spatial arrangement of the priming site and the test site, which is more in accord with the physiological question. In Table 2 the data are presented in terms of the anatomical position of the priming site relative to the test site, which is the site from which attack was elicited during the second train of pulses.

From these data it can be seen that priming was most effective when done at the test site. If the priming site was anterior to the test site, priming occurred, but was significantly less effective than at the test site. If the priming was done at sites posterior to the test site, the priming was ineffective and did not differ from the control condition in which no priming pulse train was administered. In Cats 4 and 5, in each of which there were two effective attack sites, switching the site of priming yielded the general finding. Since the anterior priming sites were effective, and the posterior ones were

TABLE 2

Reduction in Attack Latency When Priming Occurred at Sites
Posterior and Anterior to Test Site and at Test Site

Cat Number	Priming Site			Test Site			Percent Reduction in Latency
	F	L	H	F	L	H	
Priming Site Same as Test Site							
1	11.0	3.0	−5.2		same		36%
2	12.5	2.7	−3.0		same		60%
3	11.5	1.2	−3.5		same		66%
4a	13.0	2.5	−3.0		same		31%
4b	10.0	3.0	−3.0		same		34%
5a	13.0	2.5	−3.0		same		30%
5b	11.0	3.0	−3.5		same		35%
Priming Site Anterior to Test Site							
3	14.5	1.5	−2.5	11.5	1.2	−3.5	25%
4b	13.0	2.5	−3.0	10.0	3.0	−3.0	20%
5b	13.0	2.5	−3.0	11.0	3.0	−3.5	25%
Priming Site Posterior to Test Site							
1	3.0	2.0	−5.0	11.0	3.0	−5.2	7%
2	9.0	2.5	4.0	12.5	2.7	−3.0	10%
4a	10.0	3.0	−3.0	13.0	2.5	−3.0	3%
5a	11.0	3.0	−3.5	13.0	2.5		−11%

Note: The percent reduction in latency is 100 (1 − latency with priming / latency without priming). The statistical tests were based on the differences in individual latencies. The locations of the tips of the electrodes are given in coordinates from the Jasper and Ajmone-Marson atlas.

not, the data indicate that the major direction of influence is from the anterior onto the posterior sites. This conclusion is in accord with the general hypothesis of Fernandez de Molina and Hunsperger (1959), who proposed that the growling and growling-hissing patterns elicited by electrical stimulation of the amygdala developed through the activity of the hissing zone of the hypothalamus, and the activity of the hypothalamus is maintained in turn by the presence of the central gray matter of the midbrain. This hypothesis was based on the findings that the growling-hissing pattern obtained on stimulation of the amygdala was suppressed by an ipsilateral lesion placed at midbrain or hypothalamic levels. The hissing pattern obtained from the hypothalamus was blocked by bilateral coagulation of the central gray of the midbrain. Their hypothesis is in accord with both their findings and the early findings of Woodworth and Sherrington (1904), who elicited partial patterns of rage in decerebrate cats, and with Bard's (1928) findings of sham rage in hypothalamic animals. This conclusion is also in accord with the findings of Bergquist (1970), that posterior lateral lesions in the hypothalamus could block quiet attack elicited from anterior sites, and posterior middle lesions could block affective attack, while anterior and lateral lesions were generally ineffective.

It should also be stated that the direction of influence is not exclusively from anterior to posterior, since Barbara Inselman and I (1972) now have evidence that posterior sites in the hypothalamus can influence anterior sites in the preoptic region.

In a third experiment Sledjeski and I dealt with a question that is readily understood in psychological terms, but not equally readily understood in physiological terms. Does the act of attacking change the poststimulus excitability? If the cat attacked the rat during the priming train, would the latencies to attack during the test train be changed?

Observations were made on seven cats. In one cat, two sites were used. Priming and testing were always at the same site. Each trial consisted of two stimulus trains separated by a 5-second interval. There was no rat in the test cage during the first train of half of the trials and in the others a rat was present. At six of the sites, the initial train lasted 10 seconds. Since it proved difficult to elicit attack in less than 10 seconds reliably from Cats 5 and 6, the duration of the first train for them was 15 seconds. During all trials, the cage door was opened between trains and the rat was placed in a standard position on the cage floor. Twenty-five pairs of trials were conducted over three daily sessions. Occasionally attack did not occur within the duration of the priming train. Those pairs in which this happened were dropped from the computations.

The results are presented in Figure 7. The mean latencies to attack during the test trials were longer when the cat had attacked a rat during the priming train than when it could not do so. With attack the excitability was less than without attack.

The occurrence of attack during the initial train decreased, but did not abolish, poststimulus excitability. When attack occurred during the priming stimulus, the latency to the test stimulus was

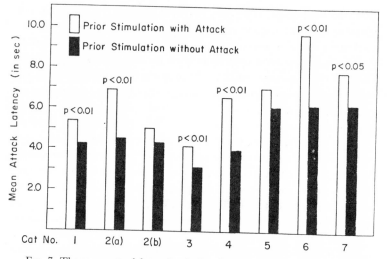

FIG. 7. The mean attack latencies during the second of two pulse trains were longer when attack was permitted during the first pulse train, indicating that the excitation from the first pulse train is less. The p values are based on t tests for paired comparisons of the latencies in the two conditions.

reduced 22%, a statistically significant reduction. When the attack could not occur during the priming stimulus, the corresponding reduction was 43%.

To translate some of the findings into the context of this symposium, it is clear that the internal state that brings about the behavior has a temporal pattern and is localized, being strongest at the site of stimulation, and though it may extend beyond its own limits, its influence has directional characteristics within the brain. Furthermore, the general behavior elicited by stimulation is less important than is the anatomical locus of excitation. These observations in general make it very difficult to assume that the arousal of a simple drive is sufficient to account for the behavioral data that have been presented.

Thus far we have considered some properties of the patterning mechanism itself. At this point we would like to look at a number of patterned reflexes which at least in part account for the cat's behavior. These patterned reflexes are found in cats from which attack is elicited and they are highly appropriate to the form of behavior in which the cat is engaged.

A number of years ago Malcolm MacDonnell and I (1966b) investigated the role of sensory systems in attack elicited by stimulation of the hypothalamus. Without going into the details of the experiments, we found that the visual system and the tactile system were of primary importance, and two tactile areas, the muzzle and the forepaws, were particularly involved. The olfactory system, contrary to our expectations, was not of critical importance.

In order to understand the nature of the deficits, we (MacDonnell & Flynn, 1966a) looked at the functioning of the cats whose sensory systems were intact and found that there were reflexes present that would be interfered with by sectioning of sensory branches of the trigeminal nerve which supplies innervation of the muzzle. Specifically, two reflexes were found. If the area of muzzle indicated in Figure 8 is touched during stimulation, the cat moves its head to bring the tactile stimulus to the lip. When the lip is touched, the mouth snaps open. The effective area for mouth opening is shown in Figure 9. In both figures the area shown is the maximum region from which the reflexes are elicited. These reflexes are customarily not present in the absence of stimulation.

The receptive field for these reflexes increases in size with increase in intensity of stimulation at an attack site in the brain. The field for mouth opening increases from the midline of the cat's lip back to the corner of the cat's mouth. This is documented in Figure 10. A particularly important feature of this phenomenon is the fact that the field on the lip opposite to the side of the brain stimulated is larger than the field on the ipsilateral side. This difference in responsiveness between the two sides of the muzzle indicates a differential excitation of the two sides of the body by the stimulation. The stimulation brings the reflex itself into play, but it affects one receptive field for the reflex more than it does the other. Other examples of the differential responsiveness of the two sides of the body will be brought out with respect to other reflexes.

A second tactile patterned reflex involves striking (Bandler & Flynn, 1972). In this case, the patterned reflex consists of a movement of the paw to strike, hold, and position a furry object with which the paw has been stroked. Light tactile stimulation produces

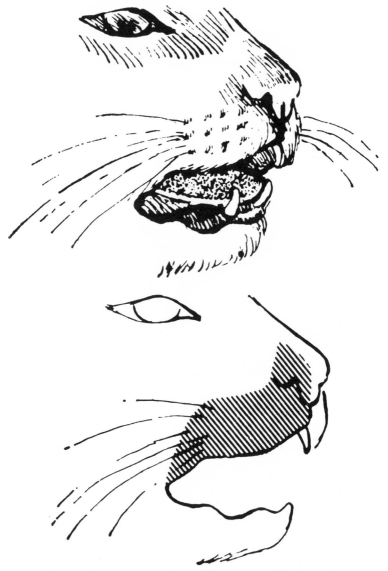

Fig. 8.   Maximum extent of the maxillary sensory field for head-orienting responses during relatively intense stimulation. A similar mandibular field has not yet been mapped in detail.

FIG. 9. Maximum extent of the sensory field for the jaw-opening response during relatively intense stimulation.

an initial flexor movement followed by extension of the forelimb and claws with a slight adduction occurring when the object is touched. The untouched forelimb is occasionally used in this final stage of grasping the furry object. Observations were made on six cats. The testing was done with the cat held in a loose-fitting canvas bag from which its head and forelimbs protruded, its head being fixed by a head-holder.

Several features of this reflex should be noted. First of all, the reflex is present during stimulation; at other times stroking the paw

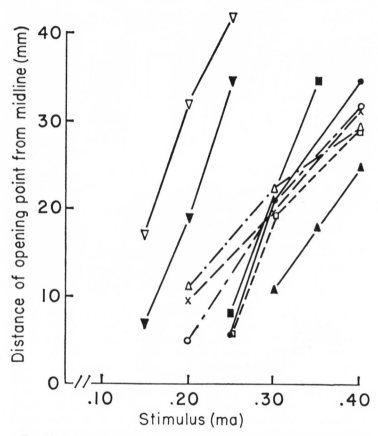

F₁G. 10. Extent of sensory fields for jaw-opening increases with intensity of stimulation. The data are from eight different cats, and all but one (the solid circles) of the curves represent the maxillary lip-line field. Each point is the mean of ten trials.

elicits little response, aside from an occasional lifting of the paw. Second, the reflex is stronger on the paw contralateral to the side of the brain stimulated than it is on the ipsilateral paw. Furthermore, the tactile, receptive fields for the reflex increase in size according to the successive tactile dermatomes. The correspondence between the receptive fields and the dermatomes is shown in Figure 11. The size of the tactile receptive fields for the reflex increases with

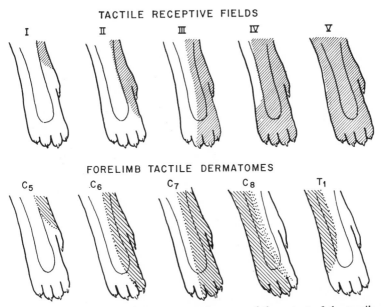

FIG. 11. The first row is a representative map of the extent of the tactile receptive fields on the cat's forelimb from which striking could be elicited during stimulation. As the intensity of hypothalamic stimulation was increased the extent of the tactile receptive field expanded from I to V (also see Fig. 2). The second row is a map of the C_5 to T_1 tactile dermatomes of the cat's forelimb, adapted from J. Hekmatpanah (1961). A comparison of rows 1 and 2 suggests that at low intensities of hypothalamic stimulation the tactile receptive field approximates the area of the C_5 and C_6 dermatomes, and as the intensity of hypothalamic stimulation was increased the tactile receptive field expanded to include the approximate area of the next successive tactile dermatomes, C_7, C_8, and T_1.

increasing stimulation to the hypothalamus. This increase and the difference between the contralateral and ipsilateral paws are shown in Figure 12. In addition, increasing the intensity of hypothalamic stimulation increased the briskness of the motor response. With low-intensity stimulation the motor response consisted of the final adduction phase of the strike. At higher intensities the complete strike sequence described above was elicited.

In a study of striking that was elicited by stimulation of the ventral quadrant of the central gray of the midbrain, an analogous

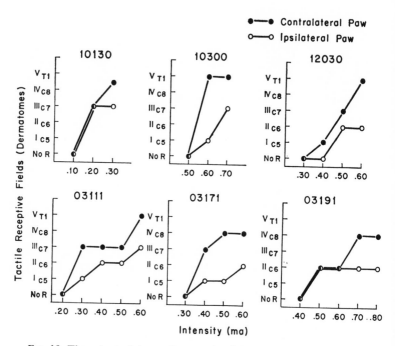

FIG. 12. The extent of the tactile receptive field for striking is indicated for each forelimb as a function of the intensity of hypothalamic stimulation. The data are from six cats. Each point is the average of ten trials and represents the greatest extent (on at least 50% of the trials) of the tactile receptive field at each stimulation intensity. All differences were significant by at least $p < .05$ (χ^2 test). Tactile receptive fields are represented on the ordinate. The intensity in ma (peak to peak) of hypothalamic stimulation is represented on the abscissa.

set of observations was made (Edwards and Flynn). Striking is a prominent feature of the form of attack in which an affective display consisting of vocalization, opening of the mouth, baring of the teeth, retraction of the lips and ears, piloerection, and sometimes arching of the back occurs. Although such a display can take place without an attack marked by striking, the latter is rarely noted in the absence of a display. Striking depends upon objects being in the environment, a moving unanesthetized rat being more likely to elicit striking than an anesthetized one.

While visual guidance appears to be an intrinsic part of the striking elicited from stimulation of the central gray matter, only the motor aspects of it have been studied thus far. The behavioral evidence for a specific facilitation of motor mechanisms involved in striking on one side of the body as opposed to those of the other side comes from the fact that the strike is always delivered by the forelimb contralateral to the side of the brain stimulated. This effect of stimulation is depicted in Figure 13. The particular limb used in striking can be reversed by stimulating the other side of the brain, so the effect is not a matter of limb preference. Cats 1, 4, 6, and 8 struck with the contralateral limb, using the left or right forelimb, depending on the side stimulated. The role of the pyramidal tract in

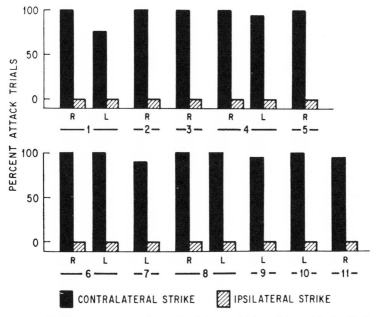

Fig. 13. The percentage of attack trials in which striking with the limb contralateral and ipsilateral to the side of midbrain stimulation occurred for each cat used in this experiment (designated by numbers). Letters refer to the side of central gray electrode placement in each cat. Eighty attack trials were conducted for each electrode placement.

striking was examined in these cats. Lesions of the pyramidal tract were found to impair flexor movements at the elbow and wrist. Despite this impairment, which in seven cats was unilateral, the impaired animals never resorted to the use of the unimpaired limb, which strongly suggests involvement of the motor system of the contralateral limb.

A more direct involvement of the visual system in a patterned reflex is demonstrated by results obtained by Bandler and me (Bandler & Flynn, 1971). The patterned reflex in this case consists of a cat's lunge toward a mouse visually presented during electrical stimulation of the brain at attack sites. Observations were made on five cats. The experiment was conducted with the cats restrained in a loose-fitting canvas bag from which its head protruded. The cat in its sack was further enclosed in a plastic box that left its head, but not its body, free to move. For each experimental trial the hypothalamic attack site was stimulated for 30 seconds. During this time a deeply anesthetized mouse attached at one end of a tongue depressor was rapidly moved toward the cat's head and directed towards the mouth. The experimenter varied the angle of presentation, exploring the cat's visual field. Movements of the cat's head introduced additional variations in the angle of presentation. The number of presentations within a 30-second period varied from 5 to 10, depending upon the cat's success in reaching the mouse. First one eye was covered and then the other, and the occurrence of lunging by the cat towards the mouse was noted. A blinder along the midline front restricted the visual fields. At least 5 minutes intervened between each pair of 30-second trials. No more than 10 trials were carried out on the same day at any one attack site.

In the unstimulated cat the visual presentation of the mouse produced no observable activity beyond a tendency in some cats to withdraw the head from the approaching stimulus. During hypothalamic stimulation, however, the cat lunged (i.e., rapidly moved its head forward) and opened its mouth at the sight of the mouse. The maximum distance at which the mouse elicited the lunge and jaw-opening was 2 to 2.5 inches (5.1 to 6.4 cm) from the cat's mouth. The lunge and jaw-opening were always followed by vicious biting of the mouse if the probe was not quickly withdrawn.

There was a higher likelihood of a lunge occurring when the mouse was presented to the eye contralateral to the site stimulated than when the mouse was presented to the ipsilateral eye. This main result for each of the five cats is shown in Figure 14. For one cat (Cat 5), however, if one site (site b) was stimulated, no difference between the two sides was found, although from this same animal the general result was obtained if a second site (site a) was stimulated.

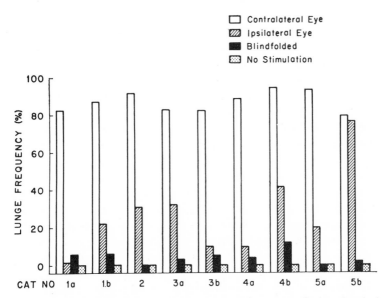

Fig. 14. The frequency of a cat's lunge toward a mouse during electrical stimulation of hypothalamic attack sites was greater when the mouse was presented to the contralateral eye than when the mouse was presented to the ipsilateral eye. The cat is indicated by a number, and the stimulated site by a letter. Sites a and b for Cats 1, 4, and 5 were on opposite sides of the brain. The lunge frequency percentages for the contralateral and ipsilateral eyes were based on at least 200 presentations of the mouse to each eye, with the exception of Cat 4, for which the frequencies were based on 110 presentations to each eye. All lunge frequency percentages for the unstimulated and blindfolded conditions were based on at least 50 presentations of the mouse. The differences between the contralateral and ipsilateral eye (except for Cat 5, Site b) were significant at $p < .001$ on the basis of χ^2 test.

The finding that the contralateral eye is more effective in mediating attack (that is, lunge and jaw-opening) is not attributable to a consistent defect in the ipsilateral eye of the cats, since in the case of three cats (Cats 1, 4, and 5) the "ipsilateral" eye yielded many responses when the stimulation was switched to a hypothalamic attack site on the opposite side. Neither is the result attributable to olfactory cues alone, since, when both eyes are occluded, the responses are very infrequent.

Furthermore, the differential sensitivity of the two eyes does not appear to be a consequence of a distortion of the optical system of the ipsilateral eye. In two cats (Cats 2 and 3) an increase in the intensity of stimulation to the hypothalamus resulted in a significant increase in the number of lunges made when the mouse was presented to the eye ipsilateral to the site of stimulation (Figure 15). Were distortion of the optical system of the ipsilateral eye the

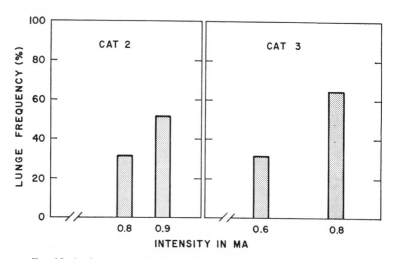

FIG. 15. An increase in the intensity of hypothalamic stimulation for two cats resulted in a significant increase in the number of lunges when the mouse was presented to the ipsilateral eye. All lunge frequency percentages were based on 200 presentations of the mouse at each stimulation intensity. Cat 3 was stimulated at Site a. The difference for Cat 2 was significant at $p < .05$ on the basis of a χ^2 test. The difference for Cat 3 was significant at $p < .001$ on the basis of a χ^2 test.

cause of the main result, an increase in the intensity of stimulation should have resulted in less, rather than more, frequent responses on the ipsilateral side.

Thus, the contralateral eye is more effective in mediating attack than the ipsilateral eye, and the effect seems to be due to a facilitation of visual mechanisms related to the contralateral eye and not simply to the exclusion of sensory information from the ipsilateral eye. The mechanisms within the nervous system whereby this effect is mediated are not known at present. The effect may be related to visual field effects, with the effective visual field of the contralateral eye being larger than that of the ipsilateral eye. This interpretation is suggested by the increased number of lunges to the ipsilateral side with increasing stimulation intensity.

We have briefly reviewed the experimental data dealing with patterned reflexes that are part of the general process of attack behavior. For the most part, those reflexes which have been found to be present during stimulation are involved in the final act of biting or striking, which we have taken as the operational definition of attack. The tactile reflexes do not require well-differentiated stimuli for elicitation. The visual lunge is also activated by a wide variety of stimuli. The visually guided strike, which occurs as a major mode of attack in those cats in which display is marked, seems (although this is not adequately documented) to be more dependent on highly differentiated aspects of the target. The force and direction of the movements of striking appear to be keyed exactly to the rat. The stimuli that trigger a reflex seem to be more differentiated as distance separates the object attacked and the attacker. The approach of the cat to rat, to the neglect of a bowl of food or a styrofoam block, implies that a differentiated stimulus is required for this aspect of attack behavior. If the neural mechanisms whereby approach occurs are understood, given that the outlines of the terminal acts are themselves established, the need for the concept of motivation as applied to attack behavior diminishes to a point where its usefulness is questionable.

In the case of attack behavior, motivation may at the neural level consist in the preparation of the sensory and motor systems to act in highly specific ways, some of them in the nature of patterned reflexes, which constitute, at least in part, overt attack behavior.

REFERENCES

Adams, D., & Flynn, J. P. Transfer of an escape response from tail shock to brain-stimulated attack behavior. *Journal of the Experimental Analysis of Behavior*, 1966, **9**, 401–408.

Bandler, R. J., & Flynn, J. P. Visual patterned reflex present during hypothalamically elicited attack. *Science*, 1971, **171**, 3972.

Bandler, R. J., & Flynn, J. P. Control of somatosensory fields for striking during hypothalamically elicited attack. *Brain Research*, 1972, **38**, 197–201.

Bard, P. A diencephalic mechanism for the expression of rage with special reference to the sympathetic nervous system. *American Journal of Physiology*, 1928, **84**, 490–515.

Bard, P., & Rioch, D. A study of four cats deprived of neocortex and additional portions of the forebrain. *Bulletin of Johns Hopkins Hospital*, 1937, **60**, 73–147.

Bergquist, E. H. Output pathways of hypothalamic mechanisms for sexual, aggressive, and other motivated behaviors in opossum. *Journal of Comparative and Physiological Psychology*, 1970, **70**, 389–398.

Chi, C. C., & Flynn, J. P. Neural pathways associated with hypothalamically elicited attack behavior in cats. *Science*, 1971, **171**, 703–706. (a)

Chi, C. C., & Flynn, J. P. Neuroanatomic projections related to biting attack elicited from hypothalamus in cats. *Brain Research*, 1971, **35**, 49. (b)

Edwards, S. B., & Flynn, J. P. The corticospinal control of striking in centrally elicited attack behavior. *Brain Research*, in press.

Fernandez de Molina, A., & Hunsperger, R. W. Central representation of affective reactions in forebrain and brain stem: Electrical stimulation of amygdala, stria terminalis, and adjacent structures. *Journal of Physiology*, 1959, **145**, 251–264.

Flynn, J. P., Vanegas, H., Foote, W., & Edwards, S. Neural mechanisms involved in a cat's attack on a rat. In R. E. Whalen (Ed.), *The neural control of behavior*. New York: Academic Press, 1970. Pp. 135–173.

Hekmatpanah, J. Organization of tactile dermatomes, C_1 through L_4, in cat. *Journal of Neurophysiology*, 1961, **24**, 129–140.

Hess, W. R. Stammganglien-Reizversuche, 10. Tagung der Deutschen Physiologischen Gesellschaft, Frankfurt am Main. *Bericht Über die Gesamte Physiologie und Experimentelle Pharmakologie*, 1928, **42**, 554–555.

Hess, W. R. *The functional organization of the diencephalon*. New York and London: Grune & Stratton, 1957.

Hess, W. R. *The biology of mind*. Chicago and London: University of Chicago Press, 1964.

Hess, W. R., & Akert, K. Experimental data on role of hypothalamus in mechanism of emotional behavior. *Archives of Neurology and Psychiatry*, 1955, **73**, 127–129.

Hess, W. R., & Brugger, M. Das subkortikale Zentrum der affektiven Abwehrreaktion. *Helvetica Physiologica and Pharmacologica Acta*, 1943, **1**, 35–52.

Inselman, B. R., & Flynn, J. P. Modulatory effects of preoptic stimulation on hypothalamically elicited attack on cats. *Brain Research*, 1972, **42**, 73–87.

Jasper, H. H., & Ajmone-Marsan, C. (Eds.) *A stereotaxic atlas of the diencephalon of the cat.* Ottawa: National Research Council of Canada, n.d.

Konorski, J. *Integrative activity of the brain.* Chicago: University of Chicago Press, 1967.

MacDonnell, M. F., & Flynn, J. P. Control of sensory fields by stimulation of hypothalamus. *Science*, 1966, **152**, 1406–1408. (a)

MacDonnell, M. F., & Flynn, J. P. Sensory control of hypothalamic attack. *Animal Behavior*, 1966, **14**, 399–405. (b)

Masserman, J. H. Is the hypothalamus a center of emotion? *Psychosomatic Medicine*, 1941, **3**, 3–25.

Masserman, J. *Behavior and neurosis.* Chicago: University of Chicago Press, 1943.

Nakao, H. Emotional behavior produced by hypothalamic stimulation. *American Journal of Physiology*, 1958, **194**, 411–418.

Pavlov, I. P. *Lectures on conditioned reflexes.* New York: Liveright, 1928.

Plotnik, R., Mir, D., & Delgado, J. M. R. Aggression, noxiousness, and brain stimulation in unrestrained rhesus monkeys. In B. E. Eleftheriou & J. P. Scott (Eds.), *The physiology of aggression and defeat.* New York and London: Plenum Press, 1971. Pp. 143–221.

Roberts, W. W., & Kiess, H. O. Motivational properties of hypothalamic aggression in cats. *Journal of Comparative and Physiological Psychology*, 1964, **58**, 187–193.

Sherrington, C. *The integrative action of the nervous system.* New Haven, Conn.: Yale University Press, 1961.

Sledjeski, M. B., & Flynn, J. P. Post stimulus excitability at attack sites in the cat's hypothalamus. *Brain Research*, 1972, **40**, 25–31.

Ulrich, R. E., Wolff, P. C., & Azrin, N. H. Shock as an elicitor of intra- and inter-species fighting behaviour. *Animal Behavior*, 1964, **12**, 14–15.

Wasman, M., & Flynn, J. P. Directed attack elicited from hypothalamus. *Archives of Neurology*, 1962, **6**, 220–227.

Woodworth, R. S., & Sherrington, C. S. A pseudaffective reflex and its spinal path. *Journal of Physiology*, 1904, **31**, 234–243.

The Environmental Causes of Aggression

RONALD R. HUTCHINSON

Fort Custer State Home, Augusta, Michigan

Though philosophers, theologians, statesmen, and combatants have all speculated upon the causes of aggression, an experimental science of aggressive behavior has only recently developed. This paper is an attempt to systematize this work by providing general, empirically based statements regarding the causes of aggression as they have thus far been established. Perhaps this can provide clues for workers interested in the biochemical and physiologic intermediaries of attack and aggression, and for social scientists interested in extending these principles to the study of complex cases for a variety of species in the natural environment.

The causes of aggression are of two principal classes: (a) the class of causal events which precede or are antecedent to instances of aggressive behavior and (b) the class of causal events which occur subsequent to aggression and which may influence the occurrence of future attack episodes. Aggression is therefore influenced by the same two stimulus classes that may influence practically all other complex overt behavior.

ANTECEDENT-STIMULUS CAUSES OF AGGRESSION

Antecedent environmental events which cause aggressive or attack behavior are of two major types. The first involves the onset or increase of intense, noxious, painful, or negatively reinforcing–type stimuli, or other previously neutral signals which have come to be paired with such events. The second class of antecedent stimuli which cause aggressive behavior are the offset or decrease of

pleasant, beneficial, biologically necessary, or positively reinforcing–
type stimuli or other previously neutral stimuli which have come to
be paired with one of these types of events. Each of these general
observations derives from a large number of experiments over numerous species using a variety of stimulus techniques by several
investigators in different laboratories. A brief summary of the empirical evidence for these statements follows.

As Figure 1 illustrates, the antecedent delivery of a physical blow
(Azrin, Hake, & Hutchinson, 1965), tail shock (Azrin, Hutchinson,
& Sallery, 1964), intense heat (Ulrich & Azrin, 1962), noxious brain
stimulation (Renfrew, 1969), airblasts (Ulrich, Hutchinson, & Azrin,
1965), footshock (Ulrich & Azrin, 1962), loud noise (Hutchinson
& Emley, 1972), and stimuli which have come to be conditional

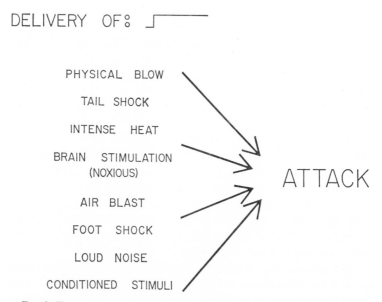

Fig. 1. Types of antecedent stimulation which have been shown to produce
attack behavior by their onset.

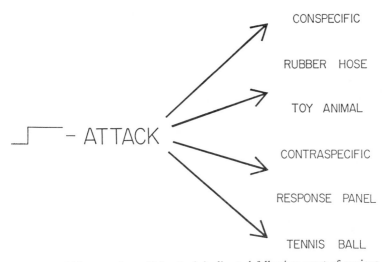

FIG. 2. Objects against which attack is directed following onset of noxious stimulation.

stimuli subsequent to pairings with one of the above (Hutchinson, Renfrew, & Young, 1971; Vernon & Ulrich, 1966) are each capable of triggering the occurrence of attack behavior. The term *attack* here means the forceful seizure or contact with another object or creature such that physical injury, dismemberment, destruction, immobilization, or disarmament occurs. The variety of attack responses which has been studied and shown to be produced by the stimuli previously described is illustrated in Figure 2. Attack caused by the onset of stimuli is directed against a conspecific (Ulrich & Azrin, 1962), rubber hose (Hutchinson, Azrin, & Hake, 1966), toy animal (Azrin, Hutchinson, & Sallery, 1964), contraspecific (Azrin, Hutchinson, & Sallery, 1964), response panel (Azrin, Hutchinson, & Hake, 1967), or tennis ball (Azrin, Hutchinson, & Sallery, 1964). By studying a variety of noxious or intense antecedent events and numerous types of target objects, the general relation between noxious events and aggression is established.

The second class of antecedent events which cause aggression involves the withdrawal or reduction of pleasant, beneficial, biologically necessary, or positively reinforcing–type stimuli. Figure 3 illustrates that experiments have employed withdrawal of food

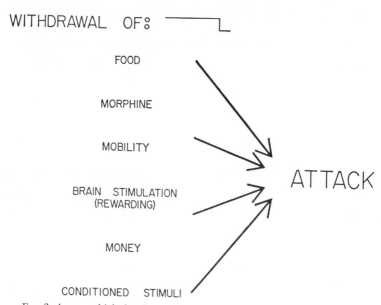

Fig. 3. Agents which, by their offset, produce attack behavior.

(Azrin, Hutchinson, & Hake, 1966), rewarding brain stimulation (Hutchinson & Buelke, in preparation;[1] Hutchinson, Gault, Renfrew, & James, in preparation),[2] monetary rewards (Hutchinson & Pierce, 1971), mobility (DeFrance & Hutchinson, in press), morphine (Boshka, Weisman, & Thor, 1966; Emley, Hutchinson, & Brannan, 1970), or the termination of signals previously associated

1. In these studies, to be published shortly, unrestrained rats had electrodes implanted in a variety of neural structures where contingent electrical stimulation supported lever pressing. Stimulus termination was promptly and recurrently followed by biting attack upon a restrained mouse. Pre- and post-test control observations confirmed that attack did not occur either during sessions without stimulation or during ongoing stimulation reinforcement.

2. In these studies, to be published shortly, experiments were conducted with both rodents and primates prepared according to *encephale isole* procedures. Stimulus termination in a variety of "reward" brain structures produced biting upon a rubber hose. Control observations showed that biting did not occur either during tests without stimulation or during ongoing stimulation.

with the delivery of one of these agents (Hutchinson, Azrin, & Hunt, 1968; Hutchinson & Pierce, 1971). That attack is the general response which occurs to the offset of beneficial or positive-reinforcer-type agents is known because a variety of attack objects have been tested in such circumstances, as is illustrated in Figure 4. Stimulus-termination-produced attack will occur against a conspecific (Azrin, Hutchinson, & Hake, 1966), a stuffed animal (Azrin, Hutchinson, & Hake, 1966), a rubber hose (Hutchinson, Azrin, & Hunt, 1968), a response panel (Kelly & Hake, 1970), or a contraspecific (Hutchinson & Buelke, in preparation).

These findings generally establish that the antecedent causes of aggression are as summarized in Figure 5, that is, the antecedent delivery or increment of aversive or negatively reinforcing–type stimuli or the removal or reduction of pleasant or positively re-inforcing–type stimuli.

The relationships so far described were initially observed in single species: rats for stimulus-onset-produced aggression, and pigeons for stimulus-offset-produced aggression. Additional studies investigated a variety of species to determine the presence or absence of these relationships across a sufficient phylic range to

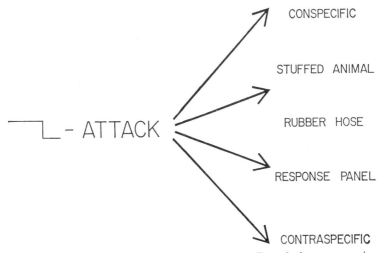

Fig. 4. Objects which are attacked following offset of pleasant or rein-forcing stimuli.

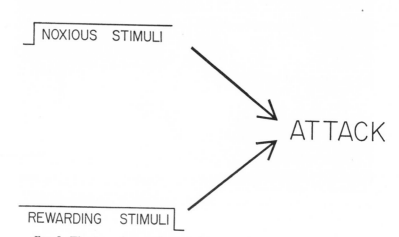

Fig. 5. The two classes of antecedent stimulation which produce attack behavior.

justify the assumption that the principles already discovered might be general and applicable to the understanding of man and his aggressive behavior. Beginning 10 years ago, a variety of species were tested for attack against at least two of three classes of target objects: conspecifics, contraspecifics, and inanimate objects.

This work, which is still being expanded, has already involved testing of more than 100 different attacker-target paired comparisons. Figures 6 through 14 are illustrations of a selected few attacker-target pairs which have been tested for antecedent-stimulus-offset-produced attack. The sampling demonstrates a phylic range from crustacia through primate mammals (Ulrich & Azrin, 1962; Ulrich, Hutchinson, & Azrin, 1965; Azrin, Hutchinson, & Sallery, 1964; Azrin & Hutchinson, in preparation;[3] Hutchinson,

3. In these studies more than thirty species were examined for attack responses against conspecifics, contraspecifics, and inanimate objects. Standard ABA designs were employed to determine the necessity and sufficiency of noxious events to produce attack in an otherwise neutral environmental background.

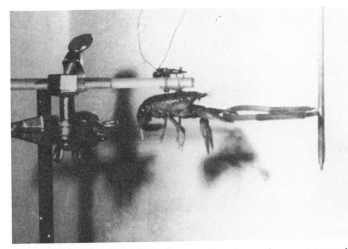

Fig. 6. Attack by a crayfish against a rubber hose subsequent to noxious electrical stimulation of the thorax.

Fig. 7. Paradigm for study of stinger extension in the common barn wasp following noxious electrical, thermal, or pressure stimuli of the thorax. Other experiments demonstrated directionality of the behavior by recording lateral movement of the abdomen toward a target placed either right or left of the preparation.

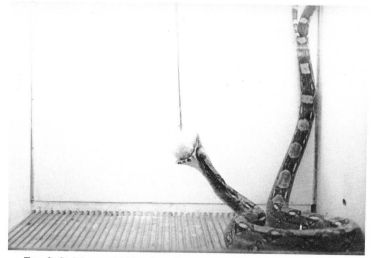

FIG. 8. Striking and biting by a boa constrictor against a suspended tennis ball subsequent to noxious electric shock delivered through a grid floor.

FIG. 9. Extended seizure and biting by alligator snapping turtles subsequent to noxious electrical stimulation from floor grids.

Fig. 10. Lunging and biting by an American alligator against a suspended tennis ball subsequent to noxious electrical stimulation from floor grids.

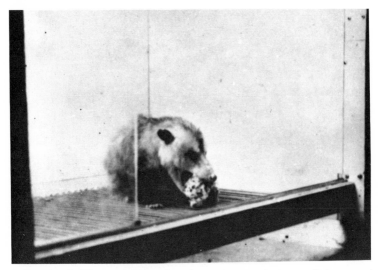

Fig. 11. Striking and biting by an opossum upon a terry cloth–covered tennis ball subsequent to noxious electrical stimulation from floor grids.

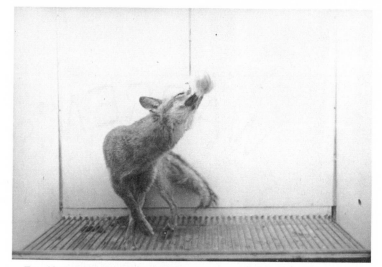

Fig. 12. Lunging and biting by a gray fox upon a suspended tennis ball subsequent to noxious electrical stimulation from floor grids.

Fig. 13. Lunging and biting of a suspended tennis ball by a ferret subsequent to noxious electrical stimulation from floor grids.

Fig. 14. Lunging and biting by a squirrel monkey upon a rubber hose following delivery of noxious electric shock to the tail or following termination of food rewards for lever pressing.

FIG. 15. Paradigm for studying pecking and wing beating by a free pigeon upon a stuffed pigeon subsequent to extinction of key pecking for food.

FIG. 16. Biting attack by an albino rat *encephale isole* preparation subsequent to termination of electrical stimulation in "pleasure centers" of the brain.

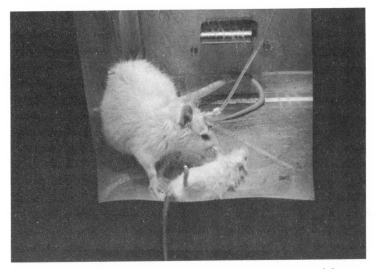

Fig. 17. Lunging and biting attack by an albino rat upon a laboratory mouse subsequent to extinction of lever pressing for electrical stimulation of a "pleasure center" of the brain.

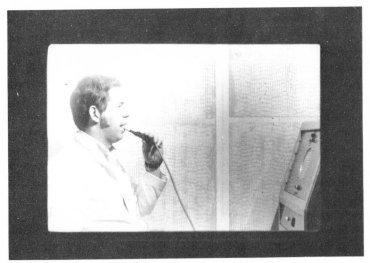

Fig. 18. Paradigm for studying jaw contractions in humans following onset of noxious auditory stimulation or following offset of positively reinforcing (monetary) stimulation.

Azrin, & Hake, 1966). Figures 15 through 18 are several illustrations of attacker-target paradigms studied for antecedent-stimulus-offset-produced attack. The range of examples spans aves to human primates (Azrin, Hutchinson, & Hake, 1963; Hutchinson, Azrin, & Hunt, 1968; Thompson & Bloom, 1966; Hutchinson & Buelke, in preparation;[4] Hutchinson & Pierce, 1971). The phylic generality of antecedent-stimulus-offset-produced and antecedent-stimulus-onset-produced· attack behaviors, as so far established, is depicted in Figure 19.

The temporal and intensive character of attack behavior bears an orderly relation to the temporal and intensive properties of the antecedent-stimulus causes of aggression. Upon occurrence of a

4. See footnote 1.

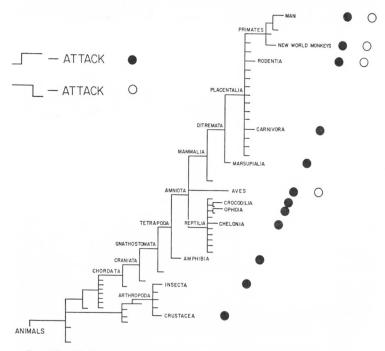

Fig. 19. Phylic span across which antecedent-stimulus-onset-produced attack and antecedent-stimulus-offset-produced attack has been confirmed.

sufficient stimulus, attack occurs immediately at full intensity and progressively decreases in amplitude over subsequent time space (Azrin, Hutchinson, & Sallery, 1964; Hutchinson, Azrin, & Renfrew, 1968; Azrin, Hutchinson, & Hake, 1966). In an environment where such sufficient stimulation repetitively occurs, attack may develop immediately preceding a discriminable and imminent stimulus episode (Hutchinson, Renfrew, & Young, 1971; Vernon

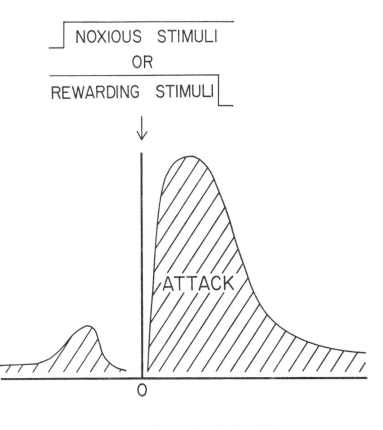

FIG. 20. The temporal and intensive pattern of attack before and after the onset of noxious stimuli or the offset of rewarding stimuli.

& Ulrich, 1966). Though the tendency to attack in anticipation of the onset of noxious stimuli or the offset of rewarding stimuli is weak relative to other behaviors (Hutchinson & Emley, 1970; Hutchinson, Renfrew, & Young, 1971), there nevertheless may be some tendency to attack which progressively increases toward the moment of stimulus occurrence, but falls sharply to almost zero the moment before stimulus change arrives (Azrin, Hutchinson, & Hake, 1967; Hutchinson, Renfrew, & Young, 1971). These relations are diagrammed in Figure 20.

The strength of attack behavior which occurs following stimulation bears a direct and positive relationship to the intensity of the causal stimulus conditions as shown in Figure 21. This relation is obtained for several measures of attack, including force of contact (Hutchinson, Azrin, & Hake, 1966), frequency of contact (Hutchinson, Azrin, & Hake, 1966), duration of contact (Azrin, Hutchinson, & McLaughlin, 1965), or probability of contact (Ulrich & Azrin,

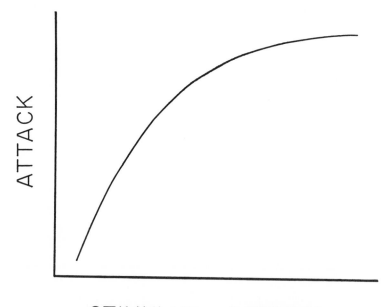

FIG. 21. The strength of attack as a function of stimulus intensity.

1962). The function has been observed in studies of antecedent-stimulus-onset-produced attack (Ulrich & Azrin, 1962; Hutchinson, Azrin, & Hake, 1966) as well as studies of antecedent-stimulus-offset-produced attack (Azrin, Hutchinson, & Hake, 1966; Hutchinson & Pierce, 1971).

Attack is also a direct and positive function of the duration of antecedent causal stimuli, as illustrated in Figure 22. This observation has been made both for antecedent-stimulus-onset-produced (Hutchinson, Azrin, & Renfrew, 1968) and antecedent-stimulus-offset-produced (Hutchinson, Azrin, & Hunt, 1968) attack. Attack behavior is a direct and positive function of the frequency of stimulation, as shown by Figure 23. This finding has been confirmed both for antecedent-stimulus-onset-produced (Ulrich & Azrin, 1962; Hutchinson, Renfrew, & Young, 1971) and antecedent-stimulus-offset-produced (Azrin, Hutchinson, & Hake, 1966) attack.

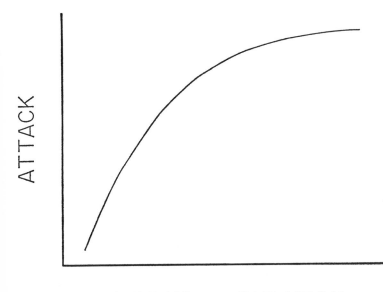

Fig. 22. The strength of attack as a function of duration of antecedent stimulation.

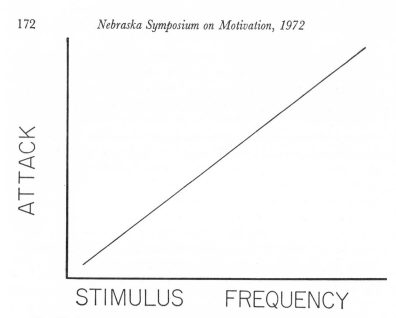

FIG. 23. Attack strength as a function of stimulus frequency. This function is modified as discussed in the text and as illustrated with Figures 24, 25, and 26.

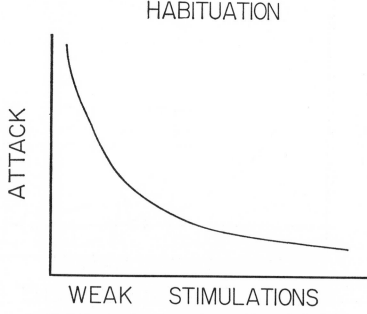

FIG. 24. Habituation of attack strength to repetitive weak stimulation.

The features of attack behavior already described are modified by certain additional stimulus features. Attack strength decreases progressively over repetitions of weak stimulation, as seen in Figure 24. This relationship has been observed to occur in attacker-target pairings studied for antecedent-stimulus-onset-produced attack (Azrin, Ulrich, Hutchinson, & Norman, 1964; Hutchinson, Renfrew, & Young, 1971) and also in studies of antecedent-stimulus-offset-produced attack (Azrin, Hutchinson, & Hake, 1966; Hutchinson, Azrin, & Hunt, 1968). This phenomenon of habituation is reduced by a period of absence of stimulation.

Attack strength also decreases as a function of weak-stimulus frequency. This effect has been confirmed for attacker-target pairs during antecedent-stimulus-onset-produced attack (Ulrich & Azrin, 1962; Hutchinson, Renfrew, & Young, 1971) and also during tests of antecedent-stimulus-offset-produced attack (Hutchin-

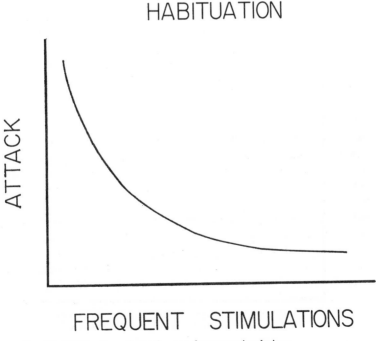

Fig. 25. Habituation of attack upon frequent stimulations.

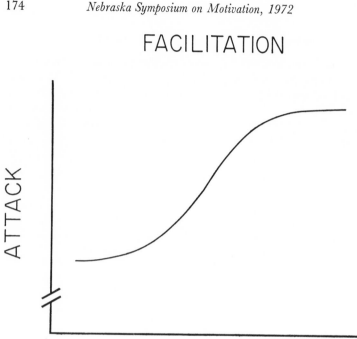

FIG. 26. Facilitation of attack behavior upon repetitive and intense stimulations.

son, Azrin, & Hunt, 1968; Azrin, Hutchinson, & Hake, 1966). Though attack strength may be constant with repetitive moderate-to-weak stimulations if they are infrequent, habituation rapidly occurs to more frequent stimulation. Figure 25 illustrates these relations.

Stimulation may also alter the temporal and intensive patterns of attack behavior through a process of facilitation. Repetitive intense stimulation leads to progressively more frequent and forceful attack episodes (O'Kelly & Steckle, 1939; Hutchinson, Renfrew, & Young, 1971). This relation, diagrammed in Figure 26, has not yet been confirmed for attacker-target studies of antecedent-stimulus-offset-produced attack.

SUBSEQUENT-STIMULUS CAUSES OF AGGRESSION

Certain events which follow or are subsequent to (in fact, sometimes contingent upon) attack may also cause increases in attack strength subsequent to these stimulus occurrences. This paradigm of response-strength generation resulting from subsequent or contingent stimulation is referred to as reinforcement or reward. Attack, a complex motor reaction sequence, can, like other complex motor behaviors, be strengthened through the process of reinforcement.

There are two classes of subsequent stimuli which can alter the future occurrence of attack behavior. The first class involves the subsequent onset and/or increment of positive, pleasant, beneficial, biologically necessary, or positively reinforcing–type stimuli or previously neutral stimuli which have come to be paired with such agents. Experiments have demonstrated several different stimuli

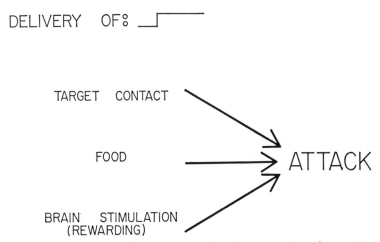

FIG. 27. Types of stimulus onset which, when occurring subsequent to attack, increase future instances of attack.

that can, by their onset subsequent to attack, reward or reinforce it. Figure 27 shows that the occurrence of target contact (Azrin, Hutchinson, & McLaughlin, 1965), food (Azrin & Hutchinson, 1967), or rewarding brain stimulation (Stachnik, Ulrich, & Mabry, 1966), when delivered subsequent to attack performance, each may lead to further attack. Naturally the reinforcement or reward capability of these three types of stimuli depends upon appropriate antecedent conditions; that is, food can only serve as a reinforcer subsequent to food deprivation, etc.

The second class of subsequent stimulation capable of strengthening future attack through reinforcement involves the reduction, termination, or continued absence of unpleasant, noxious, painful, biologically destructive, or negatively reinforcing–type stimuli or previously neutral stimuli which have come to be paired with such agents. As illustrated in Figure 28, removal of conspecific attack

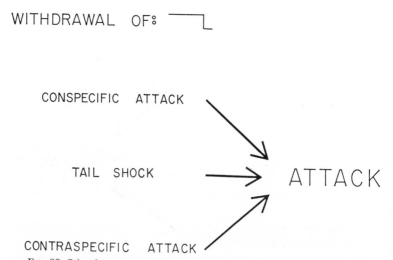

Fig. 28. Stimulus agents which, by their offset subsequent to attack, increase the future likelihood of attack.

(Scott & Fredericson, 1951; Azrin, Hutchinson, & Hake, 1963), tail shock (Azrin, Hutchinson, & Hake, 1967), or contraspecific attack (Azrin & Hutchinson, in preparation)[5] produces response strengthening. The two classes of subsequent stimuli which are causes of aggressive behavior are shown in Figure 29. The subsequent offset of noxious stimuli or the subsequent onset of positive or beneficial stimuli leads to the further occurrence of attack.

Though two classes of stimulus events, antecedent or subsequent, can cause aggression, the behaviors so produced are fundamentally different. Attack produced by antecedent stimulus-offset or stimulus-onset is accompanied by autonomic vocal and facial responses characteristic of the reaction pattern commonly referred to as anger (Hutchinson & Renfrew, 1966; Azrin, Hutchinson, & Hake, 1963; Hutchinson & Pierce, 1971). The intensity and duration of

5. See footnote 3.

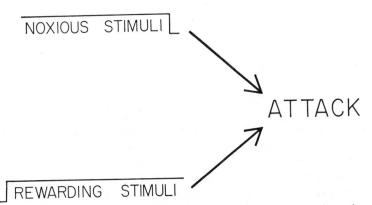

SUBSEQUENT

NOXIOUS STIMULI

ATTACK

REWARDING STIMULI

Fig. 29. The two classes of stimulus change which, when occurring subsequent to attack, increase future instances of attack.

these displays are determined by the temporal and intensive factors of the eliciting stimuli, as already discussed. Alternatively, subsequent-stimulus-caused aggression and attack is often not accompanied by signs of emotional arousal (Azrin & Hutchinson, 1967; Azrin, Hutchinson, & Hake, 1967), and only those behaviors necessary to produce the subsequent stimulus outcomes (Azrin & Hutchinson, 1967; Stachnik, Ulrich, & Mabry, 1966; Hutchinson & Renfrew, 1966) are observed.

In the stream of naturally occurring behavior, however, these two separate classes of causes are often bound up in close association. Antecedent-stimulus-produced attack may and frequently does encounter several different types of favorable consequences subsequent to its occurrence. In intense aggression where one of the combatants is severely maimed or killed, only the winner contributes to the future gene pool of the species. More immediately, antecedent-stimulus-onset-triggered aggression may cause the subsequent reduction of such stimulation and will rapidly be strengthened through reinforcement (Azrin, Hutchinson, & Hake, 1967). Attack following removal of positive stimuli where it results in the reestablishment of such stimulation will also be rapidly learned (Reynolds, Catania, & Skinner, 1963). Since attack behavior may be directed generally against animate and inanimate stimuli, it has the frequent result of destroying, immobilizing, or grossly reorganizing the environmental complex, often toward conditions which existed during more tranquil periods. Thus it is that attack is strengthened through subsequent reinforcement processes by the reciprocals of those same stimulus events which produced the behavior antecedently. These functional relationships which exist between aggression and reinforcement processes are the grist both for a post hoc explanation of why aggression exists as a phylicly general reaction and also for why great difficulty is encountered in reducing such reactions. Speculation regarding the survival value of aggressive behavior due to its ability to protect a creature against potentially destructive events or to prevent the termination of necessary and beneficial contacts finds direct and empirical confirmation in the experiments and principles here described. Additionally, these relationships between aggression and reinforcement processes state the functional outline upon which more reductionist biological accounts must come to be based. It is clear also that social scientists wishing to explain and/or therapeutize in complex social settings must develop their programs on the basis of the relationships described here.

Numerous workers have observed aggression in a variety of naturalistic settings. Sometimes this behavior takes the form of attack sequences between conspecific males during the courtship season; at other times it is observed that a mother animal attacks both conspecifics and contraspecifics that approach her offspring. In other instances it is noted that animals defend their nesting or feeding and watering sites. Some workers have noted that periods of stimulus deprivation that is, isolation, seem to result in subsequent hyperaggressiveness. In yet other instances larger species destroy and consume creatures for food. These naturally occurring attack sequences have often been complemented by naturalistic laboratory analogs. Different labels are frequently attached to the various performances, and reactions are inferred to have different underlying functional bases, for example, maternal aggression, courtship aggression, territorial aggression, isolation-induced aggression, predatory aggression, etc.

There probably are not as many functional relations or underlying separate physiologic subcircuits as there are novel incidents of aggression and attack. All of these "kinds" of aggressive behavior have common elements about them which are discussed in this paper. It is understanding these common elemental processes which allows predictions to complex cases or an efficient search for the underlying biological reactions which, in composite, produce these functional relations. To this end it will be important to discover by laboratory methods whether there are actual fundamental causes of aggression not appropriately subsumed under the general principles here described.[6]

[6] The assistance of G. Emley, E. Hallin, N. Murray, G. Pierce, B. Snowden, V. Pufpaff, S. Carpenter, S. Hunt, N. Hunter, K. Dinzik, R. Sauer, and J. Tough was essential to this work. Financial support came from National Science Foundation grant GB–18413, Office of Naval Research grant N–00014–70–A–0183–0001, National Aeronautics and Space Administration grant NGR–23–010–004, and the Department of Mental Health of the State of Michigan.

REFERENCES

Azrin, N. H., Hake, D. F., & Hutchinson, R. R. Elicitation of aggression by a physical blow. *Journal of Experimental Analysis of Behavior*, 1965, **8**, 55–57.

Azrin, N. H., & Hutchinson, R. R. Conditioning of the aggressive behavior of pigeons by a fixed-interval schedule of reinforcement. *Journal of Experimental Analysis of Behavior*, 1967, **10**, 395–402.

Azrin, N. H., Hutchinson, R. R., & Hake, D. F. Pain-induced fighting in the squirrel monkey. *Journal of Experimental Analysis of Behavior*, 1963, **6**, 620.

Azrin, N. H., Hutchinson, R. R., & Hake, D. F. Extinction-induced aggression. *Journal of Experimental Analysis of Behavior*, 1966, **9**, 191–204.

Azrin, N. H., Hutchinson, R. R., & Hake, D. F. Attack avoidance and escape reactions to aversive shock. *Journal of Experimental Analysis of Behavior*, 1967, **10**, 131–148.

Azrin, N. H., Hutchinson, R. R., & McLaughlin, R. The opportunity for aggression as an operant reinforcer during aversive stimulation. *Journal of Experimental Analysis of Behavior*, 1965, **8**, 171–180.

Azrin, N. H., Hutchinson, R. R., & Sallery, R. D. Pain-aggression toward inanimate objects. *Journal of Experimental Analysis of Behavior*, 1964, **7**, 223–228.

Azrin, N. H., Ulrich, R. E., Hutchinson, R. R., & Norman, D. G. Effects of shock duration on shock-induced fighting. *Journal of Experimental Analysis of Behavior*, 1964, **7**, 9–11.

Boshka, S. C., Weisman, M. H., & Thor, D. H. A technique for inducing aggression in rats utilizing morphine withdrawal. *Psychological Record*, 1966, **16**, 541–543.

DeFrance, J. F., & Hutchinson, R. R. Electrographic activity in the amygdala and hippocampus associated with biting attack. *Physiology and Behavior*, in press.

Emley, G. S., Hutchinson, R. R., & Brannan, I. B. Aggression: Effects of acute and chronic morphine. *Michigan Mental Health Research Bulletin*, 1970, **4**, (Fall), 23–26.

Hutchinson, R. R., Azrin, N. H., & Hake, D. F. An automatic method for the study of aggression in squirrel monkeys. *Journal of Experimental Analysis of Behavior*, 1966, **9**, 233–237.

Hutchinson, R. R., Azrin, N. H., & Hunt, G. M. Attack produced by intermittent reinforcement of a concurrent operant response. *Journal of Experimental Analysis of Behavior*, 1968, **11**, 489–495.

Hutchinson, R. R., Azrin, N. H., & Renfrew, J. W. Effects of shock intensity and duration on the frequency of biting attack by squirrel monkeys. *Journal of Experimental Analysis of Behavior*, 1968, **11**, 83–88.

Hutchinson, R. R., & Emley, G. S. Schedule-independent factors contributing to schedule-induced phenomena. In *Schedule-induced and schedule-dependent phenomena*. Vol. 1. Toronto: Addiction Research Foundation, 1970. Pp. 187–225.

Hutchinson, R. R., & Emley, G. Effects of nicotine on avoidance, conditioned suppression, and aggression response measures in animals and man. In

Council for Tobacco Research, *Conference on motivation in cigarette smoking.* New York: Academic Press, 1972, in press.

Hutchinson, R. R., & Pierce, G. E. Jaw clenching in humans: Its measurement, and effects produced by conditions of reinforcement and extinction. Paper presented at the meeting of the American Psychological Association, 1971.

Hutchinson, R. R., & Renfrew, J. W. Stalking, attack, and eating behaviors elicited from the same sites in the hypothalamus. *Journal of Comparative and Physiological Psychology,* 1966, **61,** 360–367.

Hutchinson, R. R., Renfrew, J. W., & Young, G. A. Effects of long-term shock and associated stimuli on aggressive and manual responses. *Journal of Experimental Analysis of Behavior,* 1971, **15,** 141–166.

Kelly, J. F., & Hake, D. F. An extinction-induced increase in aggressive response in humans. *Journal of Experimental Analysis of Behavior,* 1970, **14,** 153–164.

O'Kelly, L. E., & Steckle, L. C. A note on long-enduring emotional responses in the rat. *Journal of Psychology,* 1939, **8,** 125–131.

Renfrew, J. W. The intensity function and reinforcing properties of brain stimulation that elicits attack. *Physiology and Behavior,* 1969, **4,** 509–515.

Reynolds, G. S., Catania, A. C., & Skinner, B. F. Conditioned and unconditioned aggression in pigeons. *Journal of Experimental Analysis of Behavior,* 1963, **6,** 73–74.

Scott, J. P., and Fredericson, E. The causes of fighting in mice and rats. *Physiological Zoology,* 1951, **24,** 273–309.

Stachnik, T. J., Ulrich, R. E., & Mabry, J. H. Reinforcement of aggression through intracranial stimulation. *Psychonomic Science,* 1966, **5,** 101–102.

Thompson, T., & Bloom, W. Aggressive behavior and extinction-induced response-rate increase. *Psychonomic Science,* 1966, **5,** 335–336.

Ulrich, R. E., & Azrin, N. H. Reflexive fighting in response to aversive stimulation. *Journal of Experimental Analysis of Behavior,* 1962, **5,** 511–520.

Ulrich, R. E., Hutchinson, R. R., & Azrin, N. H. Pain-elicited aggression. *Psychological Record,* 1965, **15,** 111–126.

Vernon, W., & Ulrich, R. E. Classical conditioning of pain-elicited aggression. *Science,* 1966, **12,** 668–669.

Disruption of Behavioral States as a Cause of Aggression

JOHN B. CALHOUN

National Institute of Mental Health

Background and Objective

In its most overt expression, aggression takes the form of a physical attack of one individual on an associate. However, I have previously sought to formulate aggression in terms of the changes of state of reactivity that arise as a result of the stochastics of interaction among members of a group (Calhoun, 1963b, pages 24 to 46 specifically). Here it was shown that, on the average, one-half of all contacts between two individuals must be neutral in character, one-fourth gratifying, and one-fourth frustrating. After either a gratifying or frustrating encounter the individual enters a refractory state during which it cannot interact sufficiently appropriately to fulfill another's need for social intercourse. From this perspective,

> an aggressive act is merely one in which an individual in a refractory state of either gratification or frustration behaves inappropriately with respect to the requirement of fulfilling the need for social intercourse felt by another. An individual thus frustrated in his attempts at effective social intercourse is frustrated simply in the sense of failing to have his behavior rewarded. An aggressive act becomes synonymous with a negative sanction. An aggressive act may assume the form of violent action but is just as effective in a more mild and sublimated form, so long as the individual in the social need state recognizes the behavior of the one with whom he sought interaction as being inappropriate to the fulfillment of his own needs. [Calhoun, 1963b]

This formulation presupposes that one individual can only be aggressive toward another during times when it is in a refractory state resulting from a prior interaction. However, long observation of individuals who are members of organized social groups suggests another category of conditions which predisposes one individual to act inappropriately, that is, aggressively, towards its associates. Externally this category is reflected by sudden changes in the physical environment in which the individual or the group finds itself. For example, if a group is transferred from a familiar to a strange environmental context, the incidence of fighting increases. Internally, this implies that there has been some change in the "setting" of control mechanisms which influence the expression of behavior. For this thesis to become useful in the understanding of behavior in general and aggression in particular, one must be able to define these settings of behavior control mechanisms in precise operational terms.

My attempt to gain this understanding began in 1956 and is still continuing. It has resulted in the identification of five probability functions, which taken together, I believe, are capable of explicitly defining motivation, drive, mood, and emotion. For the present purposes I will only present sufficient data to convey the reality of these probability functions, whose setting at any moment in time governs the expression of individual behavior. The presentation of these probability functions will form the first part of this paper. The second part of the paper will focus on a number of instances of aggression, involving fighting. Here the attempt will be made to interpret the episodes of fighting as related to abrupt alterations in one or more of the probability functions.

PROBABILITY FUNCTIONS INFLUENCING BEHAVIOR

1.1 Apparatuses Developed for Recording Behavior

The apparatuses described here were designed to record the duration and sequence of behavioral states of wild and domesticated strains of Norway rats. By behavioral state I mean any continuing state such as sleep or any sequence of related acts that have functional meaning for the rat such as those involved in episodes of ingestion, locomotion, courtship, etc.

RSB, Rhythms of spontaneous behavior apparatus (Figure 1). Two tunnels, intersecting each other at right angles at their midpoints, provided access to four compartments, one at each end of each tunnel. One compartment consisted of an activity wheel. A nest compartment lay at the opposite end of the tunnel that gave access to the activity wheel. A lever, whose depression presented a drop of water, lay at one end of the other tunnel, while a food hopper was

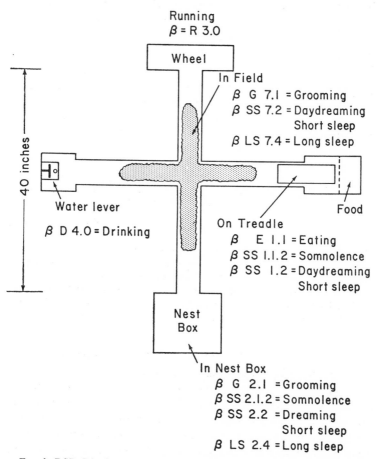

Fig. 1. RSB, Rhythms of spontaneous behavior apparatus. β = behavioral state. Although rats were not observed during data recording, a name is given to each β to denote the general kind of state or activity characterizing the individual at each place. See Figure 10 for graphic methodology for distinguishing several beta as derived from durations at a single place.

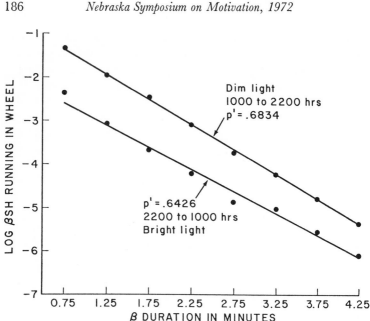

Fig. 2. Running-in-wheel beta, R 3.0. $\beta SH = \beta s/\text{Subject}/\text{Hour}$. During 10,149 rat hours 72 rats engaged in 9,857 episodes of running in the wheel. Most (5,968) of these lasted no longer than .5 minutes. Running proper (3,875 βs) falls within the range of .6 to 4.5 minutes. The remaining 86 episodes of running, that lasted between 4.6 and 20.0 minutes, had a p' of approximately .61. The mean running time of the above theoretical least squares best fit curves are 1.353 and 1.427 minutes for dim and bright light respectively. The T statistic with 12 degrees of freedom comparing the two curves is 2.46, $p < .05$.

located at the other end of this tunnel. The following events were recorded on an Esterline-Angus strip-paper recorder: each depression of the water lever, each revolution of the wheel, each entry into or exit from the nest box, each positioning of a rat on a treadle before the food hopper, and each departure from it. Four identical RSBs were constructed. The lighting in the room containing the four RSBs was maintained on a regimen of 12 hours of bright light and 12 hours of dim light daily in conformity with that characterizing the habitats from which the animals were removed. All light cycles were dim light 1000 to 2200 hours, and bright light during the 2200 to 1000 hours. Only one rat was placed in an RSB. Subjects were drawn from several diverse physical and social settings where they had lived for at least several months. Each subject was left in an RSB for 7 days. Seventy-two subjects met the criteria of living through the whole 7 days in an RSB with no breakdown of the recording devices. The start and stop times, to the nearest tenth of a minute, were noted visually and successively transferred to punched cards and magnetic tape for later computer analysis. Although only four gross behavioral states were directly recorded, computer analysis of the durations at compartments, or in the tunnel between them, permitted identification of additional discrete behavioral states (betas). For example, in the nest box five discrete behavioral states could be recognized on the basis of their durations (see Figure 10). Those lasting less than one minute we designated as *reorientation*; those lasting from 1 to 10 minutes we called *grooming*; those from 10 to 20 minutes, *somnolence*; those from 20 to 96 minutes, *short sleep*; and those longer than 96 minutes, *long sleep*. A distinct equation described the frequency of behavioral states as a function of their duration within each of these ranges. Unless otherwise mentioned, data presented will have been derived from use of the RSB.

STAW, Socialization training apparatus, water. As previously described (Calhoun, 1967, Figure 1), this consisted of two short parallel channels of wire screen. Each channel could accommodate one rat, and a rat in one channel could detect the presence of another rat in the adjacent channel. A mechanical lever at the blind end of each tunnel presented one drop of water in a cup with each press of the lever. The weight of a rat on the hinged floor closed a microswitch. Through appropriate circuitry the STAW could be made to operate in either of two modes. Mode 1 was designated COOP (for cooperation). This mode required the presence of two rats, one in each channel, for the levers to unlock. Departure of one of the two rats caused a locking of the lever being pressed by the other rat. Mode 2 was called DISOP (for disoperative). This mode required the presence of only one rat for its lever to unlock. When another rat entered the opposite channel, both levers locked. STAWs were placed in larger environments, where normally 2 to 32 rats had access to a single instrument.

Activity alleys. Two somewhat similar models were constructed. Their common attributes included: (a) a light-proof channel, 6 to

8 inches in diameter, 12 to 14 feet long; (b) a door at one end to which a nesting compartment for one rat could be attached; (c) a smoked-glass lighted panel forming the opposite end. Movement out into the alley was monitored by counters and paper-strip recorders. Four alleys were operable at any one time, with one rat per alley. See pages 229–232 for summary of pages 188–229.

1.2 The Terminator Probability, p'

Any ongoing behavioral state, beta or β, eventually terminates and is then replaced by another behavioral state. If the time of initiation and of termination of many βs of a particular kind are recorded it is noted that they vary in length. When such durations are tabulated into several equal-length class intervals, all of the distribution, or most of it, is characterized by each longer duration having a lower β count. Figure 2 presents such sets of data for running in the wheel as a β over the range of .6 to 4.5 minutes duration. Where the number of βs as a function of their duration is describable by a negative exponential curve it may be shown that, regardless of how long the β has already lasted, there is a constant probability, p', of the β terminating in the next unit of time, t. For our studies with rats a t of 1.0 minutes has been consistently used.

Derivation of p'. Let:

β_j = the number of behavioral states (motor activity, rest, or sleep) continuing for at least a jth duration.

N_j = the number of behavioral states terminating at the jth duration.

p'_j = the probability of a behavior terminating at the jth duration.

Then:

$$\beta_{j-1} - \beta_j = p'_{j-1}\beta_{j-1} \tag{1}$$

$$N_j = p'_j\beta_j \tag{2}$$

$$N_j - N_{j-1} = p'_j\beta_j - p'_{j-1}\beta_{j-1} \tag{3}$$

Where $(j - 1) - j = t = 1.0$ minute and $p'_j = p'$, a constant independent of j.

It follows that:

$$N_j - N_{j-1} = p'(\beta_j - \beta_{j-1}) \tag{4}$$

$$N_j - N_{j-1} = -p'(\beta_{j-1} - \beta_j) \tag{5}$$

$$N_j - N_{j-1} = -p'(p'\beta_{j-1}) \tag{6}$$

And by analogy to Equation 2:

$$N_{j-1} = p'\beta_{j-1} \tag{7}$$

Substituting Equation 7 into Equation 6:

$$N_j - N_{j-1} = -p'N_{j-1} \tag{8}$$

Therefore:

$$p' = (N_{j-1} - N_j)/N_{j-1} \tag{9}$$

Programs were written to calculate p' from any set of N_j, the the equations for the related negative exponential curve and tests of significance of observed to theoretical. For example, the two curves in Figure 2 differ significantly even though the p' values are not too different: .683 for the dim-light hours versus .643 for the bright-light hours. Lower p' values produce longer mean β durations.

p' values were similarly calculated for the other βs recorded by the RSB; see Table 1. For 8 of the 9 sets, p' is lower during the bright than the dim hours. This suggests that lowered metabolism during the bright-light hours, when rats spend more time in sleep, influences the origin of the signal which determines p'. The following tentative model may help to understand the nature of p': for a particular β there is an assembly of randomly firing neurons. Simultaneous firing of some fixed number of neurons, that are members of this assembly, suffices to generate a signal capable of terminating the β. There is some small capacity temporarily to recruit or reject neurons from participation in the assembly. Such alteration in the number of neurons in an assembly can only vary within narrow limits as evinced by the β specific narrow range in p' between dim and bright hours. Since p' varies much more between βs, giving such extremes as .0094 for long sleep, LS 2.4, and .6912 for drinking, D 4.0, neuronal assemblies among the βs must vary widely in number.

TABLE 1

VARIABILITY OF THE p' TERMINATOR PROBABILITY
FOR THE $N = 72$ GROUP OF RATS

Beta	Bright 12 Hours	Dim 12 Hours	Range in minutes for p' calculation
D 4.0	.68767	*.69124*	1.6 to 5.0
R 3.0	.64262	*.68339*	0.6 to 4.5
G 7.1	.319	*.368*	1.1 to 8.0
G 2.1	.28208	*.31760*	1.1 to 7.0
E 1.1	*.19680*	*.15208*	2.1 to 8.0
SS 1.2	.09513	*.09908*	16.1 to 72.0
SS 7.2	.03961	*.04923*	8.1 to 72.0
SS 2.2	.02562	*.02972*	16.1 to 72.0
LS 2.4	.00943	.00982	224.1 to 576.0

The constellation of stimuli characteristic of the alley represents a novel environmental context to a rat first placed in an activity alley. During the first 2.5 hours within the alley, activity is normally markedly elevated (Figure 3). This increased activity results entirely from an increase in the number of trips out into the alley that are initiated. Rates of travel were found to be constant, and independent of the distance of the trip termination. Thus the distance of the trip becomes equivalent to the duration of the trip. The slope of the curve for the first $2\frac{1}{2}$ hours of "emotional hyperactivity" does not differ from that during the next three 12-hour nocturnal periods after adjustment to the surroundings. That is to say, the average length of a trip is the same during both the initial phase of "emotional hyperactivity" and the following phase of adjustment to surroundings. Thus the probability, p', of terminating a behavior may remain unaltered despite a marked increase in the probability, $\hat{p}$, of initiating that behavior. $\hat{p}$ is discussed later (Section 1.6).

Upon initial exposure to the activity alley, the number of trips initiated out into the alley per half hour is 20 times that during the adjusted phase of 3-day residence in the alley. During the next 2.5 to 3 hours after introduction into the alley there is a negative exponential decline in the frequency of initiating trips out into the alley (Figure 4). The change in frequency of initiating trips in part arises from an increase in the $\hat{p}$ (β-initiator probability) function. Such trips represent a behavioral state, β. However, during such "emotional hyperactivity" the durations of other beta become

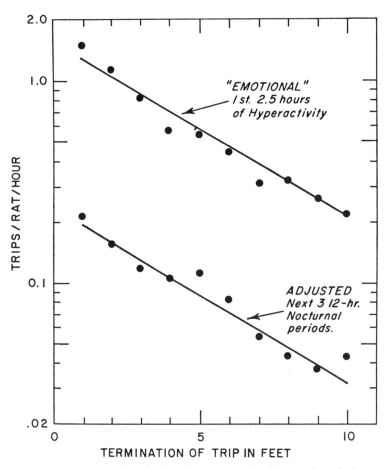

Fig. 3. Frequency of terminating trips at successive distances from the home compartment in the unstructured Ferguson Alley. (From Calhoun, 1963b)

extremely short; their respective p' values essentially become 1.0. Under such circumstances there is little that the rat can do in the barren alley except engage in consecutive episodes of undirected motor activity. My thesis (Sections 2.2, 2.3) holds that in a social context an increase in the novelty or strangeness of external environmental stimuli will permit this diffuse motor activity to be channeled into aggressive attacks on associates.

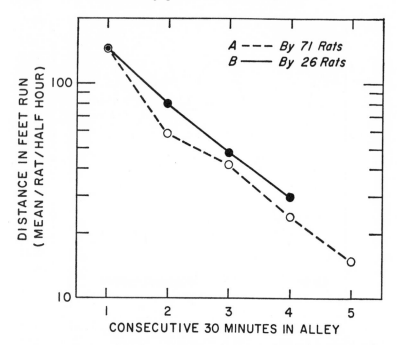

Fig. 4. Hyperactivity in a strange environment: Curve A represents the mean activity level of 71 rats immediately after first exposure to the Ferguson Alley. Curve B similarly gives the mean response of 26 rats to the NIH Emotional Activity Alley. (From Calhoun, 1963b)

Limitations to the effectiveness of p'. The lower p', the longer will be the duration of the β, other factors being equal. As may be seen in Table 1, p' is generally slightly lower during the bright hours when rats are less active. In effect, p' reflects the probability of a signal, s', being generated that has the capacity to terminate the ongoing β. In some cases, such as for the "short sleep" in the RSB field, SS 7.2, shown in Figure 5, p' varies markedly over the 24 hours. For others, such as the drinking beta, D 4.0 (Figure 11), p' remains relatively constant. Even relatively large fluctuations in p', such as for the β SS 7.2 (Figure 5) produce only minor changes in the mean durations of the behavioral state. β SS 7.2 has a minimum duration of about 16 minutes. If this kind of β is initiated it will last for at least 16 minutes before the p' terminator probability function becomes

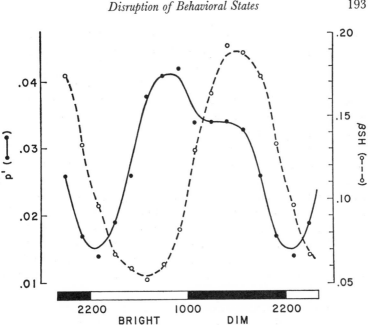

FIG. 5. Some circadian cycles pertaining to the behavioral state of "short sleep" in the field, SS 7.2. βSH = Beta/Subject/Hour. The curves are trends through 3-point moving averages.

activated. There is also an upper threshold of duration for this β that is slightly in excess of 76 minutes. For this 16-to-76-minute-duration range the 297 βs recorded during the 6 hours of maximum p' have a mean of 34.5 minutes, whereas during the 6 hours of minimum p' the mean for the 165 recorded βs is only increased to 39.6 minutes.

1.3 The Behavioral State Duration Inhibitor Probability, p_i

Examination of the data for all the behavioral states revealed that the central nervous system of rats has the capacity to reduce the average duration of behavioral states below that possible only by increasing p'. This function is designated as the beta duration inhibitor probability, p_i. For reasons not at all understood, p_i only operates appreciably with respect to: eating, E 1.1 from .1 to 11.0 minutes; short sleep in the field, SS 7.2 from 8.1 to 72.0 minutes; and for short sleep in the nest box, SS 2.2 from 8.1 to 72.0 minutes. Some of the curves for the latter two are much like that of E 1.1 in Figure 7. Focus will be placed on the "on-treadle" behavior, the shorter durations of which are designated as β E 1.1 and most likely represent episodes of eating.

Longer durations on the treadle, those lasting from about 20 minutes to 76 minutes, for all subgroups among the total group of 72 studies were characterized by a constant p'. An example is given in Figure 6 comparing socially active and socially inactive male rats. These will be discussed in more detail in the later Section 1.9 on the sequence of behavioral states. The frequency of the on-treadle behavioral state as a function of its duration over the shorter duration range apparently fails to conform to the negative exponential distribution characteristic of the longer durations. A most extreme deviation from the p'-related negative exponential distribution characterizes the bright-light hours of 2200 to 0600 for the $N = 72$ group of rats (Figure 7). Obviously p' here is not constant.

As earlier shown, where p' is constant:

$$p' = (N_{j-1} - N_j)/N_{j-1} \tag{9}$$

Where $t =$ time (i.e., duration), it follows that:

$$\frac{dN}{dt} = -p'N \tag{10}$$

Let:

$p'_i =$ a varying p'
$N_0 =$ number of β initiated, N when $t = 0$

Then:

$$N = N_0 \, \mathrm{e} \left[-\int_0^t p'_i dt \right] \tag{11}$$

$$p'_i = p_0 e^{-kt} \tag{12}$$

$$\int p'_i dt = \frac{p_0}{k} [1 - e^{-kt}] \tag{13}$$

Therefore:

$$N = N_0 e \tag{14}$$

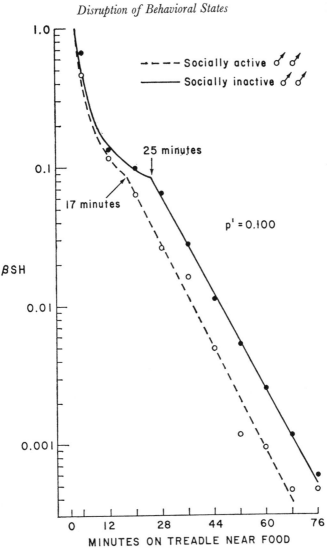

FIG. 6. The influence of degree of social activity on on-treadle behavioral states. Data encompass 3,439 rat hours for 25 socially inactive rats, and 4,319 rat hours for 30 socially active rats. For β SS 1.2 between 16.1 and 80.0 minute, p' is approximately .100 for both groups, but the βSH (β/Subject/Hour) is twice as high (.213) for the socially inactive groups as for the socially active groups (βSH = .106).

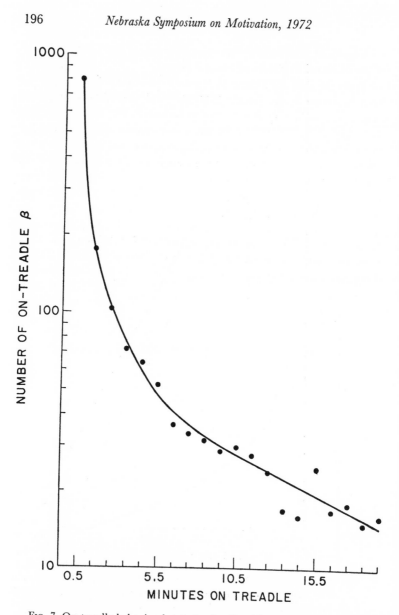

FIG. 7. On-treadle behavioral state for the $N = 72$ group of rats during the bright-light hours of 2200 to 0600. Durations of .1 to about 10.0 minutes delineate β E 1.1, while those greater than 10.0 minutes denote β SS 1.1.2.

Equations 1 to 14 were developed for me by Dr. Clifford Patlak of the National Institute of Mental Health.

From the smoothed curve in Figure 7 the sequential p'_i calculated from Equation 9 are, for the 1-minute class intervals of durations from .1 through 9.0 minutes, approximately: .78, .428, .270, .236, .185, .140, .112, .091, .085. The latter seven values lying between 2.5 and 8.5 minutes conform to a negative exponential decline in p' as a function of β duration. Given this lead, the data for the $N = 72$ group of rats were examined in more detail, contrasting the 12-hour period of 0600 to 1800 with the most constant p' to the 12-hour period of 1800 to 0600 with the most variable p_i (Figure 8).

Curve A represents the more basic pattern with only p' governing the duration of the β. The left portion of Curve A, with a p' of .1755 presumably represents eating, β E 1.1. Given a p' of .1755, 25.9% of the eatings which lasted for at least 1.0 minute would continue

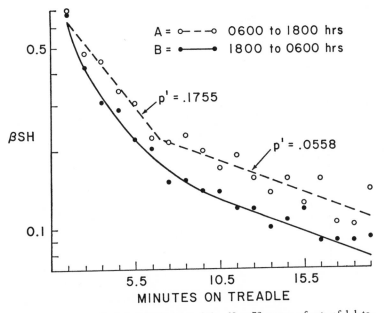

Fig. 8. On-treadle behavioral state of the $N = 72$ group of rats of 1.1-to-20.0-minutes duration. Data are divided into two 12-hour time periods providing the greatest contrasting curves. βSH = Beta/Subject/Hour.

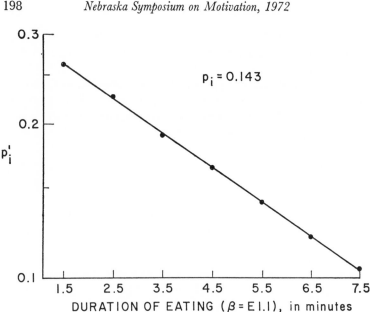

Fig. 9. Decline in the variable p', p_i', resulting from the function of a constant behavioral state inhibitor probability, p_i. p_i calculated from Eq. 15.

longer than 8.0 minutes. Some type of β did last longer than 8.0 minutes, but its p' was only .0558. With that reduced p', and if the β of 8.1 to 20.0 minutes represented a continuation of βs initiated as β E 1.1, then the ratio of βs of 1.1-to-8.0-minute to those of 8.1-to-20.0-minute duration would be .741 to .133. On this basis only 238 βs in the 8.1-to-20.0-minute range would be anticipated in proportion to the observed 1,326 of 1.1-to-8.0-minute duration. However, there were 920 observed βs in the 8.1-to-20.0-minute range.

This excess of these longer durations on the treadle suggests two means of altering behavior. First, when eating lasts longer than 8.0 minutes the CNS is able to change p' to a markedly different value. Such a marked shift in p' suggests entry into a distinctly other kind of behavioral state, most likely some kind of somnolence. Second, once such a new kind of β is established it develops its own probability of initiation, $\hat{p}$. Elevation of this $\hat{p}$ will account for the excess of on-treadle β in the 8.1-to-20.0-minute-duration range. Assuming the correctness of the above logic, the mean duration of eating would be

4.37 minutes. This represents a considerable reduction of average eating from that dictated by an uninterrupted function of a p' of .1755 for β E 1.1.

Curve B in Figure 8 suggests another major strategy of the CNS for reducing the duration of behavioral states. p_i values were calculated from the smoothed Curve B and plotted in Figure 9. p_i' declines exponentially with β duration.

Let p_i = probability of decreasing p_i' after an initial marked increase in p_i' above normal p'. As noted in the heading of this section, p_i is the beta duration inhibitor probability.

Then by analogy to Equation 9:

$$p_i = (p_{i,j-1}' - p_{i,j}')/p_{i,j-1}' \tag{15}$$

With such p_i' governed by p_i, all eating βs E 1.1 that last at least 1.1 minutes will terminate by slightly over 8.0 minutes and have a mean duration of 3.09 minutes.

In contrasting these insights derived from Curves A and B in Figure 8 it may be noted that functioning of p_i produces a 29% reduction in duration of eating.

Beyond a duration of 8.0 minutes the data in Curve B indicate that there is a transition to the somnolent β with a p' of approximately .0558, which I shall call β SS 1.1.2. The very smooth transition in Curve B from the β E 1.1 with p_i functioning to β SS 1.1.2 with $p' = .0558$ raises two very interesting issues.

1.4 Transition Balance of the Numbers of Two or More Behavioral States in the Same Environmental Context

The first issue regards the near identity in absolute numbers of the longest duration of the shorter-duration β and the shortest duration of the following longer-duration β in the same environmental context, as illustrated by the data in Figure 8, Curve A. A much more involved example of this phenomena is represented by four of the five behavioral states that take place in the nest box (Figure 10). These beta are delineated by distinctive equations describing these four beta of increasing mean duration. At each of

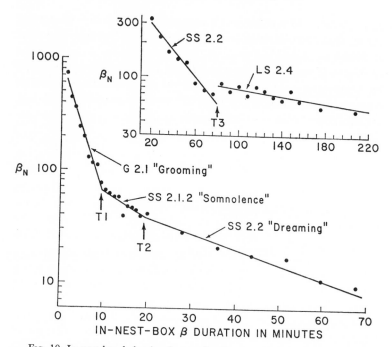

Fig. 10. In-nest-box behavioral states for the $N = 72$ group of rats. β SS 2.2 data are replicated in the upper insert figure on a contracted abscissa. $\beta_N =$ number of β by 1-minute intervals. In cases such as for β SS 2.2 where machine tallies were by 8-minute intervals, the tallied total was divided by 8 before graphing the point. It is to be noted that for β LS 2.4, long sleep, only that portion of this β is shown in which the p'', beta prolonger probability, functions (see Figure 15).

the transition durations, the numbers of the longest duration of the shorter mean duration β is approximately the same as the number of shortest duration βs of the next longer mean duration β. At the present I can deduce no basis for the origin of this harmony in number of βs at these inter-β transition durations.

The second issue involves the nonfunctioning of p' in longer-duration βs. For example, consider β SS 2.1.2 in Figure 10. All durations of this β last at least 10 minutes. This means that once such a β is initiated it will continue for at least 10 minutes before the terminator probability p' becomes functional. Similarly all β SS 2.2

that are initiated will last at least 20 minutes; and all β LS 2.4 will last at least 80 minutes before their respective p' become functional. It should be kept in mind that rats removed from their normal social setting and placed in the RSB are thus removed from changing environmental conditions, particularly represented by activities of their companions. In this absence all impetus to initiate, continue, or terminate behavioral states must result from endogenous processes.

1.5 The Behavioral State Duration Prolonger Probability, p''

Many subsets of data exhibit a reduction in the frequency of shorter-duration β during times when one might suspect that the rat might profit from continuing the behavioral state longer on the average. For example, one might anticipate that rats would drink both more often and longer during dim-light hours. Figure 11 substantiates both assumptions. Rats initiate over twice as many episodes of drinking during dim-light hours as during bright-light hours. p' calculated from durations between 2.1 and 5.0 minutes is so near identical as to contribute nothing significantly to the difference in duration of drinking. However, the greater reduction of the shorter durations, those between .1 and 2.0 minutes, during dim-light hours produce a 9% reduction of overall drinking time. Use of the word *reduction* implies a decrease from an expected value.

These expected values are obtained by projecting the slope of the p'-determined portion of the curve to intersect the ordinate. Dashed lines in Figure 11 depict such projections. Such reduction in the numbers of shorter-duration βs implies an inhibition of function of the p'-related terminator signal. It further implies that the nearer the time of an ongoing episode is from its time of initiation, the higher will be the probability that the p' terminator probability will be blocked from functioning.

Let $p'' =$ the probability of p' functioning.

Read p'' as p double prime. In general, p'' will be referred to as the beta duration prolonger probability, since the more it functions, the longer will be the average duration of the β.

With increasing duration of drinking, the observed number of β approaches that anticipated by functioning of p' fully and alone.

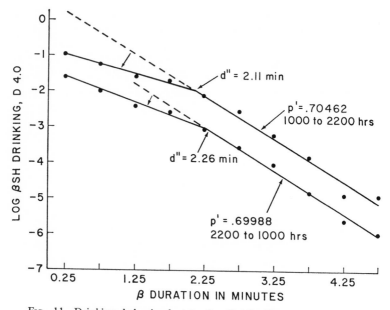

Fig. 11. Drinking behavioral state β = D 4.0. βSH = βs/Subject/Hour. During 10,149 rat hours, 72 rats engaged in 10,069 episodes of lever pressing for water that lasted no longer than 5.0 minutes. Only 60 lasted longer than 5.0 minutes. Mean duration of drinking was 1.129 during bright-light hours and 1.231 minutes during dim-light hours. βSH = .6094 during bright-light hours and 1.3654 during dim-light hours. All lines are least square best fit ones. During dim-light hours, p'' increases from .259 at .25-minutes β duration to .768 at 1.75-minutes duration. Over these same durations during bright-light hours, p'' increases from .358 to .769.

At the inflection point where the left- and right-hand portions of the curve intersect, $p'' = 1.0$. The duration at which $p'' = 1.0$ is designated d''; read as d double prime.

Dr. Samuel Greenhouse of the National Institute of Child Health and Human Development prepared for me all the equations for calculating p'', d'', and the slope of that portion of the curve where p'' functions. These equations are here omitted.

Greater insight about p'' comes from an analysis (Figure 12 and Table 2) of the drinking behavioral states of 20 rats that had lived for several months in social groups of varying size while being conditioned socially by exposure to the STAW, the "social training

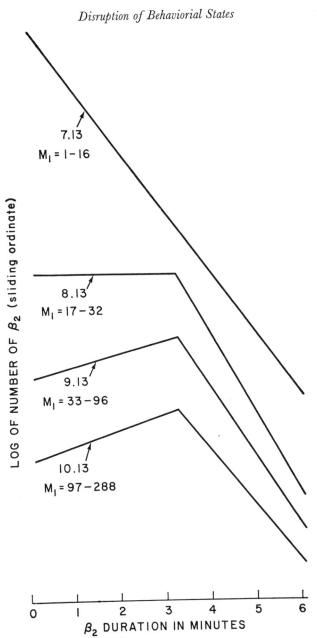

FIG. 12. Influence of increased durations (M_1) of prior nondrinking on the following durations of drinking (β_2) in isolated STAW-conditioned rats. For clarity in graphic representation the points from which the least squares best fit lines were calculated are omitted, as are also the ordinate values.

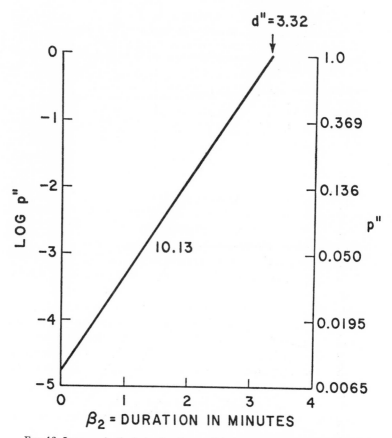

Fig. 13. Increase in the behavioral state (β_2) duration prolonger probability, p'', as a function of the duration of β_2 since its inception. Here β_2 is that sample of STAW drinking by 20 rats where the time since last drinking (M_1) varies between 97 and 288 minutes.

apparatus, water.'' (See Calhoun, 1967, pages 7 to 22, for comments about the way in which the STAW modified behavior.) The 20 rats here considered came from a study in which all male groups of $N = 3, 6, 12,$ or 24 lived under both the COOP (cooperative) and DISOP (disoperative) STAW conditions. There was a total of 20 such groups.

TABLE 2

STAW Drinking as a Function of Time since Last Drinking
(20 COOP & DISOP Rats in Total Darkness)

Data Group	Mean Drinking Minutes	d''	Number of Drinkings	M_1 Minutes since Last Drinking	p'
7.13	1.896	0.0	647	1–16	.715
8.13	2.462	3.271	542	17–32	.810
9.13	2.754	3.303	532	33–96	.766
10.13	3.022	3.325	302	97–288	.682
			2023		

At the end of this study all members of each group, except one, were removed. The STAW was then placed in the NOOP (no operative restriction to lever pressing for water) condition. The rooms were then sealed to preclude any light entering from the outside, and all internal light fixtures were switched off. All rats remained in total darkness for 60 days, except during a 2-hour period on Day 30 when the investigator entered the room to replenish food and water supplies. The objective here was to explore the effect of past social history on the rate of drift in peaks and depressions of drinking activity. Ignoring this problem, it was noted that all these rats with this long prior history of social conditioning had average durations of drinking over twice as long as any of the $N = 72$ group of rats. We are concerned here with how p'' and d'' contributed to this increase in duration of drinking.

It might also be anticipated that the longer it has been since a rat has previously drunk, the longer would be its drinking.

Let M_1 = time in minutes since last drinking.

Let β_2 = the drinking β immediately following M_1.

Four M_1 ranges were established (Table 2). Separate analyses of β_2 were made for each M_1 range (Figure 12). When M_1 is 16 minutes or less, only p' functions. The majority of such M_1 can only be composed of sequences of motor βs with only occasional inclusion of somnolence, SS 1.1.2 and SS 2.1.2, betas. However, the β_2 curves for all M_1 greater than 16 minutes do have p'' functioning. Most of these longer M_1 must contain episodes of sleeping (SS 1.2, SS 2.2, SS 7.2, LS 2.4). Thus, despite probable reduced metabolic rate during these longer intervals of nondrinking, increased periods of nondrinking do prolong the duration of following episodes of drinking. Furthermore, the longer the period of nondrinking the more p'' functions. There is also a suggestion in these data that d'' similarly increases.

The p'' increases as a function of duration of drinking is given in Figure 13 for drinking after the long duration, M_1 having a range of 97 to 288 minutes since last drinking. At initiation of drinking, p'' closely approaches zero, being only .0065. In this case, then, p'' is nearly at maximum function in prolonging β_2. It may be noted that when p'' is maximally functioning, the two halves of the curve of the log of the number of beta as a function of their duration are essentially at right angles to each other.

Effect of M_1 on the drinking β_2 duration was also examined for the $N = 72$ group of rats (Table 3 and Fig. 14). d'' increased and p'' became more functional as M_1 increased up to about 45 minutes.

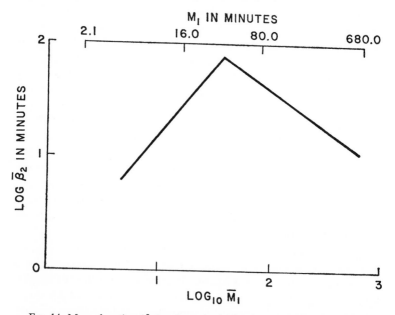

FIG. 14. Mean duration ($\bar{\beta}_2$ in minutes) of drinking in the RSB as influenced by duration (M_1) since last drinking. See Table 3 for details.

TABLE 3

MEAN DURATION[a] β_2 OF DRINKING AS A FUNCTION OF M_1, THE INTERVAL[a]
SINCE LAST DRINKING ($N = 72$ GROUP OF RATS IN RSB)

$\overline{M}_1$	Log $\overline{M}_1$	$\overline{B}_2$	N of B_2	M_1 Range
4.53	0.656	0.844	1810	2.1– 8.0
11.86	1.074	1.167	1156	8.1– 16.0
23.09	1.363	1.643	1486	16.1– 32.0
38.87	1.590	1.859	621	32.1– 48.0
61.23	1.787	1.704	436	48.1– 80.0
95.14	1.978	1.428	299	80.1–112.0
141.25	2.150	1.463	453	112.1–172.0
186.72	2.271	1.405	200	172.1–204.0
291.92	2.465	1.259	686	204.1–480.0
544.87	2.764	1.181	59	480.1–680.0
			7206	

[a] Time in minutes.

Within this range the duration of β_2 also increased. However, with increase of M_1 above 45 minutes, duration of drinking continuously declines. Most of these longer M_1 are composed of episodes of long sleep, LS 2.4. Such decline in β durations suggests that a consequence of such long sleep is to return the internal settings of the several probability functions back toward a primordial basic setting.

The likely verity of this insight finds corroboration in Figure 16. This figure shows the observed number of all of the other βs following cessation of each kind of ongoing behavioral state. Also this figure gives for each of the following βs the expected number anticipated when there are no associated biases. In every case χ^2 values of deviance of observed from expected were calculated. The sum of the χ^2 values for βs following long sleep in the nest box, LS 2.4, is only 18.3, while that for βs following all other behavioral states is much larger. For example, the sum of the χ^2 values for βs following short sleep in the nest box, SS 2.2, is 77.5, over four times that for βs following long sleep.

Finally, the generality of the importance of p'' can be judged from examining long sleep itself (Figure 15). On a circadian basis d'' fluctuates with a maximum functioning of p'' during the bright-light hours (Figure 15C) of minimum motor activity, and a minimum functioning of p'' during the opposing dim-light hours (Figure 15A).

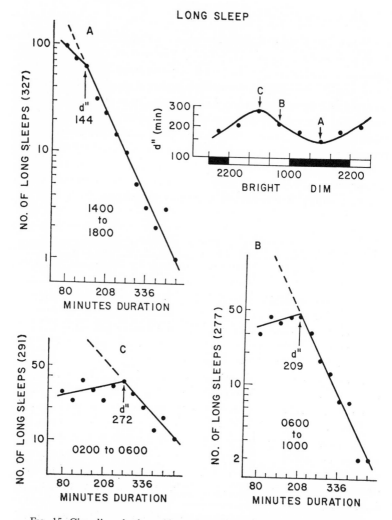

Fig. 15. Circadian rhythm of long sleep. The three insert graphs are representative of the phase changes in p'' function as it influences average duration of long sleep. Letters above the upper-right-hand graph of circadian rhythm of d'' indicate times in the cycle for the three curves describing variability in long sleep, $\beta = $ LS 2.4.

1.6 The Initiator Probability, $\hat{p}$

When the p'-related CNS signal, s', terminates an ongoing β (a β_1), according to my hypothesis, any one of the total set of behavioral states may then be initiated (designated β_2 in Figure 16), including the one just terminated. Whether a particular β will be initiated will depend upon the relative magnitude of its $\hat{p}$ (read as p caret). For example, in the present RSB apparatus, drinking βs are taken as equivalent to the duration of continuous episodes of lever pressing recorded on an Esterline-Angus event recorder moving at 6 inches per hour. Under these circumstances it is impossible to detect when a behavioral state, the same as just terminated, is initiated within a fraction of a second therefrom. Such lack of

Second β, i.e. β₂	$\hat{p}$ Covert	$\hat{p}$ Overt	First β, i.e. β₁ E 1.1	D 4.0	R 3.0	G 2.1	G 7.1	SS 1.2	SS 2.2	LS 2.4	Row totals
E 1.1	.096	.098	0 / 0	258.0 / 321.6	99.0 / 30.2	251.0 / 162.9	173.0 / 161.3	0 / 0	29.0 / 50.4	59.0 / 70.4	869.0 / 896.8
D 4.0	.293	.274	338.0 / 348.8	0 / 0	374.0 / 397.5	439.0 / 497.3	362.0 / 492.3	538.0 / 263.2	138.0 / 154.0	244.0 / 214.9	2433.0 / 2368.0
R 3.0	.122	.135	82.0 / 145.2	227.0 / 408.7	0 / 0	223.0 / 207.0	530.0 / 204.9	12.0 / 109.6	58.0 / 64.1	64.0 / 89.4	1196.0 / 1228.8
G 2.1	.162	.158	313.0 / 192.6	611.0 / 542.1	205.0 / 219.4	0 / 0	141.0 / 271.8	128.0 / 145.3	0 / 0	0 / 0	1398.0 / 1371.2
G 7.1	.149	.160	129.0 / 177.9	451.0 / 500.7	327.0 / 202.7	194.0 / 253.6	0 / 0	50.0 / 134.2	142.0 / 78.5	127.0 / 109.6	1420.0 / 1457.2
SS 1.2	.051	.052	0 / 0	186.0 / 172.1	75.0 / 69.7	101.0 / 87.2	68.0 / 86.3	0 / 0	7.0 / 27.0	28.0 / 37.7	465.0 / 479.9
SS 2.2	.047	.046	49.0 / 55.7	235.0 / 156.7	51.0 / 63.4	0 / 0	62.0 / 78.5	7.0 / 42.0	0 / 0	0 / 0	404.0 / 396.3
LS 2.4	.080	.078	104.0 / 94.9	401.0 / 267.2	60.0 / 108.1	0 / 0	93.0 / 134.0	31.0 / 71.6	0 / 0	0 / 0	689.0 / 675.8
Column totals			1015.0	2369.0	1191.0	1208.0	1429.0	766.0	374.0	522.0	8874.0

Fig. 16. β sequences and the initiator probability, $\hat{p}$. For each β_2 following a β_1 the upper number is the observed and the lower number the expected. Those sets enclosed in a heavy-lined square have the observed significantly larger than the expected. Sets outlined by a light-lined square have significantly lower observed. Circled sets by χ^2 tests do not have observed differing from expected. See text for delineation of overt versus covert $\hat{p}$. These data are for a particular subset of 50 rats of the total 72.

recognition leads to empty cells, as in the diagonal of Figure 16. Ignoring these empty cells an overt $\hat{p}$, $\hat{p}_o$, for any β_2 may be calculated simply as its row total divided by the sum of such row totals for all β_2s. Such overt $\hat{p}$ are listed in Figure 16.

Obtaining a theoretical number of each β_2 following a particular β_1 requires determination of a covert $\hat{p}$, $\hat{p}_c$, consonant with the above-stated hypotheses. On the assumption that this hypothesis is true, such covert $\hat{p}$ may be calculated by equations developed for me by Professor John Tukey of Princeton University. These have not yet been published and, because of their length, they will not be presented here. Such covert $\hat{p}$ are also listed in Figure 16. However, since the diagonal cells are missing, as well as a few others where two or more distinct βs were identified on the basis of different p' values characterizing different durations at a place (e.g., see Figure 10), an adjusted $\hat{p}_c$, $\hat{\hat{p}}_c$, must be calculated for each $\beta_1\beta_2$ cell in order to calculate the theoretical number of β_2 in that cell.

Procedurally $\hat{\hat{p}}_c$ is calculated as follows, using the data in Figure 16 as an example: In an 8×8 table like this one start with all 64 cells initially blank, but containing row and column totals. Insert in all cells of each row (except those cells lacking observed β_2 values) the covert $\hat{p}$, $\hat{p}_c$, for that row.

Let N = number of cells in a column having observed β_2.

$$\sum_1^N \hat{p}_c = \text{column total of covert } \hat{p}.$$

Then, for any ith cell in the column:

$$\hat{\hat{p}}_{ci} = \frac{\hat{p}_{ci}}{\sum_1^N \hat{p}_c} \tag{16}$$

As an example consider the column headed by $\beta_1 = $ E 1.1 and the cell where $\beta_2 = $ G 2.1.

$$\hat{\hat{p}}_c = \frac{.162}{.853} = .1898$$

Theoretical number of $\beta_2 = \hat{\hat{p}}_c \cdot (\text{Column total}) \tag{17}$

$$= .1898(1015) = 192.6$$

Light	Beta $\hat{p}_c$ Rank							
	1	2	3	4	5	6	7	8
Bright •	D 4.0	G 2.1	LS 2.4	E 1.1	G 7.1	R 3.0	SS 1.2	SS 2.2
Dim ○	D 4.0	G 7.1	G 2.1	R 3.0	E 1.1	LS 2.4	SS 2.2	SS 1.2

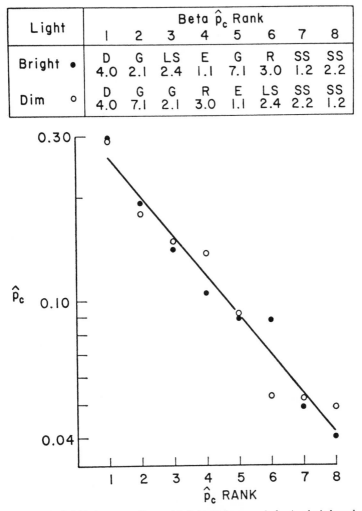

FIG. 17. $\hat{p}$ shifts between dim and bright 12-hour periods. Analysis based on 50 rats, each with 6 days of uninterrupted data. Trend line fitted by eye. Each sequentially lower $\hat{p}$ by the smoothed lines is 77% of the value of the next higher ranked $\hat{p}$ value. From dim- to bright-light hours $\hat{p}_c$ for grooming, G. 7.1, decreased from .178 to .089; $\hat{p}$ for running, R 4.0, decreased from .137 to .088; while $\hat{p}_o$ for long sleep, LS 2.4, increased from .053 to .141. See Figure 20 for circadian rhythm of $\hat{p}_o$, the overt probability of β initiation.

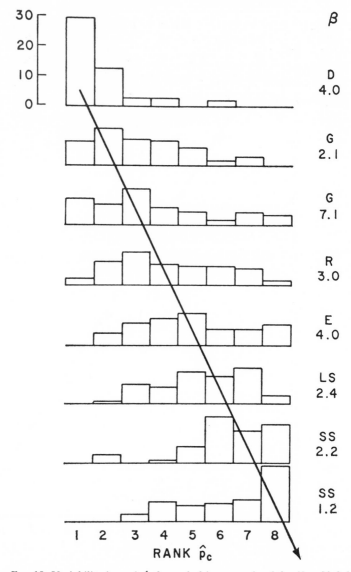

Fig. 18. Variability in rank $\hat{p}_c$ for each β in a sample of the $N = 50$ 6-day complete record rats. Bar graphs indicate the number of rats having $\hat{p}_c$ ranks 1 through 8 for each β. The arrow passes through each β graph at its most typical $\hat{p}_c$ rank.

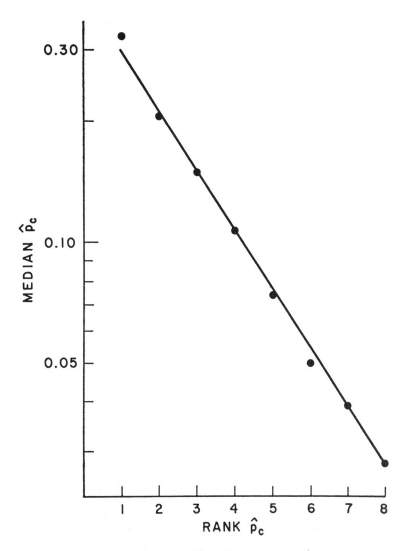

Fig. 19. Central tendency curve of $\hat{p}_c$ as a function of rank $\hat{p}_c$ based on the 19 of the 50 rats exhibiting the most uniform distribution. In each rank several betas are represented. Each successive $\hat{p}_c$ is 0.71 the prior one. Trend line fitted by eye.

All theoretical (i.e., expected) numbers of β_2 given in Figure 16 were calculated by using Equation 17.

As may be seen from Figure 16, there is a six-fold variability between extreme values for $\hat{p}_c$. This same degree of variability holds when the $\hat{p}_c$ values for dim and light hours are contrasted (Figure 17), even though there are striking rearrangements with regard to the $\hat{p}_c$ rank for the several βs. Calculations of $\hat{p}_c$ were made for each of the rats in this sample of 50 which formed the basis for the data in Figures 16 and 17. Figure 18 reveals that among the subjects there is marked variability as to which βs are associated with any given $\hat{p}_c$ rank; and yet, there is a marked central tendency for each β to have its $\hat{p}_c$ have a particular rank.

Graphs were prepared for each of these 50 rats of $\log \hat{p}_c$ as a function of $\hat{p}_c$ rank. Thirteen of these rats never exhibited one or two of the βs. Eighteen rats appeared not to have developed a uniform pattern in the sense that they had an excessively large rank 1 $\hat{p}_c$, or an excessively low last rank $\hat{p}_c$. The remaining 19 rats each exhibited a trend very much like that of the entire group (Figure 17). Ignoring the particular βs involved, the median $\hat{p}_c$ for each $\hat{p}_c$ rank was identified and plotted in Figure 19. This very remarkable orderliness in the variability of $\hat{p}_c$ across animals, coupled with the realignment of $\hat{p}_c$ across the dim-light to bright-light shift, augers

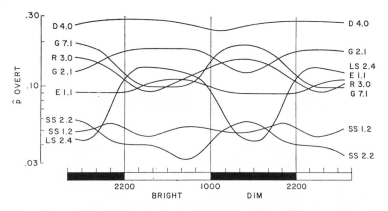

Fig. 20. Circadian variability of the overt probability, $\hat{p}_o$, of initiating behavioral states given an ongoing behavioral state has terminated. Trend lines fitted to observed data by eye. Observed points lay very close to the trend line.

for a neural basis for the necessity for such ordering. It is my belief that $\hat{p}_c$ represents the most parsimonious and precise definition of motivation.

The behavioral state initiator probability, $\hat{p}$, varies markedly over the 24 hours for several of the betas, particularly for long sleep, LS 2.4 (Figure 20). Since the sum of the $\hat{p}$ for all the betas must add up to 1.0, it follows that as the $\hat{p}$ for β LS 2.4 increases, at least some of the $\hat{p}$ for other βs must decrease. Inspection of Figure 20 reveals that at some time of day the several $\hat{p}$ are undergoing more change than at other times. Two propositions in the present thesis hold (a) that the values (settings) of the several behavioral states controlling probabilities existing at any moment in time determine the mood of the animal at that time and (b) that change in these probability values over time represents emotion. For empirical analytical purposes:

Let $\Delta\hat{p}$ = change in $\hat{p}$ over a 2-hour period.

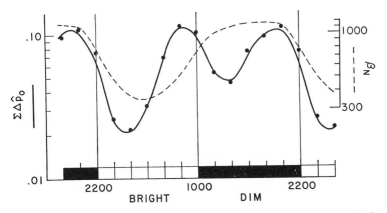

Fig. 21. Circadian rhythm in the sum of changes, between consecutive 2-hour periods, of the overt probability, $\hat{p}_o$, of initiating the eight behavioral states shown in Figure 20. Depressions in the curve indicate relative $\hat{p}_o$ stability, while peaks represent relative $\hat{p}_o$ instability.

The number, β_N, of behavioral states of running, $\beta = $ R 3.0, in the wheel was calculated for the $N = 72$ group of rats for each 2-hour period. The dashed line closely approximates these points. It was based on an analysis of 9,331 episodes of running in the wheel.

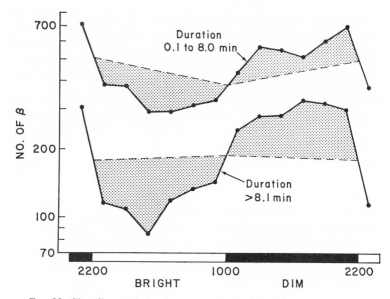

Fig. 22. Circadian variation in on-treadle βs. Stippled areas of curves are defined by lines connecting points where light changes intersect the curves. The greater variability of the initiator probability, p, for the longer-duration βs is reflected by the larger stippled areas for this curve in contrast to those associated with the upper curve for short-duration βs. Upper curve represents β E 1.1 (eating) while the lower curve represents the total of β SS 1.1.2 (somnolence on-treadle) and β SS 1.2 (day-dreaming short sleep on-treadle).

Twelve such Δp were determined for each of the behavioral states graphed in Figure 20. A $\sum \Delta p$ for the eight Δp for each 2-hour period was then calculated (Figure 21). Each $\sum \Delta p$ value represents an overall motivational emotional state. One peak in such emotion falls $1\frac{1}{2}$ hours before the shift from bright- to dim-light hours, while the other falls $2\frac{1}{2}$ hours before the shift from dim to bright light. Minimal motivational emotional states fall approximately $3\frac{1}{2}$ hours after each light shift.

These changes in emotion may be anticipated to influence the character of social interaction, including aggression. However, the frequency with which such emotional states do affect social behavior will in part be influenced by the likelihood of animals contacting each other. Running in the wheel in the RSB most closely approximates the moving about more extended physical fields in which contacts among animals occur as a result of the movement. As may be seen from Figure 21, the circadian rhythm of initiating episodes of locomotion differs markedly from that of $\sum \Delta \hat{p}$. This contrast is presented here to illustrate the many complexities of change in the total character of a behaving animal that result from variations in the five underlying behavioral control probability functions.

The number, β_N, of most behavioral states other than for long sleep (LS 2.4) varies relatively more widely than does the related probability, $\hat{p}$, of initiating the behavioral state. For example, compare the upper curve in Figure 22 for the eating beta E 1.1 with the $\hat{p}$ for this eating in Figure 20. In part Figure 22 is presented as background for the bearing longer-duration betas on the treadle have with regard to the differential aggressive tendencies between socially active and socially inactive rats. See pages 226–229.

1.7 *The Concatenator Probability,* p_κ

When any ongoing beta, β_1, terminates, according to my hypothesis, any other β, including the one just terminated, may then be initiated. How likely it is that a particular β will be initiated depends upon its covert probability, $\hat{p}_c$. If initiations of βs are solely so determined, then the observed number, β_{2B}, following a particular terminated beta, β_1, will closely approximate the theoretical number, β_{2T}. However, inspection of Figure 16 reveals that there are several instances in which the observed differed significantly from the theoretical. When the observed markedly exceeds the theoretical it indicates the functioning of a concatenating probability, p_κ, which increases above chance the likelihood that this particular β_2 will be initiated after the termination of the β_1 in question. This p_κ may be calculated as follows:

Consider a particular β_1 and an associated β_2.
Let:

β_{2B} = observed number of β_2
β_{2T} = theoretical number of β_2
R = row total of β_{2B}
C = column total of β_{2B}

It is apparent that:

$$p_\kappa = 0 \text{ when } \beta_{2B} = \beta_{2T} \tag{18}$$

$$p_\kappa = 1.0 \text{ when } \beta_{2B} = R, \text{ provided } R < C \tag{19}$$

$$p_\kappa = 1.0 \text{ when } \beta_{2B} = C, \text{ provided } C < R \tag{20}$$

It follows that:

$$p_\kappa = \frac{\beta_{2B} - \beta_{2T}}{R} \tag{21}$$

provided $R < C$ or

$$p_\kappa = \frac{\beta_{2B} - \beta_{2T}}{C} \tag{22}$$

provided $C < R$.

The necessity for these two equations for p_κ derives from the fact that β_{2B} cannot exceed either the number, C, of the β_1 which it follows, nor can it exceed the total number, R, of times this β_2 occurs.

p_κ will be positive when the observed, β_{2B}, exceeds the theoretical, β_{2T}. p_κ will be negative when the observed, β_{2B}, is less than the theoretical, β_{2T}.

Positive p_κ were calculated for all 16 instances shown in Figure 16 that the observed β_2 exceeded the theoretical. These p_κ are plotted as a function of rank p_κ in Figure 23. A negative exponential equation would adequately describe this distribution. The last four points on this graph, in particular, do not differ from the basic hypothesis that β sequences are initially at random expectation levels depending solely on their respective $\hat{p}_c$ for initiation. The χ^2 values of the difference between observed and expected for the p_κ Ranks 13, 14, 15, and 16 are respectively 2.2, .9, 1.2, and .9. See the representation of these four β_2 in Figure 25. In contrast, χ^2 values relating to p_κ Ranks 1, 2, 3, and 4 are 214.4, 480.8, 515.9 and 39.2. The very fact that a negative exponential curve describes p_κ as a function of rank p_κ, with highly significant deviances of β_2 from expected on the one end and random deviances on the other, suggests that initial deviances, by their deviance, increase the probability of concatenation. I have been able to detect no logical

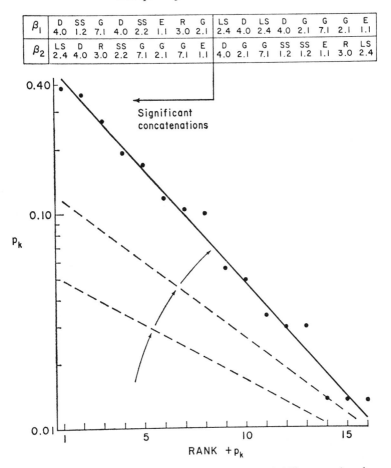

FIG. 23. Variability of the positive concatenator probability, $+p_k$, based on data in Figure 16. Arrows point toward hypothetical accentuation (reinforcement) during maturation of initial deviances of associations from chance levels. All 16 instances in which the observed β_2 exceed the theoretical are here shown. However, in comparing observed with theoretical, there is a sharp break in χ^2 values between p_k Ranks 8 and 9. Ranks 8 and above have χ^2 values exceeding 47.0, while Ranks 9 and below have values below 9.0.

reasons, either probabilistic or situational, why particular β_2 should become significantly concatenated with another particular β_1. The product of the respective $\hat{p}_c$ for associated β_1 and β_2 are

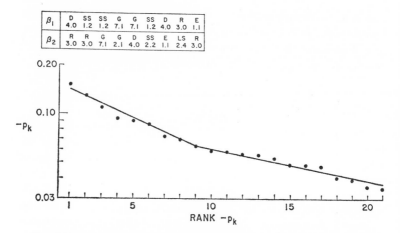

| β_1 | D 4.0 | SS 1.2 | SS 1.2 | G 7.1 | G 7.1 | SS 1.2 | D 4.0 | R 3.0 | E 1.1 | |
| β_2 | R 3.0 | R 3.0 | G 7.1 | G 2.1 | D 4.0 | SS 2.2 | E 1.1 | LS 2.4 | R 3.0 | |

Fig. 24. Variability of the negative concatenator (disjunctor) probability, $-p_k$, based on data in Figure 16. The observed number of β_2 related to the nine left most $-p_k$ are significantly less than the theoretical. χ^2 values for them vary between 21.4 and 80.7.

uncorrelated with rank $\hat{p}_K$. Similarly I can find no logical basis for the differential degree of negative concatenation among the several β_1 and β_2 pairs (Figure 24).

Regardless of the origin and persistence of positive, negative, or random associations between β_1 and β_2, it is possible to depict the overall pattern emerging from them (Figure 25). Five subgroups of rats formed the total of 50 in this analysis. Only those associations are shown in this figure that met the following criteria: (a) all groups had no significant difference between observed and expected, or (b) if a significant difference existed, most groups varied significantly in the same direction with no group varying significantly in the opposite direction. Considering that 25 of the 48 cells of Figure 16 are represented in Figure 25, one might come to the conclusion that there are innate CNS biasing processes which enhance the likelihood that certain behavioral states will more often follow certain others, while similar processes will reduce the likelihood of sequential associations of two betas below chance levels. This may be so. However, examination of the direction and degree of positive and negative concatenations (i.e., the magnitude of $+p_K$

and $-p_\kappa$) of behavioral states among the five subgroups of rats reinforces my belief that all significant deviations from an expectation of randomness of association arise from external environmental conditions affecting long times of living by individuals.

1.8 The Nature of Behavioral States

At this point it may be helpful to remark on the differences between behavioral states and their component motor acts. In the RSB, a very unnatural environment for rats, drinking is equated with a sequence of very similar acts of depressing a lever with a forepaw. Intervals between pressing usually last only sufficiently long for the rat to lean over and lap up the drop of water in the cup that arises from the well below upon release of downward pressure on the lever. Sequences of such lever pressing interrupted by long intervals of non-lever pressing constitute an episode of the behavioral state of drinking. Such a behavioral state has a direct counterpart in nature. Wild Norway rats at an open pool of water often repeatedly insert a paw into the water, raise it, lick off the water, and then dip the paw back into the water. Nest building by rats also forms a behavioral state. It consists of an uninterrupted series of trips from the nest location to a general region where material appropriate to nest construction may be found. Termination of each trip includes organizing the transported material into the nest before embarking on another trip. Thus a certain amount of variability characterizes the component behavioral acts which comprise this behavioral state.

The ethological literature includes many examples of behavioral states of courtship, prey acquisition, and nest building where the component acts or behavior become much more diverse and sequentially predictable. Although such predictability of sequential behaviors within a behavioral state may have a major innate CNS component influencing this internal ordering, such control is not required. For example, consider written paragraphs as a behavioral state. The length of the paragraph represents its duration. Each included sentence is a component behavior. Sentence content diversity represents behavioral diversity. I have examined two sets of such conceptual behavioral states: (a) Norbert Wiener's *The*

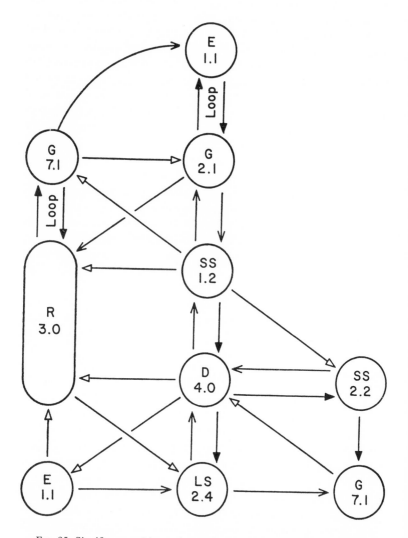

Fig. 25. Significant positive and negative β concatenations based on data in Figure 16. Arrows point from β_1 to β_2. Solid arrows point to β_2 whose observed numbers are greater than the theoretical. Open arrows point to β_2 whose observed are less than the theoretical. Arrows with unclosed heads point to β_2 whose observed do not differ from the theoretical.

Tempter and (b) an anthology of 3,200 paragraphs selected for their philosophical cogency to the topic of "population and mental health." The log of the number of paragraphs as a function of their duration revealed the activity of both p' and p'' probability functions. Wiener's simpler prose produced a curve much like those in Figure 11 representing conditions of drinking by rats less subjected to the deprivation and social conditioning affecting the character of drinking curves shown in Figure 12. The behaviorially more complex paragraphs from the anthology were most like the curve in Figure 12 where M_1 equals 33 to 96 minutes.

I might add that the jocular overtone of Wiener's novel was punctuated with one episode of verbal violence. In this paragraph the lead character (Wiener?) was bemoaning the fact that he had not received a Nobel prize. This paragraph's length so far exceeded all others as to fall completely outside the equations describing the remainder of the distribution. Later (Section 2.9), when I focus more specifically on aggression, a situation with many parallels to Wiener's episode of violence will be described which caused most dominant rats to go berserk.

If behavioral states do become relatively permanently concatenated, their combined duration will then comprise a suprabehavioral state whose p' and p'' will be a function of the several p' and p'' of the contained behavioral states. This applies also to random sequences. If one takes the hypothesis that dream sleep, specifically what for rats denotes short sleep in the nest box, SS 2.2, represents a neurological equivalence of sequences of motor betas lacking motor manifestations, then one could treat all durations of non-sleep (i.e., those not interrupted by the betas SS 1.1.2, SS 2.1.2, SS 1.2, SS 2.2, and LS 2.4) and treat them as a behavioral state. Mr. Garrett Bagley of our staff wrote a computer program to do this with the data for the $N = 72$ group of rats. Such simulated short sleep was characterized by a p' intermediate between "somnolence" (β SS 2.1.2) and "dream sleep" (β SS 2.2) that occurred in the nest box. I am therefore led to the conclusion that the neural mechanisms determining p' and p'' for discrete behavioral states can be joined together to form another behavioral state with quite other manifestations and implications than those of the different kinds of behavioral states from which it was formed.

1.9 Differential Concatenation among Subgroups

The $N = 50$ group of rats, which was selected out of the larger $N = 72$ group to investigate the problems of initiation and concatenation of behavioral states, was in turn comprised of seven subgroups. I suspected that the different histories of these subgroups might provide insights into the process of control of behavioral states. These groups, all of the albino domesticated Osborne-Mendel strain of *Rattus norvegicus*, were as follows:

1. Females, $N = 9$. The mean age in days at rat introduction into the RSB was 288, with a range of from 206 to 319 days. Up until this age all had lived as members of the second series of populations described in Calhoun (1962b) in a complex physical and social environment. Drinking in this environment was ad lib at a bar containing six mechanical levers. Five of the females (subgroup 1.1) had many self-inflicted scratch wounds; four (subgroup 1.2) had few such wounds. For the present purposes, Subgroups 1.1 and 1.2 are combined as just females.

2. High-velocity males, $N = 10$. The mean age in days at introduction into the RSB was 410, with a range of from 316 to 452 days. Environmental setting was the same as for Group 1. Velocity (Calhoun, 1963b, 1967) is a measure of degree of activity and alertness in those portions of the environment where status interactions more often take place. High-velocity males are socially dominant and/or territorial. Each had a history of considerable success in agonistic encounters. Their behavior was mostly compatible with species survival.

3. Low-velocity males, $N = 6$. The mean age in days at introduction into the RSB was 374, with a range of from 230 to 429 days. Environmental setting was the same as for Group 1. All these males had a long early history of lack of success in status interaction. Related to this failure was the fact that they withdrew physically and psychologically. They spent much more time resting or sleeping in places of reduced social contact. Per unit of time active they engaged in fewer social interactions than did high-velocity males. Their behavior deviated in many ways from normality.

4. Old males, $N = 13$. The mean age in days at introduction into the RSB was 652, with a range of from 633 to 667 days. From weaning to 468 days of age they had been part of an experiment on aging and had lived in groups of five in metal cages, 7 × 12 × 17 inches. At 468 days of age they were transferred to 2.4 × 5.0-foot pens with sawdust floors. Here drinking was in STAWs where the levers were on NOOP (no restriction to conditions of levers being locked). Of this group, six were experimental (Subgroup 4.1). Up until placement in the sawdust-floored pens they had been on a dietary sequence in which normal diets were interspersed with various types of deficient diets. The remaining seven, the control Subgroup 4.2, were always on an adequate diet. For present purposes, Subgroups 4.1 and 4.2 are combined simply as old males. Male rats of this age have a long history of being socially active in the sense of involvement in status interactions. However, they had always lived in such small groups that one would not anticipate much inhibition of social involvement such as characterized the low-velocity males of Group 3.

5. *Young males, N = 12*. The mean age in days at introduction into the RSB was 64.3, with a range of from 52 to 73 days. From weaning all lived in groups of eight in the 2.4 × 5.0-foot pens described for Group 4. These males were of an age characterized by extremely infrequent involvement in fighting, either among this age class, or as resulting from attacks by older associates when rats live in age-structured populations.

There were 23 socially active males. High-velocity males and old males, because of the great similarity of their history with regard to social involvement, may be grouped together to increase sample size. The number of socially inactive males was 18. Low-velocity males resemble young males with regard to their relative lack of involvement in status interactions involving fighting.

It may be noted that the Ns of each of these two pooled groups are less than that indicated in Figure 6 and Table 4. For greater precision of analysis only those rats were accepted for the p' and p'' analyses where their records consisted of six consecutive 24-hour periods without interruption due to apparatus failure.

For each of the five major groups listed above matrices (as exemplified in Figure 16) of observed and expected number of β_2 following just terminated β_1 were prepared. Chi square values were

TABLE 4

Differential Concatenation of Behavioral States, Socially Active and Socially Inactive Rats

| | | Observed > Expected | | | | | Observed < Expected | | | |
| | | Socially Active | | Socially Inactive | | | Socially Active | | Socially Inactive | |
β_1	β_2	OBS	EXP	OBS	EXP	β_2	OBS	EXP	OBS	EXP
		More ± concatenations by socially active rats								
G 7.1	R 3.0	306	131.3	91	40.2	G 2.1	59	149.2	35	50.5
E 1.1	G 2.1	192	98.7	83	62.5	R 3.0	39	85.6	26	29.2
G 2.1	E 1.1	141	79.8	77	54.6	G 7.1	74	134.5	41	47.5
R 3.0	G 7.1	197	127.9	56	38.9	LS 2.4	27	53.4	15	24.5
D 4.0	SS 2.2	159	97.2	51	39.0	R 3.0	113	207.1	95	123.3
Total		995	534.9	358	235.2		312	629.8	212	275.0
$\Sigma \chi^2$		505.3		141.1			165.7		24.7	
		More ± concatenations by socially inactive rats								
SS 1.2	D 4.0	135	71.5	353	206.5	R 3.0	9	35.2	3	44.9
SS 1.2						G 7.1	25	43.9	10	43.6
Total		135	71.5	353	206.5		34	79.1	13	88.5
$\Sigma \chi^2$		58.9		127.6			28.4		66.0	

prepared regarding the difference between observed and expected for each of the 48 cells for each group (total 240 Chi squares).

Three cells in Figure 16 are particularly instructive with regard to the origin of significant concatenations. These cells are: (a) $\beta_1 = $ E 1.1, $\beta_2 = $ D 4.0; (b) $\beta_1 = $ R 3.0, $\beta_2 = $ D 4.0; (c) $\beta_1 = $ R 3.0, $\beta_2 = $ G 2.1. In each of these cells of the $N = 50$ group the observed numbers of β_2 are very close to that expected. Chi square values are respectively .3, 1.4, and 1.0, suggesting completely random association between β_1 and β_2 in these examples. However, in every case the females had the observed differing significantly from the expected, while in one of the four other groups the difference was significant in the opposite direction, thus canceling out significant deviation from the expected in the overall sample. In all other cases where there were two or more groups with significant deviations from the expected for a particular cell, all were in the same direction.

Comparisons between the socially active and the socially inactive males suggest how prior experience with aggression may influence the degree to which behavioral states become concatenated (Table 4). After behavioral states (β_1) having a high motor component, the following β_2 of socially active males deviate more widely, both positively and negatively, from the expected than is true of the socially inactive males. In contrast, socially inactive males have much stronger concatenations following the "day-dreaming" short sleep (β SS 1.2) on the food treadle. Another way of stating this is that socially active rats are more traditional or predictable following strongly motor behavioral states, while greater predictability of upcoming behavior following day-dreaming characterizes socially inactive rats.

Figure 6 and Table 5 contrast day-dreaming short sleep for these two groups. Socially inactive rats are 2.0 to 2.7 times as involved in day-dreaming, both with regard to number of times initiated and the total time per day spent in this behavioral state. My designation of long durations on the treadle as day-dreaming is purely interpretative. It derives from the following logic: In complex social and environmental settings rats were noted stretched out for long periods with eyes often open. This is a quite different stance than the curled-up, eyes-closed position presumed to represent sleep. Since most rats in such contexts usually retired to nest boxes for most long

TABLE 5

"On Treadle" Behavioral State, E 1.0

		Relative Degree of Social Involvement	
β in Minutes	Statistic	Socially Inactive (25 rats)	Socially Active (30 rats)
0.1 to 1.0	β_N	1483.0	952.0
1.1 to 8.0 "Eating" E 1.1	β_N[a] β_d[b] βSD[c] MSD[d]	854.0 3.694 5.96 22.0	1122.0 3.690 6.24 23.01
8.1 to 24.0 "Somnolence" E 1.1.2	β_N β_d βSD MSD	806.0 15.30 5.625 86.0	781.0 14.31 4.34 62.11
24.1 to 80.0 "Dream Sleep" E 1.2	β_N β_d βSD MSD	395.0 34.17 2.755 94.10	189.0 33.70 1.050 35.39
Total Rat Hours from Which Above Data on β Were Derived		3439.21	4319.36

[a] β_N: Number of β in total hours analyzed (see bottom row) for entire group of rats
[b] β_d: Mean duration of β in minutes
[c] βSD: Number of β per subject per day (i.e., 24 hours)
[d] MSD: $\sum$ of minutes in β per subject per day (i.e., 24 hours)

absences from the field comparable to the SS 2.2 and LS 2.4 in the RSB, I assume that these absences constitute dream and long-sleep states. Thus, I deduce that the stretched-out-relaxed episodes in the field of complex environments away from nest boxes is comparable to the β SS 1.2 in the RSB field. Both are designated as day-dreaming as an approximation to a more conceptually active state likely characterizing these episodes of reduced motor activity.

By *conceptually active* I mean a neural representation of prior motor states. See above discussion (in Section 1.8) of simulated short sleep. If such SS 1.2 behavioral states do represent neural images of prior sequences of motor states, the more time spent in day-dreaming by socially inactive rats should enhance the fixation of positive and negative concatenations in a similar manner as they develop after motor behavioral states for socially active rats (Table

5). I have not yet been able to formulate any precise hypotheses about the origin and implication of an increase in presumed day-dreaming short sleep. However, the accentuation of this behavioral state among two quite divergent groups (the young, and the low-velocity withdrawn), who in their current life less frequently engage in aggression, suggests a relationship between reduced involvement in aggression and creativity.

1.10 Summary of Probability Control of Behavioral States

When an animal lives in an environment where the context varies over time, that is to say, the incidence and pattern of stimuli fluctuate, the elicitation and continuation of behavioral states will be modified by these fluctuations. However, if an animal is removed from a varying environment and placed in a constant one the course of behavior over time must be solely controlled by endogenous mechanisms. The theory developed here holds that the character of behavior over time in a constant environment can be largely accounted for by five probability functions, p', p_i, p'', $\hat{p}$ and p_κ. These five probability functions control the initiation, continuation, and concatenation of behavioral states. A behavioral state (designated as beta, β) is formed by a sequence of similar or interrelated acts, physiological states, or behaviors that form a meaningful whole, and which as an assembly are controlled by the five probability functions.

1. p' is a β duration terminator probability. Each β has a specific p'. During any specific episode of a particular β its p' is essentially constant. It designates the probability of the β terminating in a next unit of time, t. t is empirically set at 1.0 minutes for purposes of calculation and analysis. Thus, once a β is initiated there is a constant probability of its terminating in the next unit of time, t, no matter how long it has already continued. p' reflects the probability over time, t, of origin of a signal capable of terminating the beta. Functioning of p' alone leads to a negative exponential equation describing the number of β, β_N, as a function of beta duration (e.g., see Figure 2). Average duration of the β increases with decrements in p'. Thus the higher the need state the lower p' will become. However, a lower p' can only influence average duration of the β. In a high-need state, with p' only functioning, an initiated β may

last a short time or a long time. Furthermore, for each β its p' can vary insufficiently to accommodate all variations in need state.

2. p_i is a behavioral state duration inhibitor probability. When an individual has a surfeit of a particular behavioral state one means of reducing time in this state is to decrease its average duration. Beta duration will be very short if p' approaches 1.0. The central nervous system has the capacity initially after inception of the β to increase p' toward 1.0, or at least much higher than its normal value. p_i, from that initial point of elevation of p', is the probability of reducing p' to its normal value. p_i declines exponentially over time such that at the maximum duration of the beta p' will have been reduced to a minimal value (see Figure 9).

3. p'' is a behavioral state prolonger probability. When the need arises for an increase in beta duration beyond that possible from decreases in p', the p'' probability becomes functional. p'' represents the probability of the circuit functioning over which the p'-related signal must pass in order to terminate the beta. When it is functioning, p'' at the moment of inception of the beta has a value less than 1.0. It may be at least as low as .005 at this time. As the beta continues p'' approaches 1.0. The beta duration at which p'' equals 1.0 is designated as d''. Beyond d'' only p' controls the probability of the beta terminating. Below d'' the probability of the beta terminating is formed from the product of p'' and p'. That is to say: Below d'', duration of the beta is governed by the probability of the circuit being functional over which the signal capable of terminating the signal must pass and the probability of the signal being generated, given the circuit over which it must pass is functional.

Many behavioral states, in the absence of external stimuli precipitating their termination, have a minimal duration of continuation before p' becomes functional. In such cases p'' equals zero until this minimal duration is reached. For example, in rats the behavioral state of long sleep, LS 2.4, always lasts about $1\frac{1}{2}$ hours before p'' increases and p' becomes functional.

To reiterate, in the absence of external disruptive stimuli, duration of a behavioral state is solely governed by the three probabilities, p', p_i and p''.

4. $\hat{p}$ is the probability of initiating a behavioral state, given an ongoing β has terminated. Every β has a unique $\hat{p}$. Since at the

termination of any β, the $\hat{p}$-generating system for every β is functional, it follows that a particular β can follow itself. Such a following of one β by itself appears externally to be a single episode of this β continuing. $\hat{p}$ is in general subject to limitation by environmental context. A rat isolated from associates cannot engage in courtship. A person who has developed the behavioral state of composing prose will less likely do so in the absence of pencil, typewriter, or an audience. Under such circumstances $\hat{p}$ will rapidly approach zero, or if functional the overt expression of the behavioral state must become quite different from its former manifestation.

5. p_κ is the concatenator probability. Purely as the result of the functioning of the $\hat{p}$ for the several behavioral states, each β will at times be observed to follow each other β. Over some extended period of living, the situational context, or chance increased following of one β by another specific one, will culminate in eliciting the functioning of a positive concatenating probability that will thereafter enhance the likelihood of the persistence of this concatenation. The longer it persists the higher will the frequency of this concatenation become. When a particular concatenation persists, the following member of the pair must follow some other β less frequently than anticipated by the chance functioning of its $\hat{p}$. This leads to dissociations, or negative concatenations, between certain pairs. Mutual positive concatenations between two betas represent a behavioral loop. Similarly, two betas may become mutually negatively concatenated to form a sink manifested by rarely seeing one of the two betas follow the other.

In the interest of parsimony I propose that all major behavioral attributes of an animal may be designated by these five probabilities:

Motivation becomes synonymous with $\hat{p}$, the probability of initiating a behavioral state.

Drive becomes synonymous with the functioning and interaction of p', p_i, and p'' in continuing a behavioral state once it is initiated.

Stereotypy or traditionalism becomes synonymous with the functioning of p_κ in producing positive and negative concatenations of behavioral states beyond the degree of association arising from the functioning of the $\hat{p}$ of the several beta.

Mood is the outward manifestation, at any instant in time, of the settings (values) of the five probability functions.

Emotion is a manifestation of any change in mood, any change in the values of the several behavioral control probabilities over time.

Personality is the pattern of motivation, drive, stereotypy, mood, and emotion over some extended time.

Aggression in Relationship to the Behavior Control Probability Functions

2.1 Theoretical Stance and Present Intent

I have proposed that the five probability functions discussed above permit the most parsimonious and precise basis for describing behavior and personality. To the extent that aggression is a behavioral state, a viewing of it from the perspective of these probability functions may help us to understand aggression better.

Over the past 25 years I have had the opportunity to observe in depth the behavior of wild and domesticated strains of mice and rats who were members of socially organized groups or populations. Without attempting to be quantitative I wish to draw on this experience. Situations will be described in which some alteration in frequency or intensity of fighting developed. In each case some comment will be made relative to the theory of behavior control probabilities.

2.2 Heightened Aggression upon Exposure to a Strange Environment

Figure 3 and related text in the present paper describe the marked elevation of diffuse motor activity that follows introduction into a strange environment. This elevation represents strong emotion in the sense of drastic increase of $\hat{p}$ for locomotion, and marked reduction of $\hat{p}$ for other behavioral states. In one study (Calhoun, 1956), two groups of C57/BL mice resided in adjoining, nearly identically structured habitats. The smaller and longer-established colony included three adult males, $4\frac{1}{2}$ months old at the time of the incident here recorded. Previously these three males had exhibited only rare instances of mild aggression that seldom resulted in wounds. The adjoining pen contained four pairs of adults that had been introduced 23 days earlier with their newborn young. These pairs, having lived their prior lives in small cages, had not yet become well organized socially. A small passage was opened to permit access between the two pens. Very soon the three males from the longer-established colony invaded the pen adjoining their home one. Degree of locomotion became highly accentuated. They viciously attacked members of the colony they invaded. Then these three males attacked each other, causing severe wounding, although they had previously lived amicably together. This suggests that aggression is accentuated when mice are in a state of emotional hyperactivity.

2.3 Invasion of Personal Space

One colony of Balb C albino mice was established in a large 16-cell universe (Calhoun, 1971, Marsden, 1972). At optimum utilization of the physical space the population consisted of 150 adults who were members of 14 socially organized groups. One territorial male controlled the space predominately utilized by each group. Often each such a territorial male could be observed alone in the floor space that could be designated as his territory. Being alone in that way permitted such individuals to experience the configuration of surroundings unimpeded by other mice. My presumption is that an animal extends his ego boundaries to include that portion of the physical environment where it associates more frequently with its characteristics in the absence of associates. Such a personal space is like an activity alley to which prior accommodation has already been made. I have earlier shown (Calhoun, 1967) that the more an activity alley is structured the higher will be the elevation of emotional hyperactivity. Invasion of a territorial mouse's personal space, then, has the effect of increasing the intensity of strange stimuli, and since strangeness of the environment aggravates the likelihood of aggression, the basis for territorial defense becomes apparent.

Such spontaneous attack presumes an innate linkage between such environmental stimulation, resultant arousal of emotional hyperactivity, and the elicitation of aggression. It is just from such a situation as described above that we might anticipate the evolutionary origin of a genetic basis for aggression and territorial defense. In an animal's established home range the environmental context remains relatively stable and familiar. One of the more repeated environmental changes would, in fact, be incursion of one animal's home range by a stranger of the same species. Given that strange stimuli elicit hyperactivity, it would be of survival value to attack and extrude the stranger from the resident's personal space. To make such extrusion effective requires linking the arousal of hyperactivity with a neural circuit that enhances expression of aggression under appropriate circumstances (i.e., the presence of another animal).

Completing this line of reasoning requires interpretation of why hyperactivity is associated with environmental change. In the lives of most land vertebrates sudden environmental changes often do occur. Survival from flood, fire, and predators is enhanced by flight, often rather blindly, from the presented threat. Flight represents diffuse hyperactivity.

2.4 Social Velocity and Aggression

Cursory observation of rats or mice who are members of long-established groups reveals that individuals differ with regard to their degree of locomotor activity and alertness. In our studies we regularly utilize standardized observational procedures to develop a quantitative index of this activity and alertness, which we call *social velocity* or simply *velocity*. Major focus in obtaining such indices is placed on that portion of the field where status interactions more often take place. In an optimum-sized group of N_0 individuals velocity varies from 1.0, as a relative value for the most active animal, to $1/N_0$ for the lowest-velocity individual.

Let:

R = Rank; highest ranked animal has $R = 1.0$.
$v_R^{(r)}$ = velocity of the Rth ranked individual relative to $v = 1.0$ for the highest ranked individual.

Then:

$$v_R^{(r)} = \frac{(N_0 - R) + 1}{N_0} \tag{23}$$

Regardless of the increase in group size above the optimum, the velocity of the lowest-ranked individual remains a constant,

$1/N_o$. However, as N becomes greater than the optimum, the relative velocities of all other members will decline. At $N = N_o^2$ the velocities of all individuals approach the minimum of $1/N_o$.

The theory of velocity (Calhoun, 1963b, 1967), supported by empirical data, derives from the stochastics of interaction among members of a group which leads to a differential in the likelihood that an animal seeking gratification from social contacts will be rewarded in its efforts. The greater the proportion of these intents that are frustrated, the more the animal's behavior will deviate from the norm and the more it will withdraw, both physically and psychologically. This dual withdrawal is reflected in comparable decreases in velocity measures. The amount of wounding from fighting increases with decrease in velocity. This reflects the decrease in social rank with decrease in velocity. Territorial and dominant animals have high velocity scores. Animals with very low velocity gradually cease becoming involved in social interactions, even when they are active. As a consequence they lose the characteristic of fresh wounds derived from fighting. This loss of social involvements has major consequences with regard to the settings of the behavior control probability functions. Appreciation of these changes and their impact on behavioral states is facilitated by further consideration of the manner in which changes in the physical environment alter behavior.

2.5 Withdrawal from Reality Testing following Long-Term Solitary Confinement (i.e., Stimulus Deprivation and Limitation of Behavior)

The outstanding response of any animal to being confronted with a strange setting is the initiation of a markedly heightened degree of movement through the available space. This diffuse hyperactivity (Figure 4) is distinct from intentional exploration. Normally it lasts only for a few hours, with gradual decline to normal levels of motor activity. This abrupt increase, then gradual decline of activity, appears to be requisite to adjustment to a new setting. It may be observed with equal clarity in rats or mice placed in a new setting or in children at their first day at nursery school. However, it may also be observed that some individuals react in the extreme opposite direction. Except for perhaps an initial extreme burst of activity, a kind of violence, they lapse into a state of continuous inactivity in which they avoid most aspects of the new environment.

In order to investigate this process of adjustment to a new environment we constructed an experimental setting permitting the recording of the behavior of rats in it. This simply consisted of a long alley with a home compartment at one end, into which the rats were introduced. The alley could either be left barren or structured with various items to make it more unfamiliar. Each of 500 rats, encompassing a wide range of exposure to physical and social environments, were given several 2-hour trials in it. Analytical emphasis was placed on the degree of avoidance of entering the new environment, or if entry was more than the initial one, the rate of decline of hyperactivity. For our present concern we will focus solely on the former, conditions which foster avoidance of entering the strange environment.

In one study a large group of weanling rats were placed in solitary confinement and allowed to remain there for 3 months until physically adult. Their cage was just sufficiently large for them to lie down comfortably or to stand up and eat or drink at the sources provided them. Food and water could be provided without opening the cage. The cages were so constructed that they could not see out. Only a little light through cracks at the top edge of the cage provided a light intensity appropriate to these nocturnal animals. Thus normal locomotion and the many other response opportunities available to rats in a more natural setting were excluded. Toward the end of the confinement period two groups of rats were taken out each day in a rehabilitation program in which each individual was given an opportunity each day to adjust to a richer environmental setting. At the end of this 10-day rehabilitation program each rat was given four 2-hour exposures to the alley test environment (Calhoun, 1963b, pages 17 to 18 and 175 to 184 in particular).

Most members of each of the two groups of rats given somewhat different rehabilitation training entered the alley on each of the exposures to it and exhibited a relatively normal decline in hyperactivity (Figure 4) until they adjusted to this new environment. It must be noted that the degree of avoidance of the alley was greater than that of most rats which had enjoyed a continuous history in a much richer physical and social environment. In contrast, most of the rats entering the test environment directly from the long-term confinement completely avoided entering it. This was equally true of the fourth day's trial and the first, and whether the experimental alley environment was simple or complex. On the first exposure a few of these previously totally confined rats dashed out into the alley, ran its full length, then dashed back into the home compartment, which simulated the conditions of the confinement cage, and never emerged again. In other studies of extreme confinement we have also noted this tendency toward an initial episode of violent movement through the strange environment before completely retiring from it.

We have, therefore, come to the conclusion that any long-term deprivation of stimulus input and of elimination of expression of normal behaviors produces an animal with a heightened tendency to avoid contact with any environment exceeding the complexity of that to which it had been confined. Since our rehabilitation training program did counteract some of the consequences of long-term confinement, a word is in order about our philosophy and technique. The environments into which the rats were placed during rehabilitation were relatively simple and, equally important, provided no opportunity for physical withdrawal from exposure to the stimuli present. Each such environment also provided the opportunity for making a motor response somewhat similar to, but still somewhat more complex than, that in their confinement cage. In essence our strategy was to force exposure to a slightly different environment within which the individual could profit from a choice it made.

From a theoretical point of view, the following interpretation helps give perspective to the above. Every behavioral state, including various categories of sleep, has its roots in adjustments to external circumstances. Every such adjustment involves a reality testing which culminates in the incorporation of the adjustment into an existing behavioral state, the initiation of a new behavioral state, or a rejection of the circumstance (a rejection of the novel stimuli constellation as having no relevance to the continuing organism). If the novel stimuli represent an order of magnitude not greatly exceeding that to which prior adjustment has been successfully accomplished, then these stimuli will elicit a phase of emotional hyperactivity, whose initial expression and following reduction is requisite to completion of reality testing. However, if the stimuli characterizing the novel situation markedly exceed, quantitatively, those inherent to contexts encountered in recent history, then one of two consequences follows. First, the p' (behavioral state terminator probability) of diffuse motor activity is greatly reduced, causing an exceptional prolongation of the initial, or first few, instances of initiation of this behavioral state. Such a change is the hallmark of violent behavior, or "going berserk," discussed below (Section 2.9). Second, a more extreme accentuation of the novelty of stimuli will cause an overloading of the adjustive, reality testing mechanism. By *overloading* is meant that the p (behavioral state initiator probability function) goes to zero. When this happens an animal behaviorally "freezes." It may be that only the p for locomotor activity approaches zero. However, the p for such behavioral states as eating or drinking may also go to zero, in which cases the animal will die from hunger and/or thirst (*e.g.* low v rats in the RSB).

2.6 Withdrawal from Reality Testing following Social Rejection

Most of our studies with rodents involve environmental settings designed to simulate the complexity existing in nature. Furthermore, in most of our studies we allow the population to increase until a state of overcrowding exists. Under these conditions there is a central tendency for the number of individuals representing what is the optimum number for that setting to preserve for themselves the favorable way of life existing before the optimum number was exceeded. In this process many individuals are rejected by their more dominant and established associates. The essence of this rejection involves the interruption of behavioral states of socially lower-ranking individuals where the behavioral state involves an attempt at social intercourse such as is involved in courtship or the establishment of a role in the hierarchy. In these rejections there is both an interruption of action cycles and a frustration or punishment of normal behavior. There are two major consequences of such rejection. Behavior becomes more deviant, more abnormal and inappropriate. The rejected individuals withdraw both psychologically and physically. Their psychological withdrawal is evinced by reduction of variability and complexity of responding to both their physical and social environment. Their physical withdrawal is exhibited by a marked reduction in motor activity. The degree of motor activity by an animal we have called *velocity* (Section 2.4). It is relatively easy to obtain quantitative measures of this velocity. In our studies we have thus been able to select our animals at the opposite ends of the velocity spectrum. High-velocity rats are the territorial or dominant individuals exhibiting a normal repertoire of sexual and other social behavior, while the low-velocity rats are the most rejected members of the population.

When placed in the home compartment of the strange environment represented by the activity alley cited above, most of the high-velocity rats entered it and exhibited the more normal pattern of initial hyperactivity with a gradual decline to the customary level. In contrast, a much higher proportion of the low-velocity rats withdrew from or totally avoided entry of the alley on one or all of their exposures to it. I have, therefore, concluded that rejection from social involvement has the same consequences as physical confinement.

The profound impact of such *social confinement* on rats is provided in a parallel study in which a smaller set of high- and low-velocity rats were removed from their social milieu and each placed in an apparatus (the RSB) which for a week recorded the starts and stopping and sequence of a small repertoire of behavioral states including eating, drinking, locomotion, grooming, and sleeping. As anticipated from the interruption of action cycles in the prior social setting, the motor behavioral states of the low-velocity rats were of shorter duration and the episodes of sleeping longer. Furthermore, the sequences of behavioral states for the low-velocity rats were much more random. These two findings indicate that social confinement culminates in an organism much less capable of engaging in complex patterned behavior.

Furthermore, 3 of the 12 low-velocity rats died in the apparatus. They either refused to eat or drink. The eating and the drinking situation was slightly different from that in their prior setting. Their death in the face of a slightly altered environmental setting indicates that their capacity to adjust to new sets of environmental stimuli had become so restricted that even thirst and hunger were insufficient to elicit response.

2.7 Violence following Social Rejection

The kind of aggression involved in territorial defense has survival value either to the individual or the group. It preserves assurance of increased likelihood of a continued availability of resources and an equanimity of life style including protection of young during their critical phases of maturation. However, occasions do arise which override normal behavioral controls and precipitate types of aggression detrimental to the the individual, the group, or both. An example of the development and beneficial consequence of normal aggression, culminating in territoriality, is discussed in Section 2.3 above. Certain conditions built into this environmental setting, however, culminated in violence.

This physical environment (Calhoun, 1969) was designed to eliminate or drastically reduce five major mortality factors. First, resources were provided in a superabundance. The amount of food and water, the number of places they could be procured, and the number and distribution of retreat spaces sufficed to provide resources for a population of adults in excess of 3,000 before shortages of them should have been a limiting factor. Second, predation was eliminated. Third, excessive temperature was eliminated, thus precluding death from inclement weather. Similarly, the indoors habitat also precluded stress from rain and wind. Fourth, emigration was precluded by the elimination of all routes of egress. Fifth, the maintaining of population as a semiclosed system reduced the possibility of introducing epidemic disease; in fact, we observed little indication that any factor other than aging contributed significantly to mortality. It might be added that the distribution of resources and other configurations of the environment enhanced the ease with which males could establish territories and females could find protected places in which to rear their young. These combined conditions established an initial phase of population growth in which most members of most litters conceived survived to adulthood. Under these conditions the population increased from the four pairs introduced to a point when there were 620 weaned individuals. During this resource exploitation phase the population doubled every 55 days. At this point of reaching $N = 620$ the doubling time of population abruptly increased to 145 days. At this time of phase shift in rate of population growth there were only 150 fully adult mice. These formed 14 well-organized social groups that controlled all of the desirable physical space as well as all social space. All the effective social roles possible in this setting were then filled. The adults filling these roles were just entering the physical prime of their lives, and most possessed the behavioral capacity to maintain their favorable roles for several months.

Most of the 470 juvenile and subadult mice had enjoyed a favorable early history, one that provided them with the capacity to assume adequate roles in mouse society, provided they were able to find empty niches or take over roles held by adults. Many of the younger males had experienced such an excellent early history of good mothering and adequate early behavioral development. However, as they approached adulthood they found all social roles filled with older mice. In their attempts to find a role in mouse society these maturing mice were very intensely and forcefully rejected by their established associates. After this phase of rejection they became extremely low-velocity, withdrawn individuals who huddled together in the less desirable places in the environment. They were essentially ignored by their dominant associates from this time on. And yet all of these very withdrawn mice soon became covered with fresh wounds and scar tissue. This damage they inflicted on each other. Just as in the case of the rats after long-term physical confinement, they could not tolerate change in their environmental setting. Since these withdrawn mice spent most of the time motionless in huddled masses, any return of one of their members after it had gone to the source of food and water amounted to an abrupt change in the pattern of ambient stimuli. Often such returns precipitated one of the resting mice into a berserk hyperactive episode of attacking its associates; but having lost the capacity to flee, the mice remained stationary even though they were being bitten severely.

2.8 Establishing Violence as a Way of Life

The abnormal aggression arising from social confinement has its counterpart following physical confinement. Whenever mice or rats are placed together for the first time in a new environment the strange setting always elicits both hyperactivity and heightened aggression. Usually both subside rapidly. However, if the individuals brought together have been living in solitary confinement for some time, the initial pattern of aggression may become fixed into a continuing one of heightened frequency and intensity of aggressive acts. The population of mice discussed above in Section 2.7 was one of five initiated at the same time with four pairs of mice each. These mice were introduced into closed physical space and the same configuration of resources and physical structures.

Subjects used as colonizers came from the National Institutes of Health breeding colony and were received at a weaning age of 22 days. Each animal was placed in a cage by itself where it had no visual or physical contact with other mice. They were left in this situation for another 22 days while the construction of the universes was being completed. Thus at introduction two variables might affect the initial history: (a) the preceding period of confinement and (b) the size of the universe. For practical purposes we can divide the results with respect to size of universe into the smaller 1- and 2-cell universes and the larger universes of 4, 8, and 16 cells. A cell is a standardized environmental unit (Calhoun, 1962a, 1971). In the smaller universes, initial heightened aggression soon subsided into a pattern of sustained, relatively subdued aggression. However, in each of the three larger universes, one of the four males became excessively aggressive. At the initiation of each day's 12-hour period of normal heightened activity, starting with the onset of dim light, one of the four males in each population began a search for his three companions. As each was found it would be herded, to the accompaniment of vicious attacks, until each was set in place at a visible location, where movement therefrom served as a stimulus for another vicious attack. Within the first 2 months after introduction, two of the males in the largest universe (16 cells) succumbed from the stress accompanying such intense attacks. Likewise, one soon died in the second-largest universe (8 cells), and after a longer time one died in the middle-sized universe (4 cells). In contrast there were no deaths for many months in the two smaller universes (1 and 2 cells). In these latter, fighting among colonizers was relatively subdued and was accompanied by an equally interesting phenomenon—self-grooming became transformed into mutual grooming. That is, each individual's identity became fused with another. In the larger universes an individual had much more opportunity to roam through space without encountering an associate. As a consequence, more extended personal spaces developed, which led to heightened aggression upon encounter. The initial accentuated aggression coupled with such developing extensive personal space presumably accounts for the persistence of violent behavior among these colonizing males inhabiting the larger universes. No such extreme aggression was ever observed to characterize territorial males born in such physical settings.

2.9 Berserk Episodes by Dominant Males

Seven populations of Osborne-Mendel rats were permitted to develop in structured habitats (Calhoun, 1962b, 1963b). Instead of permitting unrestrained population growth, artificial cohorts or tiers were permitted to survive. Every population had three basic tiers. Each consisted of 32 to 40 rats. The first was formed from pregnant females introduced into the habitats just prior to parturition. The second consisted of the first litters born to the first-tier members when they were approximately 100 days of age. After the formation of the second tier all young born for the next six months were removed prior to weaning. Then the next litters born contributed to the formation of the third tier. In some cases a fourth or fifth tier was allowed to form approximately 3 and/or 6 months after the third tier. Formation of the third and later tiers represented an ecologically abnormal tempo. In a more ecologically normal situation, litter production gets spaced so that a few litters are being born at all times during the breeding season. Thus a few juveniles and subadults of all ages are normally always present. In a population with such a diverse age structure, maturing rats rarely get attacked by older associates until well after sexual maturity has set in. In this type of situation adults are accustomed to contact with younger rats of various ages who move freely about among the adults and often encroach upon their activities. Such encroachments upon adult activity rarely elicit anything more than mild spankings; the adult rolls the young over and pummels it with all four feet, an action which brings no physical damage to the young.

However, in the tiered populations a period of 3 or more months elapsed without the adults having any interaction with weaned young. And when the weaned young did appear, a large number emerged at about the same time. In every case, most dominant and territorial males went berserk for 2 or 3 days sometime during the period when the average age of the young ranged between approximately 40 and 60 days. At any one time only two or three adult males would so behave. Their behavior took the form of slashing attacks on all associates, regardless of age or sex. Tails were often bitten, in some cases completely severed. Body wounds extended down into the muscles and might be as much as 15 to 20 mm in length. For a 2- or 3-week period the habitats would literally be dripping in blood. At any other time young rats of either sex and females of all ages were rarely wounded, and when wounded the incisions were usually in the form of slight nicks just partially penetrating the dermis.

The following interpretation is placed on these episodes of berserk violence. Dominant and territorial males were the only members of the population that had developed an effective aggressive behavioral state, even though its intensity was subdued. The relatively sudden appearance of many juvenile and subadult animals represented a drastic change in their environment. This abrupt change in the constellation of ambient stimuli provoked initiation of emotional hyperactivity that involved both diffuse motor activity and that of the aggressive behavioral state. Other rats, particularly the lower-velocity males, had already undergone a long period of suppression of expression of aggressive behavior, so that I as an observer did not detect any significant enlargement of aggression on their part.

2.10 Violence Generated by Value Conflict

In one study with Osborne-Mendel strain rats, groups of $N = 2, 4, 8, 16,$ and 32 were placed in 2.4×5-foot pens. One STAW (socialization training apparatus, water; see Section 1.1) was placed in each pen. One or more groups of each N was placed in the cooperative (COOP) and the disoperative (DISOP, a forced non-cooperation) condition. Under the COOP condition two rats could, and must, drink at the same time. Under the DISOP condition, one and only one rat could drink at any time. This meant that the STAW for a particular N had to be in use twice as much under the DISOP condition as under the COOP condition. Rats were physically mature at the time of the episode described below. Under the STAW lever-pressing-for-water situation, each rat had to meet the required condition for at least 30 minutes each day. Despite these conditions, rats maintained their 24-hour cycle of activity, with greatest activity during the dim-light hours. Focus will be placed on the $N = 16$ DISOP and COOP groups. Satisfying the water needs of the COOP rats required 4 hours of meeting the required condition. In contrast, 8 hours were required for the DISOP rats. Another restricting condition is that all rats sleep about 75% of the time. Thus any rat has only about 6 hours in any 24-hour period when it might drink. That the p (behavioral initiator probability function) for drinking has likely been activated may be detected by a rat approaching the STAW. If it encounters the STAW being utilized appropriately by one or two other rats it moves away and enters some other behavioral state. One must suspect that a stimulus situation inappropriate for continuing in a particular behavioral state, in this case for lever pressing for water, leads to p' immediately becoming 1.0, thus terminating the behavioral state before it has in any way been effectively implemented. An animal so turned away, and having entered some other behavioral state, is thus blocked from taking opportunity to enter the STAW as soon as it is vacated. Under this complex of conditions, rats in an N of 16 on DISOP of the STAW periodically experienced difficulty in securing enough water.

Despite a persisting slight water deficit for most 16-DISOP rats, it was clearly evident that every member had learned its task well. Rare indeed were the instances when one of these rats would enter an empty channel if an associate was already on the other side. Thus my term *disoperation* simply means to collaborate by staying out of each other's way.

The 16-COOP rats had learned their task sufficiently well so that no rat experienced any appreciable deficit in water intake. Two slightly different ways of dealing with the situation had developed. Starting with no rat on or at the STAW, one rat would approach and enter one side and remain just in front of the lever without pressing it. One of his associates would immediately approach and enter the other side of the STAW. The rapidity of this second rat's response indicates an awareness by it of the first rat's intent and need. As soon as both were positioned in front of their respective levers, each simultaneously began pressing. As soon as one terminated pressing, the other did likewise, and both would back out of the STAW. An even more refined procedure of initiating the paired pressing began with one rat positioning itself outside the STAW, but facing into one side. This stance served to attract another rat nearly immediately to position itself in front of the other side. Then they would simultaneously proceed into their respective channels and begin pressing. In either case, the behavior of the second rat may be termed altruistic. Both kinds of initiating cooperative behavior characterized all COOP groups.

In each group every rat had learned the role appropriate for maximizing the benefits which were possible under the respective situations imposed by the STAWs. Such a role denotes a relationship of one rat to another. Assumption of these roles reduced constraints to action and indeterminacy of action. The role of one individual complemented that of his associates and led to an increase in the probability of realizing expectancies. Dr. Joel Elkes refers to this as "increase in trust." This increase in trust can only follow from what Dr. Ernst Caspari calls "ethical behavior"—that behavior by one individual which maximizes the realization of expectancies by others.

Every COOP and every DISOP rat had developed a role of behaving ethically, appropriate to its own situation. Still, the constraint of time available for lever pressing by the 16-DISOP rats interfered with acquisition of water, since they had to confine their activities to a single side of the STAW. In contrast, the STAW available to the 16-COOP rats was more frequently vacant, because of the simultaneous use of both sides.

After a little over 3 months "on condition," one male rat among the 16-DISOP group learned to climb up on the water reservoir in its pen, jump over the electrified fence separating his home pen and that of the adjoining 16-COOP group to the top of the water reservoir in their pen, and then come down into the pen. If not immediately, then after a short while he would find the 16-COOP STAW empty. He would enter and approach the lever. Almost before he had started pressing, certainly before he could realize that pressing alone here provided him with no water, one of the COOP rats would come over and enter the other side.

To this invading DISOP male, his COOP companion's behavior was all wrong. He would immediately back out, grasp the "offending" COOP rat by the tail or hind feet, and pull it out. This happened every time the invading male entered the COOP rats' STAW. I kept returning this male to his DISOP companions, but he persisted in jumping back over into the 16-COOP pen. During the following weeks he macerated the tails and hind feet of all the COOP rats. Most lost all their toes. Seven died from these wounds. And yet the invading male was never attacked. To the COOP rats, this invading DISOP male was always behaving correctly when it entered the STAW, and their ethical standards dictated that they come to his rescue.

This is an exceptional case in which a stranger is not attacked by members of a resident group. His behavior of entering one side of a STAW was a component of the norms of behavior of the resident COOP rats. To this extent he did not represent a strange stimulus and thus did not elicit hyperactivity that overflowed into aggression. He was to this extent not a stranger. It may be presumed that the extensive wounds received by the COOP rats caused them pain, and yet this pain occurring in the context of an otherwise normal constellation of environmental and social stimuli did not suffice to elicit aggression. For the invading DISOP rat, every approach of a COOP rat into the STAW represented a drastic alteration of customary environmental stimulation. Such a drastic change in stimulus pattern sufficed to precipitate the invading DISOP rat into a degree of hyperactivity that overflowed into violent attack upon his associates.

2.11 Dissolution of Capacity for Aggression by Vitamin A

During the course of studying the first four populations of rats included in the discussion of Section 2.9 above, certain physiological anomalies were observed that suggested disturbance of vitamin A physiology (Calhoun, 1962a). These rats were fed with a pelleted Ralston Purina Company diet specifically intended for rats. This diet contained vitamin A supplementation sufficient to produce an increase from the normal 3 i.u. per g of diet to 12 i.u. per g of diet. At this increased vitamin A intake more vitamin A was stored in the liver, and the serum level of circulating vitamin A became elevated. Analysis of liver storage of 27 rats of various ages indicated that with age there is a straight-line increase of log of the amount of vitamin A stored in the whole liver as a function of the log of age. At 400 days of age 40,000 i.u. of vitamin A is stored in the liver. At about this age a sample of 7 rats gave a mean circulating level of 154 i.u. per 100 ml of serum. On the basis of the suspicion that vitamin A might be influencing social behavior, three additional populations (described in Calhoun, 1962b but not with reference to vitamin A) were initiated. They were supplied with a powdered synthetic diet which varied among populations only with respect to vitamin A. Three, 6, and 12 i.u. per g of diet were utilized. We will here only be concerned with the extremes, which will be referred to as "low" and "high" vitamin A diets. This "high" is not considered excessive at a comparable intake level for humans. Three i.u. per g of diet for rats is comparable to a daily intake of 2,500 i.u. for man. Such an intake level fully provides for all normal physiological requirements for man. Twelve i.u. per gram of diet for rats is comparable to a daily intake of 10,000 i.u. for man. The high standard of diet for most Americans, plus the current level of supplementation of foods with vitamin A, plus the wide use of vitamin pills make it highly likely that many persons must be approaching an intake level of 10,000 i.u. per day.

Tier 1 rats had the longest history under these diets. Twenty-nine Tier 1 rats on the low–vitamin A diet with an average age of 495 days at autopsy had a mean whole liver storage of 31,631 i.u. of vitamin A. Thirty-two Tier 1 rats on the high–vitamin A diet with a mean age of 490 days at autopsy had a mean whole liver storage of 41,510 i.u. of vitamin A. Both sexes are included in these averages. Of these, 18 males on the low–vitamin A diet survived to autopsy and 23 males on the high–vitamin A diet survived. For each of these males nine counts of wounds were made at 21-day intervals between 9 and 15 months of age. This is the span of prime adulthood.

Normally a wound received in fighting completely heals in less than 21 days. The average number of wounds at an examination period was 21.8 for males on the low–vitamin A diet and 13.7 for those on the high diet. These averages are based on the sum of the separate counts for four regions of the body: head, shoulder, rump, and tail. Of these four regions, the rump is the most sensitive for reflecting the degree of intense social-status interactions. At the culmination of a boxing-biting bout the loser wheels around to flee. As he does so, the winner has the opportunity to bite the fleeing rat on the rump. For this region alone the mean number of wounds was 10.97 for those on the low–vitamin A diet, but only 4.96 for those on the high–vitamin A diet.

An index of velocity was also obtained for each rat. During this time of observation, the number of social-status interactions engaged in by each rat was also recorded. At this time the total number of fully adult Tier 1 and Tier 2 males in each of the two populations was over three times the optimum for the habitat. Under this degree of crowding the average velocity of the males of these two generations was considerably lowered from that characterizing rats in a smaller, more optimum-sized population. However, the velocity of the high–vitamin A diet males was considerably higher than those on the low, or normal, vitamin A diet (Calhoun, 1963b, 1967). Despite this difference it was possible to pair rats from the two populations with respect to their velocity. For any given velocity, rats on the high–vitamin A diet engaged in only 30% as many social interactions as those on the low–vitamin A diet (Calhoun, 1967). At first consideration one might interpret these alterations as desirable ones, since the heightened level of vitamin A intake did reduce aggression and did partially counteract the suppression of activity resulting from crowding. However, a proper interpretation of the impact of elevated vitamin A intake is furthered by an examination of other behavioral changes, particularly those relating to reproduction and maternal care.

The prevalence of homosexual behavior was much greater on the part of males on the elevated–vitamin A diet. Disturbance of sexual behavior is further evinced by a decrease in age at first conception by females on the higher–vitamin A diet. The abnormality of premature conception is brought into perspective by an examination of the maturation of reproductive and maternal performance of wild Norway rats (see especially pages 260 to 275 in Calhoun, 1963a). Full reproductive performance includes the opportunity and capacity to conceive, the ability to carry young to term without resorption or miscarriage, and the ability to build nests and rear young to weaning. At 80 days of age this combined physiological and behavioral repertoire, required for producing viable young to a stage that they can enter the population, is essentially zero. Not until nearly 450 days of age does the full expression of reproductive capacity reach 1.0; that is, not until this age does the female conceive at every opportunity, carry all embryos to term, and rear all young to weaning. Thus, in an evolutionary context, in a complex social and physical environment, delay in time of conception enhances the probability that genes will be passed on to the next generation. In the present study there were 68 females on the 3-i.u. diet and 71 on the 12-i.u. diet that lived at least long enough to have one pregnancy. Only 14.7% of those on the low–vitamin A diet conceived before 80 days of age, while 42.3% on the higher–vitamin A diet conceived before this age. For both populations, most of the early conceivers were of the younger generations of the second and third tiers, whose conceptions occurred at a time when there were many older, sexually experienced males present. At the later stages of these populations, after crowding had ensued, males were seen to mount females as young as 44 days of age. One female at this very young age, that was seen to be mounted by an older male, did conceive. My interpretation is that early conceptions are primarily the result of actions by males whose capacity to integrate stimuli is impaired by changes related to reduced velocity or to the action of vitamin A. It is my conclusion that a fourfold increase in vitamin A intake above the normal level prevents rats from appropriately integrating the complex of stimuli requisite for eliciting a response or for directing it at the appropriate target object. The increased homosexual tendencies of male rats on the higher–vitamin A diet, as well as their inappropriate advances on young females, presumably have this origin.

All females were examined every 21 days for reproductive condition. These culminated in 835 examinations for the 3-i.u.-diet females and 797 for those on the 12-i.u. diet. Of the females on the low diet, 33.2% were detectably pregnant by abdominal palpation, whereas 35.8% of those on the high–vitamin A diet were noticeably pregnant. The slightly higher pregnancy rate for those on the high diet is in part accounted for by their greater inability to rear young to weaning; loss of a litter leads to an earlier opportunity to become pregnant again. Examination of nipple condition indicated that the rats were definitely lactating. Dividing the number of instances of lactation by the number of instances of pregnancy produces an index of the likelihood of pregnancies being continued through to lactation. For the low-diet rats this index was .682, but only .551 for the high–vitamin A diet rats. This means that for the entire span of the history of these two populations, females on the high–vitamin A diet exhibited a 19% reduction in capacity to continue maternal behavior for an average length of 10.5 days after parturition. This deficit became exaggerated later on. During the formation of the third tier, the females on the low–vitamin A diet reared 53.8% of their young to weaning, but those on the high–vitamin A diet reared only 24.2% of their young to this age. Whether or not young are reared primarily depends upon the capacity of females to continue their care of young through the first 2 days of their life. During the establishment of each tier, I opened nest boxes at much shorter intervals than the usual 21 days in order to determine age at birth and identity of the mother. This examination did introduce additional disturbance. Rats with less well-integrated maternal behavior desert young at this stage, or after the disturbance carry their young to diverse places rather than to a single place. When so dispersed, they are rarely reassembled and cared for. The younger the litter when this disturbance takes place, the less likely it is that the mother will continue to care for her young. When so disturbed when the young were 2 days or less of age, mothers on the 3-i.u. diet successfully reared 49.5% of their young, whereas mothers on the higher–vitamin A diet reared only 7.5% of the young after disturbance at such an early age of the litter.

I suspect that both the capacity to integrate complex sets of stimuli and to execute a complex sequence of behaviors are involved in this dissolution of reproductive and maternal behavior. Failure on the part of males on the high–vitamin A diet to become as frequently involved in status interactions is similarly presumed to arise from such impairment of perception and/or ability to continue through with complex sequential behaviors. Reduced involvement in agonistic interactions by males on the high–vitamin A diet decreased the inhibition of motor activity that arises from frustrations experienced as a consequence of such interactions. Thus the average velocity of males on the high–vitamin A diet was greater than that of males on the low–vitamin A diet.

Examination of the data for the males that were removed from their social environment and placed in isolation in the RSB apparatus (see Section 1.1) for a week provides further insight on this problem. Highest- and lowest-velocity males from Tiers 1 and 2 served as subjects. They formed a larger set of the subset described in Section 1.9 above. The 25 rats (Table 6) provided over 15,000 behavioral states, encompassing a total of 143.3 rat days. For most of the behavioral states occurring in each of the five locations in the RSB, both the high- and the low-velocity rats on the 12-i.u. diet exhibited an increase in number of behavioral states above their counterparts on the 3-i.u. diet. On the average the high diet led to a 30% increase in number of behavioral states per day. This increased number means that the average duration of a behavioral state is shortened. The shortening or fragmentation of behavioral states must arise through a combination of increase in p', a decrease in functioning of p'', and an increase in functioning of p_i.

TABLE 6

BEHAVIORAL STATES WITH LOW– AND HIGH–VITAMIN A DIETS

	Mean Number per 24 Hours per Rat			
	3-i.u. Diet		12-i.u. Diet	
Beta Place	High Velocity	Low Velocity	High Velocity	Low Velocity
Wheel	23.83	27.41	34.78	33.49
Treadle	17.91	16.13	20.66	14.00
Nest Box	29.09	22.48	30.32	48.24
Lever	23.43	25.82	30.36	27.42
Field[a]	1.45	2.38	6.20	2.01
Total	95.71	94.22	122.32	125.16
No. of rats	8	6	6	5
No. of 24 hrs	42.85	33.35	37.02	30.07

[a] Only beta in the field having durations in excess of 8.0 minutes are included. This eliminates any possibility of biasing data by inclusion of transits between two locations.

To the extent that vitamin A produces a comparable effect on the physiology and behavior of man that it does on rats, one must conclude that the current degree of elevation of vitamin A intake by man will simultaneously reduce the likelihood of involvement in agonistic relations and at the same time reduce the capacity for executing complex sequential behavioral states.

2.12 Accentuation of Female Aggressiveness in the Absence of Effective Territorial Males

The population of mice described in Section 2.7 above continued to increase until an upper number of 2,200 was attained. At the time when the population reached 620 weaned individuals, the doubling time of population increase abruptly shifted from 55 to 145 days. This shift in rate of population growth coincided with the filling of physical space with 14 organized social groups totaling 150 individuals. The great number of maturing males contesting for positions in the social system taxed the capacity of the most dominant males to continue territorial defense effectively. Gradually this capacity became so eroded that such males engaged in aggression much less frequently, and then only in a small area somewhat removed from the access ramps to the batteries of nest boxes. This reduced territorial defense provided more opportunity for maturing mice to invade nest boxes containing lactating females. Normally such females infrequently engage in aggression. However, in the absence of effective expression of territoriality by adult males, the incursion of their nest sites elicited aggression on the part of many females. This gradually extended to encompass areas about the bases of the ramps to the nest boxes. Furthermore, this accentuated female aggressiveness generalized to their own young. Between 15 and 20 days of age, at a time when their eyes were open and they were well furred and becoming mobile within the nest box, they were attacked by their mothers. Such attacks never occurred during the first, more rapid, phase of population growth. As a consequence many of these young were prematurely weaned; they moved away from the home site several days earlier than normally would have been the case.

2.13 Failure to Develop Aggressive and Other Complex Behavioral States

The young mice mentioned in the above section moved out into the larger population without having developed affective bonds with their mother. Presumably this lack of experience in developing affective bonds hindered acquisition of such bonds as they further matured. As they moved out into the environment, now reaching high densities, any attempt to engage in social interactions ran the risk of mechanical interference, some other mouse intervening. Such interruption of action cycles further hindered the maturation of social interaction. Before most of these animals had sexually matured the population had increased to its maximum of 2,200 individuals.

A further, and perhaps even more serious, inhibition of behavioral maturation arises from this increase in total numbers. Theory of social interaction (see particularly pages 101 to 121 in Calhoun, 1963b) predicts that there is an intensity and duration of interaction in an optimum-sized social group that is appropriate to optimizing gratification from social intercourse. As the group size increases above the optimum, the intensity and duration of interaction must decrease for each individual to approach this optimum level of gratification.

Let:

α = a measure of this intensity and duration of interaction
N = number of animals in the group

Then:

$$\alpha = 1/(N - 1) \qquad (24)$$

In this mouse population discussed in Sections 2.7, 2.12, and 2.13, the cessation of most rapid population growth, when the number of adults reached 150 and there were 14 social groups, indicates that the optimum-sized social group was about 10.71 adults. With a population increase to 2,200 individuals, and to the extent that there remained social groups, the average size of the group increased to 157.14. This means that α declined from .10298 to .0064. In other words, at the heightened stage of population size, intensity and/or duration of interaction was reduced to about 6%

of its normal level. Although such reduction probably was not this great because of the physical and psychological withdrawal of many of the individuals born somewhat earlier, nevertheless the reduction must have been sufficient to impair markedly the maturation of complex behavior requiring continuation in time for full expression.

Although we do not know the exact degree to which these three factors contributed to the lack of maturation of normal social behaviors, the fact remains that most of the last 1,000 animals born during the period of suppressed rate of population growth failed to develop essentially any aggressive and reproductive behaviors. Gradually the older, and behaviorally more normal, mice aged and because of aging and prior social stress ceased reproducing. Autopsy of four populations with similar histories to the above were conducted at times varying from 4 to 7 months after cessation of population growth. Most of the later-born females had never conceived. We have referred to these mice as the "beautiful ones." Since they essentially never engage in aggression, the males that are so categorized have excellent pelage and appear in excellent physical condition. At the present date of this writing, 807 days have elapsed since the last mouse surviving to weaning was born. The population has slowly declined to about 220 individuals with an average age in excess of 870 days (roughly comparable to 87 years in human maturational terms). Because of the obvious senescent condition of these survivors there is essentially no likelihood that breeding will start again when the population has decreased to the former optimum of 150. At several times during the course of the decline of the population, mice were removed and assembled as small optimum-sized groups. Results from these studies indicated that only a few had retained partial capacity for organizing social groups or for reproduction, even when transplanted to otherwise optimum conditions.

Our final conclusion from this study is that removal of normal mortality factors permits the survival of so many individuals as to disrupt the control mechanisms through which there is a sufficient self-control of numbers of population compatible with survival of the species. The destruction of these control mechanisms leads to a dissolution of the capacity of individuals to develop those complex repertoires of behavior reflected in aggression and reproduction.

In terms of the model proposed of probability functions that control behavioral states, p' must become elevated, p'' becomes relatively nonfunctional, and p_i becomes accentuated. At the same time the concatenator probability, p_κ, becomes also essentially nonfunctional. It may be noted that this overriding of social control mechanisms produces individuals much like those resulting from increased intake of vitamin A.

2.14 *The Role of Vitamin A in Inhibiting Behavioral Development*

The Tier 3 rats, mentioned in Sections 2.9 and 2.11 above, emerged into a population structure much like that mentioned in the last section which culminated in the "beautiful one" type of mice. However, these studies on rats were culminated when the Tier 3 rats were only 6 or 7 months of age. This precluded directly determining whether or not their later life in a complex setting would be characterized by reduced aggression and failure to reproduce. However, there are pieces of information that will help to put this puzzle together. In the first series of studies with rats, the ones where the rats were on the Ralston Purina vitamin A–supplemented diet, there were also Tier 3 rats in each population that were also about 6 months old at the time of termination of these populations. At this time I was just leaving for a period of field study in Nova Scotia. Dr. Kyle Barbehenn had recently joined our group as a post-doctoral fellow. He had had extensive previous experience in studying small mammals in their normal ecological setting. He had further worked in mammalian physiology laboratories with domesticated rats. However, he had no prior experience with experimental studies of social behavior in structured settings. Without biasing him with my knowledge of these populations, I asked him to kill off all members of each population except for four males and four females in each. I merely asked him to select the four "best" males and the four "best" females of Tier 3 from each population. This he did by his own criteria, which turned out to be excellent physical health and lack of wounding. One population was excluded because of some prior extreme social disruption that accompanied an accidental suffocating of several dominant males during one period of handling. During several months after this drastic reduction from nearly 100 rats to 8, none of the females in two of the populations ever became pregnant. One female in the third group came into the situation pregnant, presumably from the advances of an older male; beyond this none of the females in this group became pregnant. Studies of aggression were not made, but judging from the loss of reproductive capacity, it is likely that these rats had also experienced a failure to develop capacity for aggression.

In the second series of studies with rats on synthetic diets at the 3-i.u. and 12-i.u. levels of vitamin A, assays of vitamin A storage in the liver were made at the termination of the population. Thirty-four Tier 3 rats on the 3-i.u. diet with a mean age of 201 days had a mean whole liver storage of 15,216 i.u. of vitamin A, while 37 Tier 3 rats on the 12-i.u. diet with a mean age of 184 days had a mean whole liver storage of 20,999 i.u. of vitamin A. Each of these two levels is approximately twice that anticipated by an increase in vitamin A storage with age, leading to the level of storage cited in Section 2.11 for Tier 1 rats. This observation leads to the conclusion that development under conditions which foster failure to develop complex behaviors, including aggression, causes enhanced storage of vitamin A, and that furthermore it is this enhanced storage which facilitates fragmentation of behavior to the point that behaviors will not be engaged in that would otherwise stress the animal.

2.15 Effect of Change in the Probability of Initiating Behavioral States on Aggression

According to the formulations presented in this paper, emotion is equated with the degree of change in the several probability functions that control the initiation, termination, and concatenation of behavioral states. One such emotion is reflected by the elevation of inception of episodes of diffuse motor activity in the presence of less frequently encountered or novel stimuli. Several instances were presented that indicate that an elevation of such emotion is usually accompanied by increased aggression. Figure 20 shows that the $\hat{p}$ behavioral initiator probability function for all behavioral states fluctuates over the 24-hour cycle. The sum of the changes in $\hat{p}$ between consecutive 2-hour periods (Figure 21) may be taken as an index of a general emotional state. When this index is high, there is considerable instability of $\hat{p}$ of the several behavioral states. Likewise, when this index is low, there is considerable stability of $\hat{p}$ (i.e., low emotionality). If my hypothesis is correct, there should be an elevation of aggression during times of $\hat{p}$ instability. The data in Figures 20 and 21 are based on rats from complex social settings isolated in the RSB apparatus. The observational data from the complex settings for these rats was not sufficiently quantified on a time period basis to test this hypothesis. However, later studies with mice do provide a lead to test this idea. These mice were on the same dim-to-bright-light schedule as the rats. If the mice had the same circadian rhythm of change in $\hat{p}$ and in amount of locomotor activity, the data on aggression in the mice may be taken as a test of the hypothesis. Although there is no direct evidence to assume this identity of cycles between the rats and the mice, general observations strongly suggest the likelihood that this identity exists.

One of our current studies was designed to explore the effect of group size on social velocity and social interactions. Groups of 4, 8, 16, and 32 CA F_1 hybrid male mice were placed in 4-cell universes. (The initiation of this study is briefly described on pages 331 to 335 of Calhoun, 1971). All mice were dyed with codes to permit individual identification. On each of 12 days for each of the universes, five 45-minute periods of observation and recording of behavior were conducted. Two of these observation periods (Table 7) came at times of marked difference of the index of $\hat{p}$ change shown in Figure 21. Focus will here be placed on the two groups where $N = 8$ and $N = 16$, since the apparent optimum group size for a 4-cell universe apparently lay between these two.

Any aggression involves some participation by two individuals. Thus, in counting total aggressive involvements a tally was given for each individual involved in any encounter. At the same time that status interactions were recorded, note was made of the identity of animals engaging in each of several behaviors that did not involve interaction with other mice. Excluded from these counts of individual behavior are those relating to movement through space that contributed to velocity scores. Table 7 shows that during the period of $\hat{p}$ instability many more individual behaviors were noted. At this time I do not have the sum of the velocity scores available, but I strongly suspect that the mice actually were less engaged in moving

TABLE 7
Effect of $\hat{p}$ Stability on Aggression

Time	$\hat{p}$	Total Aggressive Involvements[a]	Total Individual Behaviors (Nonaggressive)	Total
Period 2: 1005 to 1050	Unstable	596 (.386)[b]	949 (.614)	1545
Period 5: 1345 to 1430	Stable	336 (.346)	635 (.654)	971
Total		932	1584	2516

Note: $\chi^2 = 3.86$; $p = .05$
[a] Total aggressions half this number.
[b] Proportion of row total.

about the environment at the time of increased involvement in individual behaviors of a non-locomotor nature. Despite this deficit of availability of a major component of total behavior, Table 7 reveals that, in relation to the number of individual behaviors engaged in, mice are significantly more aggressive during times of $\hat{p}$ instability.

REFERENCES

Calhoun, J. B. A comparative study of the social behavior of two inbred strains of house mice. *Ecological Monographs*, 1956, **26**, 81–103.

Calhoun, J. B. A "behavioral sink." In E. L. Bliss (Ed.), *Roots of behavior: Genetics, instinct, and socialization in animal behavior*. Darien, Conn.: Hafner, 1962. Pp. 295–315. (a)

Calhoun, J. B. Population density and social pathology. *Scientific American*, 1962, **206** (2), 139–148. (b)

Calhoun, J. B. The ecology and sociology of the Norway rat. *U.S. Department of Health, Education, and Welfare PHS Monograph*, 1963, No. 1008. (a)

Calhoun, J. B. Social use of space. In W. V. Mayer & R. Van Gelder (Eds.), *Physiological mammalogy*. Vol. I. New York: Academic Press, 1963. Pp. 1–187. (b)

Calhoun, J. B. Ecological factors in the development of behavioral anomalies. In J. Zubin & H. F. Hunt (Eds.), *Comparative psychopathology*. New York: Grune & Stratton, 1967. Pp. 1–51.

Calhoun, J. B. Design for mammalian living. *Architectural Association Quarterly*, 1969, **1** (3), 24–35.

Calhoun, J. B. Space and the strategy of life. In A. H. Esser (Ed.), *Behavior and environment: The use of space by animals and men.* New York: Plenum Press, 1971. Pp. 329–387.

Marsden, H. M. Crowding and animal behavior. In J. F. Wohwill & D. H. Carson (Eds.), *Environment and the social sciences: Perspectives and applications.* Washington, D.C.: American Psychological Association, 1972. Pp. 5–14.

Personality and Aggression[1]

DAN OLWEUS

University of Bergen, Norway

Before embarking on the main theme of my paper, personality and aggression, I should like to make some general reflections of a theoretical nature. Hopefully, these considerations will serve to highlight some central points in the following presentation.

In trying to get a condensed representation of the organization of psychological theories and their elements, it may be helpful to use a general conceptual scheme in the form of a truncated pyramid (see Figure 1). The pyramid in Figure 1 contains four different levels, but dotted lines are used to indicate the possibility of adding further levels, if desirable. The lower levels, I and II, generally have reference to observable data or variables, while the higher levels indicate theoretical variables, constructs, or concepts.

More specifically, the lowest level of the pyramid may be thought of as referring to data that are directly observable—by an experimenter, by óther people, or by the subject himself. In addition, data on this level are generally limited to specific situations and occasions, for instance, the responses to particular test items on a certain occasion for one individual or a group of individuals. Also Level II may be regarded as an observational level but referring to data or variables that are more general and abstract. The variables on this level are formed by some process of generalization such as summing or otherwise finding a typical tendency across situations, measuring instruments, and/or occasions. Of course, one might reserve only one or perhaps three levels for more directly observable data, but

1. The author's research reported in this paper has been supported by grants from the Swedish Council for Social Research and the Norwegian Research Council for Science and the Humanities. I wish to express my thanks to Hugh Allen, visiting researcher at the University of Bergen, for suggestions of language improvements.

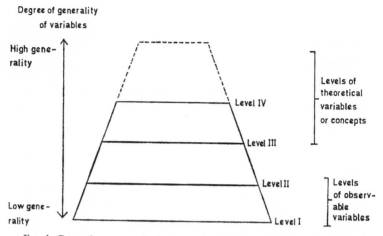

Fig. 1. General conceptual scheme for the analysis of psychological theories.

use of two levels seems appropriate to illustrate the main idea of the reasoning.

In moving higher up the conceptual pyramid one comes across variables which are not only more general but also of a different kind. In the figure they are designated by the generic term theoretical variables. Names such as intervening variables, hypothetical constructs, mediating variables, and symbolic concepts are used interchangeably or with some difference in meaning to indicate variables on these levels. Variables or constructs of this kind cannot be directly observed and they are, in fact, constructed or created by the individual theorist. Even if not observable, theoretical variables, or at least part of them, must be connected to observational variables by means of operational definitions or some other less formal procedure. If such links are not established, the theory will have no contact with reality and its consequences cannot be tested by empirical data. In most psychological theories some form of hierarchical organization of the theoretical constructs is discernible, and consequently, two levels of the pyramid are reserved for theoretical variables, Level IV being more general and comprehensive. For some theories, however, additional theoretical levels may be required for an adequate representation.

Two central aspects of this conceptual scheme should perhaps be emphasized. First, the levels of the pyramid are used to represent variables with different degrees of generality or abstraction. As one moves from lower to higher levels the variables become more general and less concrete—in a sense, more removed from observable reality. At the same time there occurs a shift (in Figure 1, located between Levels II and III) from more observable data to variables of another kind, namely, theoretical variables created by the theorist. Second, the more general variables are also more comprehensive, and consequently, fewer concepts are needed on higher levels. To end up with few, and hopefully in some sense more fundamental, variables is, of course, the goal of all theory construction, and this is sometimes referred to as the principle of parsimony: the theory should make use of fewer variables or concepts (Levels III, IV, etc.) than the empirical data or variables (Levels I and II) it purports to explain. This circumstance is symbolized in the figure by the fact that the pyramid becomes more and more narrow as one moves towards its apex.

In order to give a rough illustration of the use of this general conceptual scheme I will indicate how it could be applied to a trait-theoretical approach based on factor analysis. On the two lower levels one would find, for example, rating data or responses to inventories, tests, or subtests. Factors in general are to be regarded as theoretical constructs and consequently belong to the theoretical levels, for example, first-order factors on Level III and possible second- or higher- order factors on still higher levels. However, if the structural model of psychoanalysis is chosen as an illustration, it would seem reasonable to place the concepts of ego, id, and superego on Level IV (possibly V) and different ego, id, and super-ego functions or structures on Level III. Manifestations of these constructs, for example, in projective tests, dreams, or behavior, belong to the two lower levels.

It is my hope that this admittedly sketchy presentation has nevertheless succeeded in conveying the general ideas contained in the conceptual scheme. Only a few more points should be mentioned briefly. Even if data and relationships on lower levels could be, in principle, "explained" by any type of theoretical network on higher levels, it is often true that there is some form of interplay between different levels. More specifically, particular types of data easily lead to the construction of certain kinds of theoretical variables. Conversely, the use of particular theoretical constructs will have consequences with regard to the selection of data for study and analysis. This interdependence between levels may generally be said to have both positive and negative effects. Finally, it should be pointed out that the type of conceptual analysis presented above is not limited to psychological theorizing but should be also applicable to all other disciplines that make use of empirical data for hypothesis testing.

Some Theoretical Issues

The previous conceptual analysis will now be used as a point of departure for a few reflections in regard to aggression. In addition, it may be seen as a general background for my own theorizing and research in this area.

The term aggression has been used in widely different meanings by different authors. Some define aggression in a rather limited way, approximately equivalent to attack behavior in an interpersonal situation (e.g., Buss, 1961; Kaufmann, 1965). Here it is obvious that the term is located on the observational levels, I and II. Other authors, for example, some psychoanalysts (Hartmann, Kris, & Loewenstein, 1949) and the ethologist Konrad Lorenz (1966), use the term aggression in a very broad sense as a general motivational construct. These writers also postulate a specific aggressive energy, which can be transformed and neutralized. In this way, self-assertiveness and many other activities that seem to be very loosely connected with attack behavior are regarded as manifestations of aggression or as expressions of an underlying aggressive instinct or drive. As used by these theorists, the term aggression is clearly a theoretical variable or construct and as such has its proper place on one of the higher levels of the pyramid (Levels III, IV, etc.).

Thus far it has only been pointed out that the same term, aggression, has been given different conceptual status by different authors. And it can rightly be asserted that one usage is not necessarily better than the other. However, some writers—and this is true of Lorenz as well as several psychoanalysts—have used the same term indiscriminately to denote both a theoretical construct and observable data such as attack behavior, that is, within the same theoretical system. This course of action makes things very confusing and, in fact, largely prevents a meaningful analysis of the phenomenon.

The main point of the preceding discussion is that it is important to specify what type of conceptual status is attached to a certain term or variable within a particular theoretical system. And, evidently, the same term cannot properly be used within a particular theory to denote at the same time observable data (Levels I and II) and theoretical constructs (Levels III, IV, etc.). If certain observable variables are regarded as manifestations of a theoretical concept, it should be made clear that the observable data are indicators or estimates but not identical with the concept itself.

Now let us look at a concrete example of interpersonal interaction in order to clarify some other points. Suppose a man is severely frustrated and verbally attacked by his employer. The man in question feels a strong inner tendency to defend himself and answer back to the employer, but at the same time he is afraid he might lose his job in case he did. So he listens to the employer's accusations and says nothing in the way of protest.

This situation, as it applies to the frustrated man, has been graphically described in Figure 2, which represents an adaptation of the previous conceptual scheme to the present example.

For illustrative purposes, we can make use of a miniature "theory" relating only two variables: the theoretical variable

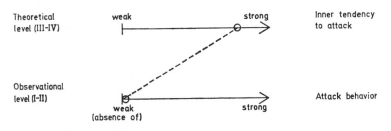

Fɪɢ. 2. Graphic illustration of example in the text.

"inner tendency to attack" and intensity of verbal (and/or physical) attack behavior as an observable variable. From the description of the example it is evident that the frustrated man feels a strong tendency to attack his employer, and consequently he has been located far to the right on the theoretical level in the diagram. His complete absence of attack behavior, however, places him far to the left on the level of observable behavior.

This example is an illustration of the fact that there is often no simple one-to-one correspondence between a theoretical variable and what might seem a natural counterpart in manifest behavior—that is, on an observational level. In some areas of psychology, and perhaps in personality and clinical psychology particularly, the relationships between theoretical variables and observable behavior can be rather complex. A simple linear model for relating variables on different levels to each other is often not very adequate, as will be further illustrated by part of my own empirical research. However, in other branches of psychology, such as perception and psychophysics, a linear, or at least monotone, model may be quite satisfactory for most purposes.

In the reported example, the discrepancy between the man's inner tendencies and his actual behavior suggests the need of at least one additional theoretical concept, such as some kind of controlling or *inhibitory tendency* or factor. Everyday experience as well as data from controlled studies seems to indicate the fruitfulness of introducing inhibitory mechanisms or some similar concept in a theory of aggression.

The importance of keeping the theoretical variables separated from the observable data, which was previously emphasized, is also illustrated by the present example. It is evident that a complete absence of attack behavior or other overt aggressive actions may under certain conditions be associated with strong inner tendencies to attack. Even more, the absence of attack behavior in situations that, so to say, call for such behavior may sometimes be an indication of very strong, but inhibited, inner aggressive tendencies. In psychoanalytic formulations the defense-mechanism reaction formation has been used to explain (part of) this type of relationship. The previous line of reasoning also suggests that it may be wise not to confine oneself too much in the study of aggressive phenomena.

That is, our attention should not be focused exclusively on attack behavior or similar forms of gross overt behavior; under certain conditions the absence of such behavior in some individuals may be a very relevant piece of information that has predictive value for overt aggressive behavior in other situations.

Implicit in the related example and the previous discussions lies also a distinction between *situational and personality, or habitual, determinants* of an individual's behavior. It is quite possible to imagine people who, in the situation of the frustrated man, would not have been quiet and submissive but would have attacked the employer in some way or other, in spite of the risk of losing their jobs. Behavioral variations between individuals in the "same" or similar situations may, then, be partly explained by reference to differences in the individuals' more stable or habitual reaction patterns. Consequently, if the frustrated man in the example generally had low inner restraints or inhibitions against displaying overt aggressive behavior and/or if he had a very violent temper, he might well resort to some form of attack behavior, despite the fact that the situational restraints against such behavior were very strong.

On the other hand, the situational factors may also vary. For instance, if the man was frustrated and attacked, not by his employer but by his subordinate, this would, in all probability, have changed the situation essentially. For one thing, it is quite possible that he would have experienced the frustration and attack as less severe, and consequently the situation would have created less strong inner tendencies to attack the frustrator. At the same time, the situational restraints against overtly attacking the subordinate would probably have been much weaker; he did not run a risk of losing his job in this situation. However that may be in the particular case, the main point of the present argument is that situational as well as habitual components, both as regards aggressive and aggression-inhibitory variables, must be taken systematically into account in an analysis of aggressive phenomena.

All the distinctions made in the previous section—*between theoretical and observable variables, between aggressive and aggression-inhibitory tendencies, between situational and habitual components*—will be further elaborated and discussed in my own conceptual scheme for the determination of aggressive responses.

Problems of Definition

As previously pointed out, the term *aggression* or *aggressive response* has been given very different meanings by various authors. Problems of definition obviously exist and I shall touch upon some of them before stating my own working definition.

A natural starting point for a discussion of the term aggressive response is the formulation presented by the so-called Yale group in the well-known monograph *Frustration and Aggression* (Dollard, Doob, Miller, Mowrer, & Sears, 1939, p. 11): "Aggression is . . . defined as an act whose goal-response is injury to an organism (or organism-surrogate)." It is furthermore said (p. 10): "Verbs such as destroy, damage, torment, retaliate, hurt, blow up, humiliate, insult, threaten, and intimidate refer to actions of an aggressive nature." In the previous definition, aggression is thus regarded as a response directed toward the infliction of injury or noxious consequences. The injury mentioned may be of a mental as well as a physical nature and the target of aggression may be animate as well as inanimate.

The Yale group definition has been the subject of considerable controversy. Some have criticized it for being too broad, among other things, and it has been argued that the term aggression should be limited to overt behavior or actions that are actually directed to an animate individual. Others have considered such a delimitation unduly narrow and find it quite natural to include reactions that are in a sense nonovert, such as responses to a projective test or a negative evaluation in a questionnaire or on a rating scale.

Most writers agree, however, that *unintentional or accidental injury* to an organism should be excluded from the category of aggressive responses. But opinions have differed on the general question as to whether *intent* or some similar construct should be included among the criteria of an aggressive response. Attempts have been made (e.g., Buss, 1961) to give the term an entirely behavioral definition, without such concepts as intent or its equivalent, goal-response, but several critics (e.g., Bandura & Walters, 1963; Kaufmann, 1965) have pointed to the difficulties and limitations of such an approach. Many authors (e.g., Berkowitz, 1962, 1965; Feshbach,

1964) thus find it meaningful to include intent or some similar term as a general criterion of an aggressive response. A difficulty with such a definition may reside in the problem of identifying the intent on the part of the aggressor. Of course it happens that the purpose of an act is explicitly expressed, but often it is not and accordingly must be assessed on the basis of the context and the antecedent conditions. Thus, in order not to treat accidental injury as an aggressive response, some form of judgment about the aggressor's intent or expectation must often be made.

It has also been pointed out that not all intentional aggressive responses are necessarily equivalent from a functional point of view. In this respect a distinction has been made between *angry or hostile aggression* and *instrumental aggression* (Berkowitz, 1962; Buss, 1961; Feshbach, 1964). In the latter case, the primary aim is not to injure or cause discomfort to another organism, as in hostile aggression, but to achieve some other, nonaggressive goal by means of "the delivery of noxious stimuli" (Buss, 1961). A robber who assaults a stranger, for instance, in a sense intends to inflict injury, but this is generally not his goal, simply a means of getting at the victim's money. The use of violence as a way of achieving economic or political goals can in general be regarded, at least in part, as an example of instrumental aggression, between groups or nations. The instrumental aspect of aggressive responses was largely excluded from consideration in the original frustration-aggression hypothesis (Dollard et al., 1939).

The distinction between hostile and instrumental aggression is important both in principle and in practice. There seem to be aggressive responses without instrumental value and, conversely, instrumental aggression with no hostile intentions toward the victim on the part of the aggressor. Nevertheless, it should be pointed out that these two forms of aggression are often found together (Feshbach, 1964): responses that may be regarded as instrumentally aggressive in many cases also involve an aim to produce injurious consequences. Accordingly, as I see it, a definition of the term aggressive response should be broad enough to include both hostile and instrumental aggression. At the same time it should be clear, however, that certain relatively pure forms of instrumental aggression, as when a dentist or a surgeon inflicts injury in order to cure his patient, must be considered of minor interest in a theory of aggression. In such cases, where the delivery of noxious stimuli is part of and, in fact, a necessary component of a socially defined and valued role, the possibility of an underlying hostile intent against the patients can for the most part be disregarded, I think. If it should be found, however, that people, or some portion of them, in these professions derived special satisfaction from this particular aspect of their role behavior, their choice of profession would become more interesting from the perspective of an aggression theory.

In the light of the previous discussion it should be obvious that several different definitions of the term aggressive response are possible. And, in fact, it seems difficult, not to say infeasible, to formulate a definition that does not involve certain problems or drawbacks. The apparently easy question of definition thus has turned out to be quite complicated and cannot be decided upon in any simple, straightforward way.

When reflecting upon a working definition of the term aggressive response, personally I find it important not to make it too narrow— for instance, to restrict it to the delivery of noxious stimuli to an animate individual. A narrow definition obviously involves the risk of omitting or failing to catch essential, but possibly more subtle, reactions or behaviors, as often observed in the field of clinical psychology. On the other hand, a very broad and vague use of the term, as exemplified by Lorenz and some psychoanalysts—where almost any activity or striving may be considered a form of aggressive response—leads to conceptual problems, besides difficulties regarding operationalization in empirical research.

The strategy that I have adopted implies using a relatively wide definition of the general term *aggressive response*, combined with certain specifications. An aggressive response is then defined as any act or behavior that involves, might involve, and/or to some extent can be considered as aiming at, the infliction of injury or discomfort; also manifestations of inner reactions such as feelings or thoughts that can be conceived to have such an aim are regarded as aggressive responses.

This definition thus includes instrumental aggression ("involves, might involve") and hostile aggression ("aiming at the infliction") as well as combinations of these two forms. As previously mentioned, however, certain relatively pure forms of instrumental aggression may attract little interest. In general, primary attention will be directed to hostile aggression and to such instrumentally aggressive acts as can also be considered to have injurious consequences as a goal or subgoal. And, as in the Yale group formulation, the injury or discomfort may be mental as well as physical in character. Moreover, an aggressive response as here defined may be directed to animate or inanimate objects, to particular situations or events, and, in fact, it may have no identifiable target at all. Aggressive responses may consist of different forms of overt behavior such as physical or verbal attacks as well as inner reactions or, more properly, reports or other manifestations of such reactions, for example, in projective tests, inventories, and rating scales. Furthermore, whether a response is to be regarded as aggressive is not dependent on the result or effectiveness of the response. An attack, for instance, that does not reach the intended target is nevertheless considered an aggressive response. Finally, acts that result in injury clearly by accident will not attract great interest, although they are not formally excluded from the definition.

It should be evident that the different responses included in this general definition need further specification. Such specification can be made in several ways—for instance, along the lines suggested in the comments on the definition. I also find it essential to state the kind of data source from which a response or response variable is obtained: (a) if an individual's responses are performed in an actual situation as noted or recorded by an observer or experimenter, (b) if they have reference to behavior or reactions reported by other people, who know the individual in question, (c) if they are reported by the subject himself, and finally, (d) if the responses are secured in a projective technique (see Bronfenbrenner & Ricciuti, 1960).

Of course it cannot be taken for granted that there is a direct correspondence or equivalence between aggressive responses from different sources of data. To say that you want to give a person a good beating may not be the same as doing it. And if overt aggressive behavior in a particular situation is to be predicted, it may be found that aggressive responses in a certain projective test relate to the "criterion" data quite differently from self-report data. To complicate things further, even different types of aggressive responses within a particular measuring instrument or situation may show different types of relationships with "criterion" data. This argument, then, chiefly implies that responses categorized as aggressive may be quite different both as regards functional value and predictive capacity. A natural first step in a research program is, thus, to separate various subclasses of aggressive responses, within as well as between different sources of data. Their degree of functional and predictive equivalence has then to be established in empirical research, guided by theoretical analysis.

By using specification procedures of this type as a complement to the general definition of an aggressive response, the possible drawbacks associated with a relatively wide definition can be clearly counteracted. Needless to say, from a theoretical point of view there are many advantages to be gained from the use of a comprehensive, uniting definition.

Perhaps one more point should be stressed in this context. The stated definition concerns aggressive responses, that is, inner reactions or behaviors that can be observed, recorded, or reported in one way or another. As will be more fully developed in a later section, I conceptualize such responses as the result, among other things, of an interaction between aggressive and aggression-inhibitory tendencies, although the latter tendencies may be equal to zero in a particular individual and situation. This conceptualization applies to inner reactions as well as to overt behavior. Thus, reports of inner reactions should not be regarded a priori as direct indicators of, for example, underlying aggressive tendencies. In a particular situation an individual may have strongly activated aggressive tendencies that are masked by still stronger aggression-inhibitory tendencies. And the predominant subjective experience may be tension and anxiety. It may be concluded, then, that these relationships—between various classes of aggressive responses and the theoretical variables in the conceptual framework—must be subjected to closer analysis, in the same way as was previously asserted regarding the relationships between different classes of aggressive responses. Some factors of relevance for such analyses will be pointed out in the presentation of my own conceptual scheme.

CAUSATION OF AGGRESSION

After this discussion of some definitional problems in connection with the terms aggression and aggressive response, I should like to touch upon the issue of the origin, or causation, of aggression. This general question can obviously be divided into several subquestions, and in this context I will restrict myself largely to the problem of *short-term causation*: that is, what factors lead to an aggressive response or, rather, to an instigation to an aggressive response at a given moment? The primary concern is here the question of instigation to an aggressive response and not whether the instigation is or is not expressed in the form of an aggressive response. Next, brief attention will be paid to factors that may create a strong inner disposition or habitual tendency to react with aggressive responses. Finally, the need of considering both situational and dispositional factors regarding the determination of aggression-inhibitory tendencies or mechanisms will be emphasized.

Two main approaches to the issue of short-term causation may be distinguished. In one, aggression is conceptualized as a constantly operative, internal drive or instinct seeking outlet. In the other, an instigation to an aggressive response is mainly assumed to be a function of certain stimulus conditions such as frustration and threat.

The *instinct* approach—represented by the psychoanalytic theory of aggression (Hartmann et al., 1949) as well as that of Lorenz (1966)—can be said to imply an energy model of motivation. As previously suggested, these two related positions hold that there is a specific aggressive energy which is continually operative in the organism. This leads to the building up of tensions that the individual tries to discharge in one form or another. If discharge of aggressive energy has not been possible for some time, the internal drive is assumed to build up until the individual actively seeks an opportunity for tension reduction. According to this conception, frustrating and threatening situations serve the function of releasing aggressive energy rather than producing instigations to aggression. Sometimes aggression is said to be "spontaneous" (Lorenz).

These two instinct theories of aggression are open to serious criticism. Without going into detail, I should like to raise the following objections. The key terms and concepts are not adequately defined, nor are they connected to empirical referents in a satisfactory way; in fact, some parts of the theories seem impossible to test empirically. The relational or syntactic rules linking the theoretical concepts are not adequately specified, which leads to difficulties in deriving consequences and predictions from the theoretical superstructure. The purported empirical evidence is meager, often poorly controlled, as a rule obviously open to other interpretations, and in some cases quite incorrect (Lorenz). Finally, the theories seem to have little explanatory value besides vague and sweeping generalizations, nor have they stimulated empirical research on aggression to any marked extent.

In this connection it is of interest to note that a number of leading ethologists (e.g., Barnett, 1967; Hinde, 1967) have been very critical of Lorenz's theoretical position and have completely rejected the notion of an aggressive instinct. Likewise there has been leveled very weighty criticism of the psychoanalytic tension-reduction view of motivation (e.g., Holt, 1965, 1967), and interesting, recent formulations of a psychoanalytic model have been proposed (Holt, 1966) which have very little in common with the old instinct theories.

As already mentioned, most psychological theorists (except the majority of psychoanalysts) have not relied upon an instinct conception of aggression. Instead there has been quite general agreement on the point that instigations to aggression should be viewed primarily as responses to certain stimulus conditions. Differences of opinion exist, however, as to which conditions ought to be considered crucial as well as their conceptual and operational definitions. It should be pointed out that this *"reactive conception"* of aggression, contrary to a prevalent misconception, does not presuppose any assumptions about whether the antecedent-consequent relationship is of innate or learned origin. Nor does it imply that biological or genetic factors lack importance in the determination of an individual's aggressive reactions or disposition. In this respect it is only argued that the conception of a biological influence in the form of constantly active aggressive drive should be rejected for a number of reasons.

The most influential of the reactive theories of aggression is the frustration-aggression formulation presented in 1939 (Dollard et al.).

In this monograph the assumed relationship between frustration and aggression was stated in the form of a broad generalization: "the proposition is that the occurrence of aggressive behavior always presupposes the existence of frustration and, contrariwise, that the existence of frustration always leads to some form of aggression" (Dollard et al., 1939, p. 2). Two years later the second part of the proposition was modified by one of the authors of the original monograph (Miller, 1941). The new statement reads as follows: "Frustration produces instigation to a number of different types of response, one of which is an instigation to some form of aggression" (p. 338). According to this conception, frustration is thus considered the main antecedent of an instigation to aggression. And by frustration is meant "an interference with the occurrence of an instigated goal-response at its proper time in the behavior sequence" (Dollard et al., 1939, p. 7).

In their important monograph, Dollard and his colleagues ingeniously formulate principles concerning many different aspects of aggressive behavior. Regarding the strength of instigation to aggression, which is of main interest in this context, the following propositions are presented: the strength of instigation to aggression varies directly with (a) the strength of instigation to the frustrated response, (b) the degree of interference with the frustrated response, and (c) the number of frustrated response-sequences. It is thus maintained that the strength of instigation to an aggressive response can be reliably predicted on the basis of specified antecedent conditions.

The frustration-aggression hypothesis has received great attention and has also drawn the fire of several critics. The majority have found the main proposition, even in its modified form, too sweeping and simple. Others have rightly pointed to the fact that the important class of response called instrumental aggression has been excluded from consideration.

There have also been objections to the ambiguity of the concept frustration. For some investigators the term refers to external blocking operations (see, e.g., Buss, 1961); for others frustration is thought of as the internal reaction resulting from the blocking or interference (Brown & Farber, 1951; Amsel, 1958). And those who use the word in the latter sense partly differ in their conception of the antecedents of this internal state. Accordingly, it comes as no surprise that experimental studies concerning the effects of frustration do not present unambiguous results. In fact, there have been findings suggesting that frustrations may increase as well as reduce aggressive responding, or have no effect at all (see, e.g., Bandura, 1969; Berkowitz, 1962, 1969). Although such results seem to signify that there are several other "natural" responses to frustration, in addition to or instead of an instigation to aggression, the negative results should not be accepted without considering the possibility of alternative explanations. In this context it seems reasonable to make reference to the demand characteristics and artificiality of many laboratory studies (see, e.g., Orne, 1971) as well as to the possible activation of aggression-inhibitory tendencies (Olweus, 1969). In addition, the diversity of conditions used to define frustration must be kept in mind.

This emphasis on alternative explanations should not be taken to imply that I regard instigation to aggression as the only natural response to frustration, nor that frustration, or even particular kinds of frustration, is the only antecedent condition of an instigation to aggression. Nevertheless, in my view there is very suggestive evidence that certain forms of what may be legitimately called frustrations can lead to, or increase, an instigation to an aggressive response. This conclusion is based on evidence from controlled studies with adults and children (for review, see, e.g., Berkowitz, 1962, 1969), as well as from clinical experience and everyday observations. The preceding conclusion, however, must immediately be supplemented with an admission that much more work is needed in order to clarify the conceptual and operational meaning of the term frustration (for a modified frustration-aggression theory, see Berkowitz, 1969).

When discussing possible antecedent conditions of aggressive instigations, such factors as *threat* and *attack* or noxious stimuli must also be considered, as has been proposed by several authors (e.g., Buss, 1961; Feshbach, 1964; Kaufmann, 1965). Threat and attack can only with considerable difficulty, if at all, be conceptualized as frustrations but nevertheless are often found to elicit aggressive responses (see, e.g., Buss, 1961). The same applies to different kinds of pain stimuli, which are generally considered a very reliable antecedent of fighting behavior in a wide variety of animal species (for a review, see, e.g., Boelkins & Heiser, 1970). Possibly, all these conditions could be subsumed under the general category of aversive stimuli, as has been proposed by Berkowitz (1969), leaning on Amsel (1962). Anyhow, there are, in conclusion, a number of external and/or internal conditions or stimulus patterns leading to aggressive instigation at a given moment: on the basis of available evidence concerning human subjects, I primarily consider what may somewhat loosely be called frustration, threat, and attack as such conditions. At the same time, it should be stressed that conditions of this kind may not only lead to an instigation to aggression; in certain circumstances and/or individuals they may also result in an activation of aggression-inhibitory tendencies, entailing conflict with the aggressive instigation.

The preceding discussion is largely concerned with what was previously (p. 269) called hostile aggression and combinations of hostile and instrumental aggression. By the way, the same applies to my own conceptual scheme for the determination of aggressive responses, to be presented in a subsequent section. General principles of relevance for the instrumental aspect of aggressive response patterns are treated by Bandura and Walters (1963) and Bandura (1969).

Next, brief consideration will be paid to another aspect of the problem concerning the causation of aggression. Now the more immediate factors, the situational determinants of aggressive instigations, are temporarily out of focus, and the interest will be concentrated on factors of importance for the development of more *stable aggressive reaction tendencies or dispositions.* The discussion will thus deal with potential constitutional and environmental factors associated with individual differences in these respects or, in the terminology to be used later, with the determination of the strength of an individual's habitual aggressive tendencies. Maybe it should be pointed out that, at least for human subjects, there is not necessarily an equivalence between strong habitual aggressive tendencies and frequent overt aggressive behavior. It is quite possible for an individual to have strong tendencies of this kind that are blocked by inhibitory tendencies in a number of situations, with weak aggressive responses as a result. The research studies, however, have for the most part used the extent of overt aggressive behavior as their point of departure. It should also be emphasized that the research approaches taken to this issue are rather heterogeneous and the results do not always form neat, coherent patterns. Accordingly, the studies permit few clear-cut, precise conclusions, and more research obviously needs to be done in this area.

First, it may be generally stated that both constitutional, or genetic, and environmental factors seem to be of importance. It is well known that the frequency and intensity of aggressive behaviors can be markedly increased by natural as well as artificial selection of animals. The effects of selective breeding on specific behavioral characteristics such as fighting behavior have been amply proved in a large number of species. It has also been demonstrated that aggressive behavior rests on a firm genetic foundation in dogs, for example (Scott, 1958). For humans, it has been suggested (Patterson, Littman, & Bricker, 1967) that a genetic influence on aggression may in part stem from genetic effects on general activity level. This assumption is based on the fact that a positive relationship has often been found between children's general activity level and amount of aggression; and individual variations in level of activity are salient already at birth and seem to remain relatively stable for many years.

Of course genetic factors do not operate in a vacuum but always in combination with particular environmental conditions. Such interactions, however, may be highly complex and little precise knowledge pertinent to this issue is at present available, particularly in the area of human aggression (see, e.g., Becker, 1962; Zigler, 1970). Nevertheless, on the basis of animal research (see also Clemente & Lindsley, 1967) it seems a very reasonable strategy to adopt an "interactionist" position (Zigler, 1970), despite the fact that human data of relevance so far are largely missing.

The role of early social experiences in shaping later behavior patterns has been examined in a large number of animal studies (for reviews, see Becker, 1962, and Boelkins & Heiser, 1970). The findings generally attest to the great importance of early periods of life for a "normal" development in the sphere of aggression. Taken together, these studies also suggest both that there may be an un-learned basis for aggressive response patterns and that early learning or training experiences may strongly affect the frequency and intensity of aggressive behaviors in animals.

More directly relevant to the question of how strong aggressive dispositions may develop in humans, particularly boys, are a number of nonexperimental child-rearing studies, aptly summarized by Becker (1964). One general finding is that parents who frequently use power-assertive child-rearing methods such as physical punishment and threat tend to have highly aggressive sons. Since it is also found, however, that the use of punitive disciplinary techniques is associated with a hostile, rejecting parental attitude toward the child, it is difficult to know if the demonstrated relationship is chiefly the result of punishment, of parental hostility, or a combination of punishment and hostility. The obtained association between power-assertive, hostile parents and highly aggressive children can be explained in several ways, and Becker (1964) suggests the following three mechanisms: (a) physical punishment, especially in a rejecting context, is frustrating and leads to hostility and frequent instigations to aggression; (b) a physically punitive parent is setting a model of aggressive behavior for the child, which at the same time may imply a partial sanctioning of aggressive responses from the child; and (c) possibly, there may be a direct reinforcement of aggressive behaviors to others by hostile-punitive parents. On the other hand, it has also been consistently found that warm parents tend to use love-oriented techniques such as praise, reasoning, and withdrawal of love and that they generally have children with a low incidence of aggressive behavior.

Another broad dimension of child rearing that has attracted considerable attention concerns the extent to which parents place demands and restrictions on their children, with reference to aggression as well as to other behavior sectors. This aspect of parental behavior has been called a restrictiveness-versus-permissiveness dimension, and the strictness of enforcement is also generally included in its definition. Regarding habitual aggressive behavior, this dimension seems to interact with that of parental hostility versus warmth. Hostile-permissive parents have highly aggressive children, while the combination of parental hostility and restrictiveness seems to create strong inner aggressive tendencies and resentment in the children but usually little overt aggression, except in certain relatively safe areas (Becker, 1964). Parental warmth, on the other hand, is usually found to be associated with low overt aggression in the child, in a restrictive as well as a permissive context. Differences in other sectors of the child's behavior may be prominent, however.

The previous summary of research is admittedly sketchy and it has not been possible to pay sufficient attention to alternative hypotheses as to the direction of the causal relationships or to differences of results depending upon divergent operational definitions. The main purpose, however, has been to demonstrate that such conditions as frequent and/or severe frustrations, parental attitudes and child-rearing patterns, and the presence of aggressive or nonaggressive models during childhood and adolescence very likely play a significant part in the development of an individual's more habitual aggressive tendencies and behavior patterns. In addition, largely animal research suggests that genetic factors related to such dimensions as general activity level and "temperament" may also be of importance, in combination with particular environmental conditions.

As regards the development of inhibitory tendencies or mechanisms, very little research explicitly directed to this issue has been conducted. However, several studies referred to in the previous paragraphs are obviously, but often indirectly, relevant. Again, it may be concluded that such factors as parental warmth, models of controlled behavior, and parents' punishment practices and restrictiveness seem to play an important role, directly or via variables such as ego control and frustration tolerance. Also in this respect, it appears natural to presume an influence of genetic factors, related to such variables as general sensitivity and anxiety proneness.

As will be more fully expounded in subsequent sections, I regard inhibitory tendencies or mechanisms of great importance in a theory of aggression. In my view, such tendencies are conceptually and often also empirically independent of the individual's aggressive tendencies and, accordingly, cannot simply be estimated as the reverse of the amount of aggressive behavior displayed. Furthermore, several reasons of a conceptual nature as well as some empirical research suggest the fruitfulness of considering both situational and habitual aspects of aggression-inhibitory tendencies, in the same way as was previously proposed for the aggressive tendencies.

A Conceptual Framework

My own attempts to deal with certain aspects of a theory of aggression will now be presented briefly, as well as some related empirical research. (A more detailed account has been given in Olweus, *Prediction of Aggression*, 1969.) The theoretical framework to be presented is naturally linked up with the preceding analyses and discussions; in fact, they have paved the way for it. Nevertheless, I should like to make a few introductory remarks to point out some special features of interest.

For one thing, my conviction that both situational and habitual determinants of an aggressive response must be taken systematically into account is reflected in the structure of the conceptual scheme. In this connection it may be noted that in theoretical writings as well as empirical investigations there is a tendency to emphasize one of these components at the expense of the other. The Yale group formulation (Dollard et al., 1939), for instance, only dealt with situational determinants of the strength of instigation to aggression. Variations in dispositional tendencies were not specifically considered. Implicitly they were treated as some sort of error variance, to be distributed equally over conditions in experimental research. A heavy stress on situational determinants is also salient in the writings of several social-learning theorists (Bandura, 1969; Mischel, 1968). On the other hand, trait-psychological or "dimensional" approaches, based, for example, on factor analysis, tend to disregard the importance of situational factors (see, e.g., Mischel, 1968). In the case of research on anxiety, it has been argued (Spielberger, 1966, p. 19) that experimental studies as a rule do not take both these aspects into account at the same time. A similar statement can, no doubt, be made concerning empirical studies in the area of aggression.

Furthermore, the significance of cognitive factors is emphasized, among other things, by inclusion of the construct *cognitive appraisal of the situation* in the conceptual scheme. This circumstance leads to the consequence that effects of situational factors are incorporated in the theoretical network in a somewhat unusual way.

Finally, it should perhaps be mentioned that some important aspects of a general theory of aggression are not considered in my conceptual scheme—for instance, the question of the more temporary effects of expressing or not expressing activated aggressive tendencies in overt behavior (see also p. 272). There seems to be little difficulty, however, in incorporating these and other parts of a more comprehensive theory of aggression into an extension of the theoretical framework.

Let us start with the diagrammatic representation of my conceptual scheme, reproduced in Figure 3. On the far left of this figure the general term *situation* will be seen. It is used here in a wide sense and refers to both external and internal conditions or stimulus patterns. These stimulus patterns are perceived, judged, and evaluated by the individual; the term *cognitive appraisal* is used to denote these cognitive processes. The appraisal process is often rapid and immediate and need not be conscious or clearly formulated. This generally complex process is decisive for an individual's interpretation or appraisal of the stimulus situation. It is consequently of major importance in determining which of the individual's reaction tendencies will be activated.

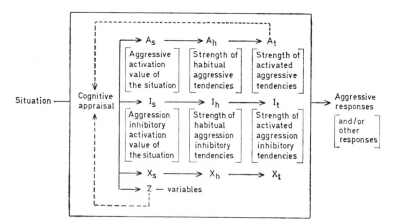

FIG. 3. Conceptual scheme for the determination of aggressive (and/or other) responses.

Furthermore, the individual is conceived of as being equipped with certain internal reaction tendencies (denoted A_h, I_h, X_h) which are assumed to be relatively constant for a given individual across different occasions and situations. These tendencies function as dispositions both to appraise certain stimulus situations in a particular manner and to respond to such appraisal with relatively consistent reactions, at a certain strength. These reaction tendencies are termed *habitual tendencies* and may be regarded as dispositional tendencies (cf., e.g., Klein, Barr, & Wolitzky, 1967), that is, tendencies that are activated or brought into play by certain classes of situations. Reliable interindividual differences are expected in these variables—as indicated by the words "strength of" in the conceptual scheme. The aggressive (A) and aggressive-inhibitory (I) tendencies are of particular interest in the present context, but to indicate the possibility of other important tendencies such as achievement and affiliation, the general term X has been inserted in the scheme.

In order to be more precise about the habitual tendencies of main interest, the following specifications may be stated. An individual's *habitual aggressive tendencies* constitute a disposition to appraise certain classes of situations as frustrating, threatening, and/or noxious; an appraisal that gives rise to an activation value above a certain minimal level entails activation of the individual's tendencies to inflict injury or discomfort. And similarly, an individual's *habitual aggression-inhibitory tendencies* constitute a disposition to appraise his own aggressive tendencies and/or responses as dangerous, unpleasant, distressing, or inappropriate; an appraisal that gives rise to an activation value above a certain minimal level entails activation of the individual's tendencies to inhibit, avoid, or deprecate the expression of aggressive tendencies. (For the definition of an aggressive response, see p. 270.)

As already indicated, certain stimuli or stimulus situations are required to activate an individual's habitual tendencies. It is also presumed that *different situations may be appraised to have different activation values* (this aspect being generally denoted by the subscript s: A_s, I_s, etc.). While various stimulus situations obviously may be experienced as differently aggression provoking, for instance, by one and the same individual, it is also clear that the "same" stimulus situation can be appraised as differently provocative by two individuals, varying in strength of the habitual aggressive tendencies. It is tentatively assumed that, by and large, there is a *positive covariation between the strength of the individual's habitual tendencies* (A_h, I_h) *and the magnitude of the activation value* (A_s, I_s) *for a given situation.* This means, for instance, that a certain frustrating situation is generally appraised as more frustrating, that is, having greater aggressive activation values (A_s), for individuals with strong habitual aggressive tendencies than for those in whom such tendencies are weaker. And if the situation is made more frustrating, all values of A_s are expected to increase, but individuals with stronger habitual aggressive tendencies will still tend to have greater activation values. In this context it should be borne in mind that the habitual tendencies $(A_h, I_h, \text{etc.})$ of a particular individual have been assumed to be relatively constant across different situations.

If a given situation, thus, is appraised to have an activation value that exceeds a certain minimal level, the individual's habitual reaction tendencies are activated and a state of activated tendencies arises (activated tendencies are denoted by the subscript t). As suggested above, *the strength of the activated tendencies* $(A_t, I_t, \text{etc.})$ *is a function both of the activation value of the situation* $(A_s, I_s, \text{etc.})$ *and the strength of the habitual tendencies* $(A_h, I_h, \text{etc.})$. Without specifying in detail, this relationship is assumed to be largely monotone increasing. An increase in the situational activation value for a particular individual leads to stronger activated tendencies, and individuals with stronger habitual tendencies are presumed to have higher $A_t\text{-}/I_t$ values for an $A_s\text{-}/I_s$ value of a certain magnitude than individuals in whom such tendencies are weaker. (See Olweus, 1969, for a more detailed presentation.)

It is also expected that both the situational (s) and habitual (h) components vary quite considerably and that the strength of the activated tendencies may be determined predominantly by the s (situational) or the h (habitual) component. If the activation value of a situation is low, however, there will be no or little activation of the habitual tendencies; a certain minimal level must be exceeded for an activation to take place.

It should be remembered that the activated tendencies are internal reaction tendencies, so that a state of activated aggressive tendencies is not equivalent to aggressive responses. *Whether and to what extent aggressive responses materialize will be determined primarily by the mutual relationship between the activated aggressive and aggression-inhibitory tendencies.* Other factors of importance are the external conditions and the variables denoted by Z in Figure 3.

The last-mentioned factors call for a brief comment. By external conditions is meant a situation that makes possible the expression of activated aggressive tendencies, in the relative absence of activated inhibitory tendencies. Terms such as releasers or releasing cues (Berkowitz, 1962) have been used for this or similar aspects of a situation. In the present context they are of secondary interest.

The Z variables are intended to represent a number of personality variables, apart from those mentioned, that may influence the strength and form of an individual's responses. This category of variables may comprise factors such as intelligence, verbal capacity, and physical resources as well as variables that are conditioned by age, sex, and cultural environment but are not directly channeled into the aggressive or aggression-inhibitory tendencies. Some of these variables may also be important for an individual's appraisal of the situation, as indicated by the dashed arrow between Z variables and cognitive appraisal in Figure 3.

The main points in the conceptual scheme may now be *summarized.* Following a process of cognitive appraisal, a particular situation is assumed to have a certain activation value (A_s, I_s, etc.) for different internal habitual reaction tendencies (A_h, I_h, etc.) in an individual. If these activation values exceed certain minimal levels, there arises a state of one or more activated tendencies (A_t, I_t, etc.), the strength of which is a joint function of the situational activation value and the strength of the habitual tendencies in question. The mutual relationship between the activated tendencies in conjunction with certain other personality variables (Z) and the external conditions determines the strength and form of the individual's aggressive (and/or aggression-inhibitory) responses.

This conceptual scheme probably sounds rather abstract and it may be difficult for one to apply the present concepts to concrete situations. So, for an illustration let me once more make reference to the sketchy example presented in the introduction to the paper (p. 265) and graphically described in Figure 2. In this example a man was frustrated and verbally attacked by his employer. He felt a strong inner tendency to answer back to the employer but he did not, presumably for fear he might lose his job. For this man the situation obviously had a rather strong aggressive activation value (A_s) that led to an activation of his habitual aggressive tendencies (A_h). At the same time, however, the man perceived the situation and an expression of his activated aggressive tendencies (A_t) in attack behavior as dangerous. In the present terminology, the situation was appraised to have a strong aggression-inhibitory activation value (I_s), entailing activation of the man's habitual aggression-inhibitory tendencies (I_h). And the latter tendencies were not very low, at least for the man in question. In the present example, thus, the activated inhibitory tendencies (I_t) were clearly stronger than the activated aggressive tendencies (A_t), resulting in an absence of attack behavior or other overt aggressive responses. The modifications introduced into the example (p. 267) could also be readily accounted for by use of the present concepts. Hopefully, this brief ex post facto "explanation" will serve the function of suggesting that the conceptual framework can be applied to a great many situations in the field of aggression—to common everyday experiences as well as to situations arranged and controlled by an experimenter.

Maybe one more point should be stressed. The conceptual scheme includes only one type of habitual aggression-inhibitory tendencies (I_h). Possibly, it might be fruitful to differentiate the inhibitory tendencies into predominantly external and internal types, for instance. Similarly, it is conceivable that an individual's habitual aggressive tendencies might be partly different for different classes of situations. Up to now, however, it has not been found essential to consider the possibility of distinctions of this kind. Subsequent research may necessitate such considerations.

An Empirical Application

Having described the general frame of reference, I will now make use of the theoretical variables in a study of the relationship between projective test data and typical aggressive behavior in an interpersonal situation. Briefly, this is done by relating the projective test data and the data on the interpersonal situation via a number of assumptions to some of the theoretical variables. As a result, two main predictions are obtained concerning the probable relationship between the subjects' aggressive responses in the test and ratings of their overt aggressive behavior.

Testing Situation

First, however, a short description of procedure. Forty-four middle-class schoolboys, aged 12 to 14 years, were tested in small groups with a specially constructed projective test consisting of four incomplete stories. All test stories were given the same basic structure: they portray two persons in conflict with each other, a male adult and a boy of roughly the same age as the subject; furthermore, the adult puts the boy in a frustrating and somewhat threatening situation, but it is clear from the context that the boy is partly responsible for the situation. The subject's task was first to write down answers to three questions and then to work out a conclusion to the story.

The test was constructed with the aim of activating chiefly the aggressive and aggression-inhibitory tendencies of the subjects. Accordingly, the analysis of the response material was undertaken with two main groups of scoring categories, one for measuring aggressive responses, denoted ProjA, and another for indications of aggression-inhibitory responses, denoted ProjI. Several empirical analyses by means of Guttman's scalogram technique strongly suggested that the test responses could be meaningfully and consistently ordered according to these two dimensions. In this context it should also be mentioned that the projective response data were differentiated into a relatively large number of subcategories so as to permit separate analyses of particular aspects of the material. Thus, a distinction was made, for instance, between variables relating to the hero's internal reactions and variables relating to behavior (see Olweus, 1969, Chap. 3, for scoring rules, etc.). By and large, however, these different aspects of the response material were related to the behavior data in a fairly similar way, and consequently the following presentation will be limited to the more comprehensive composite variables (ProjA and ProjI).

It should also be pointed out that the projective response material could be scored with great accuracy, the interscorer reliability centering around .90 (product-moment correlations) for different variables investigated.

On the basis of a rough comparison with other research situations reported in the literature, the activation values (A_s, I_s) of the present test, administered in a slightly anxiety-provoking testing situation, were provisionally classified as moderate for the group as a whole. Although this judgment was considered to some extent subjective, it could be asserted on the basis of the test responses that the activation values of the situation had been sufficiently high to activate the habitual aggressive and aggression-inhibitory tendencies (A_h, I_h) in most of the subjects. Perhaps it should be pointed out that such broad categorizations of the situational activation values for the most part seem to be precise enough, at least in the present state of knowledge.

Interpersonal Situation

Data on the subject's tendency to start fights with peers were also secured. This type of data refers, strictly speaking, to a number of interpersonal situations over some time and concerns the individual's overt aggressive behavior, denoted OA. Ratings of this variable were made on a 7-point scale by four boys selected at random from each of the three classes. The interrater reliability— expressed here as the mean correlation between all *pairs* of raters— was found to be unusually high ($\bar{r} = .77$). This fact means that the subject's position regarding tendency to start fights could be assessed with great certainty.

The peer-relation situation was deliberately included in the research design, because its aggression-inhibitory activation value (I_s) could be assumed to be generally low, clearly lower than in the testing situation. Several reasons in conjunction suggest that the habitual aggression-inhibitory tendencies (I_h) for most of the subjects will be activated to only a slight extent in such a situation. The aggressive activation value (A_s), on the other hand, could be provisionally characterized as generally moderate.

Assumptions and Predictions

Now I will go back to the main assumptions leading up to the two predictions. For lack of space the assumptions must be presented very briefly, without proper consideration of the underlying rationale or the supporting evidence from other studies. In this context it should also be pointed out that the present and a number of additional predictions can be made on the basis of the more general, quantitative model that has been developed in my book on aggression (see Olweus, 1969, chap. 12). The central assumption of this model is that the strength of an individual's aggressive responses, Y, is a monotone-increasing function of the difference between the strengths of the activated aggressive and aggression-inhibitory tendencies: $Y = f(A_t - I_t)$.

A basic point in what follows is that individuals with different strengths of the habitual aggression-inhibitory tendencies (I_h) are assumed to have partly different internal dynamics. This premise is manifested in the fact that different assumptions in certain respects are made for individuals with lower and higher levels of habitual aggression inhibition. It is consequently important to obtain an empirical estimate of the strength of the individual's habitual aggression-inhibitory tendencies.

On the basis of the general assessment of the test and the testing situation, the assumption (I) was made that the strength of the individual's aggression-inhibitory responses (ProjI), by and large, is positively related to the strength of his habitual aggression-inhibitory tendencies (I_h). This assumption thus implies that boys with stronger habitual aggression-inhibitory tendencies under the given conditions are generally expected to give more aggression-inhibitory responses in the test than boys in whom such tendencies are weaker.

In the present study the stated assumption was used only to make a rough division of the subjects into two groups with different levels of habitual aggression inhibition, denoted the Low I_h-group and the High I_h-group. It should be observed, however, that the terms Low and High do not indicate extreme groups in a distribution of I_h values; the total variation in the sample was used.

For the group with low aggression-inhibitory tendencies, the

Low I_h-group, two assumptions (II and IV)—both quite natural—
were formulated. On the basis of the general assessment of the test
situation and the interpersonal situation respectively, it was assumed
that the individual's aggressive test responses (ProjA) as well as his
overt aggressive behavior (OA), by and large, are positively related
to the strength of his habitual aggressive tendencies (A_h). When
combined via the A_h variable, these assumptions give rise to
*Prediction I, for the Low I_h-group: the strength of the individual's aggressive
responses in the test (ProjA) is positively related to the strength of his overt
aggressive responses (OA)*. In other words, boys in this group who
give many aggressive responses in the test are generally expected to
start fights with peers more often than boys with fewer aggressive
test responses.

The stated assumptions and the ensuing prediction are graphically illustrated in Figure 4. Concerning these diagrams it should be
made clear that the use of straight lines in the assumptions is not a
necessary condition for the prediction. Any other fairly monotone
relationship would give the same prediction.

For the group with higher aggression-inhibitory tendencies, the
High I_h-group, a largely positive relationship between overt aggressive
behavior (OA) and the strength of habitual aggressive tendencies
(A_h) was also assumed (V). Because of the generally low aggression-
inhibitory activation value of the interpersonal situation, the boys'
habitual aggression-inhibitory tendencies will probably be activated
to only a slight extent. Consequently, it is natural to assume for this
group, too, that boys with stronger habitual aggressive tendencies,
by and large, will start fights more frequently than boys in whom such
tendencies are weaker.

In regard to the testing situation, however, a different assumption (III) was made. On the basis of clinical considerations (see,
e.g., Schafer, 1954) and some empirical studies (Berkowitz & Holmes,
1960; Clark, 1955; Saltz & Epstein, 1963; Siegel, 1956; see also
Becker, 1964, and Megargee, 1966) it was assumed that the strength
of the individual's aggressive responses (ProjA), by and large, is
negatively related to the strength of his habitual aggressive tendencies (A_h).

This last assumption may require some elaboration. The line of
reasoning leading up to it is roughly as follows. An individual with

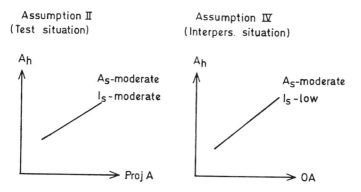

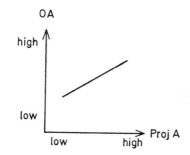

ProjA = strength of aggressive test responses

OA = strength of overt aggressive responses

A_h = strength of habitual aggressive tendencies

I_h = strength of habitual aggression-inhibitory tendencies

A_s = aggressive activation value of the situation

I_s = aggression-inhibitory activation value of the situation

FIG. 4. Assumptions II and IV and Prediction I concerning the relationship between strength of aggressive test responses (ProjA) and strength of overt aggressive responses (OA), for the group with low habitual aggression-inhibitory tendencies (Low I_h-group).

strong habitual aggression-inhibitory tendencies (I_h), who under the given conditions responds to an aggressive provocation with relatively few aggressive responses (ProjA), is assumed to have strong aggressive tendencies which, however, are heavily blocked by aggression-inhibitory tendencies. Frequent heavy blocking or conflicts of this type are in themselves frustrations and can be assumed to be associated with strong habitual aggressive tendencies (A_h). These tendencies may be readily activated but are generally not expressed, except in situations with low aggression-inhibitory activation values, that is, in relatively safe contexts. On the other hand, an individual in this category who responds to an aggressive provocation with stronger aggressive responses (ProjA) can be assumed to have less strong conflicts and anxiety or guilt feelings associated with his aggressive tendencies. The circumstance that such an individual is more able to express his aggressive tendencies in an aggression-activating situation probably means that his relation to and control over these tendencies is more adequate. It is then reasonable to assume that he also has lower habitual aggressive tendencies (A_h).

A combination of Assumptions III and V results in *Prediction II, for the High I_h-group: the strength of the individual's aggressive responses in the test (ProjA) is negatively related to the strength of his overt aggressive responses (OA)*. In other words, boys in this group who give relatively few aggressive responses in the test are generally expected to start fights with peers more often than boys with more aggressive test responses. Prediction II and the relevant assumptions are illustrated in Figure 5.

Empirical Analyses

Before briefly reporting on the empirical tests of the predictions, it should be pointed out that the relationship between projective test data and overt behavior is generally considered a very complex and thorny question. That this judgment is no exaggeration is also evident from the highly inconsistent results found in the literature (see, e.g., Buss, 1961; Kagan, 1960; Murstein, 1963; Olweus, 1969). The present attempt to relate aggressive responses in the projective

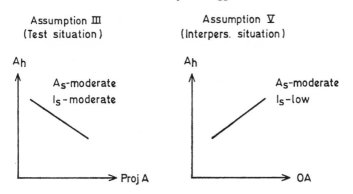

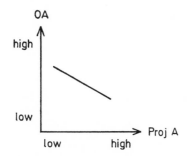

Proj A = strength of aggressive test responses

OA   = strength of overt aggressive responses

A_h = strength of habitual aggressive tendencies

I_h = strength of habitual aggression inhibitory tendencies

A_s = aggressive activation value of the situation

I_s = aggression inhibitory activation value of the situation

FIG. 5. Assumptions III and V and Prediction II concerning the relationship between strength of aggressive test responses (ProjA) and strength of overt aggressive responses (OA); for the group with high habitual aggression-inhibitory tendencies (High I_h-group).

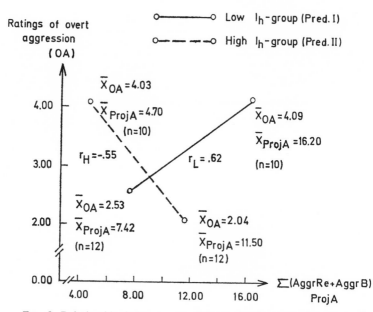

Fig. 6. Relationship between one of the projective aggressive composite variables, denoted $\sum$ (AggrRe + AggrB), and ratings of overt aggression, OA. The total sample ($N = 44$) has been divided at the median of the projective aggression-inhibitory variable ($\sum$ InhRe + DefIt) into a Low I_h-group (Prediction 0—0; r_L) and a High I_h-group (Prediction II 0---0; r_H). The mean in the variable $\sum$ (AggrRe + AggrB) for the total sample is $\bar{X} = 9.91$ and the standard deviation $s = 5.26$. For the variable OA the corresponding values are $\bar{X} = 3.09$ and $s = 1.58$. For details about variables and procedure in constructing the diagram, see Olweus, 1969, chap. 3 and chap. 9.

test to overt aggressive behavior should be seen against this background.

The two predictions—for boys with lower and higher levels of habitual aggression inhibition respectively—were tested by means of product-moment correlations. The coefficients for the Low I_h-group were positive and ranged from $+.55$ to $+.80$ for different combinations of projective subvariables (cf. p. 287; the overt aggressive variable was the same in all analyses). For the group with higher aggression inhibitions the correlations were negative and centered around $-.45$ or $-.50$. It is thus quite clear that the stated predictions receive strong empirical support from the statistical analyses. The correlations between the aggressive test variables and the ratings of overt aggressive behavior for the two I_h-groups lie in the predicted directions, positive and negative respectively, and in the majority of cases are high or very high. The groups are relatively small but the risk of the correlations obtained having arisen as a result of random variation must be judged extremely slight. The relationships are theoretically meaningful and appear very consistently in different combinations of variables. Furthermore, only slightly lower coefficients appeared when the relationships were calculated from either half of the projective test, that is, on the basis of two incomplete stories instead of four. This circumstance also attests to the validity of the results obtained.

The relationship between one of the projective aggressive composite variables (ProjA) and overt aggressive behavior (OA) is illustrated in Figure 6. Here the correlation is $+.62$ for the Low I_h-group (solid line) and $-.55$ for the High I_h-group (dotted line).

Two more things should be pointed out in this connection. The correlations reported are *not* multiple correlations with an optimal weighting of the component variables. Furthermore, a number of empirical as well as theoretical analyses concerning the influence of such variables as intelligence level, verbal productivity, verbal fluency, and school marks did *not* provide a basis for setting up alternative hypotheses that might wholly or partly explain the correlations obtained.

IMPLICATIONS

Several of the more important implications of this study will now be pointed out, a few of them in some detail. The stated predictions and their empirical verification rest on a complex network of theoretical, test-technical, and statistical premises or assumptions. As the empirical analyses have clearly verified these predictions, it can be said that the assumptions involved have also received general support. It is, of course, perfectly possible that some of the constituent assumptions are nevertheless only partly correct and that certain modifications might lead to still better results than those obtained in the present study. Further research data will provide clues to what may need modifying.

An essential feature of the previous analyses is the distinction between situational and habitual components or determinants. In the investigation reported, the habitual tendencies, which are assumed to be approximately constant for a given individual even if the stimulus conditions vary, form the basis for the predictions. At the same time, however, the situational components are decisive for whether and to what extent the tendencies will be activated. Both aspects are thus essential in the formation of the main assumptions (I to V). And the importance of taking both of them into account is demonstrated indirectly but very convincingly by considering the correlations between the aggressive test responses and the overt aggressive responses for the two I_h-groups combined. The high positive and negative correlations for the Low I_h- and High I_h-group respectively disappear and *the correlations for the total group are instead close to zero* (from $-.04$ to $+.16$ for different variables). Clear relationships within different subgroups can obviously cancel out if one attempts to relate aggressive responses in different situations without regard to theoretical considerations of the type suggested.

Turning to the research literature on aggression, it may be generally stated that the situational determinants of aggressive instigations—corresponding in part to the aggressive activation value of a situation in the present conceptual framework—have attracted a good deal of research interest (see also p. 274). The aggression-inhibitory components of a situation in general have received less attention, although there are a number of studies which have taken this aspect into careful account (for a review, see Wheeler, 1966). But systematic considerations of situational determinants in conjunction with habitual components, particularly as regards the aggression-inhibitory tendencies or some similar construct, have been largely missing in the area of aggression. To my knowledge, very few studies have been conducted on the basis of such or a similar view (e.g., Feshbach, Stiles, & Bitter, 1967; Feshbach & Singer, 1971). The results obtained, however, generally attest to the importance of taking all these aspects into simultaneous account. On the basis of the previous analyses it would also seem reasonable to conclude, more specifically, that a good deal of the obscure and contradictory results concerning the relationship between projective aggressive responses and overt aggressive behavior can be explained by the circumstance that the samples employed have included subgroups with quite different strengths of the habitual aggression-inhibitory tendencies.[2] Basically the same argument can be applied to a number of studies concerning the effects of frustrations, threats, model exposure, and similar conditions.

In my own empirical study the relationships between aggressive responses from the different sources of data (see p. 271) were found to be clear and distinct only when the boys' inhibitory tendencies were taken into account. The results obtained are, in fact, a good empirical illustration of what has been called Meehl's paradox[3] (Meehl, 1950; Horst, 1954). In order to explain his line of reasoning Meehl makes use of two hypothetical dichotomous test items, each of which correlates zero (phi-coefficients) with a criterion such as schizophrenic versus normal. Although each item, taken singly, has zero validity, joint consideration of the responses to both items—the pattern or configuration of responses—turns out to give perfect validity in the hypothetical example. As shown by Horst (1954), the configural scoring method proposed by Meehl is a special case of a nonlinear combination of item scores.

In my study the presence of this type of relationship can be demonstrated not only by means of phi-coefficients but also, without dichotomizing the "criterion" variable, by an analysis of variance technique. If the aggressive and aggression-inhibitory test variables, ProjA and ProjI respectively, are dichotomized close to the median, a fourfold table with roughly equal frequencies in the cells is obtained. The variable to be predicted, the "criterion" variable, is the amount of overt aggressive behavior, OA. This table then permits a study of the predictive power of two different factors (ProjA and ProjI), separately and in combination, as regards the boys' aggressive responses in the interpersonal situation. An analysis of variance revealed that both main effects, that is, the separate effects of each factor, were negligible, the F values being in fact close to zero. The combined effect of the two factors—the interaction effect—however, was very

2. Strictly speaking, this conclusion also presupposes that the aggression-inhibitory activation value of the projective test situation or the interpersonal situation in question has been great enough to activate the inhibitory tendencies in not too small a fraction of the sample.

3. I am indebted to Finn Tschudi, University of Oslo, for calling my attention to this fact.

prominent, with a highly significant F value of 16.26 for one combination of test variables studied ($df = 1$ and 40; projective variables: $\sum$ (AggrRe + AggrB) and ($\sum$ InhRe + DefIt); see Figure 6; ratings of overt aggression used as dependent variable in all analyses). When the index omega squared (Hays, 1963; Hoffman, Slovic, & Rorer, 1968) was used to estimate the proportion of the total variance in the boys' overt aggressive responses that can be predicted from each of the factors or their combination, the following results were obtained: practically 0% of the variance could be predicted on the basis of either factor taken singly, but their interaction accounted for roughly 26% of the variance. This finding is thus a clear indication of *configural or pattern effects* in the material.

The above relationships could also be expressed in a way more directly analogous to Meehl's example. It would then be stated that a combination of low projective aggression response and a low projective aggression-inhibitory response *or* a high aggressive response combined with high aggression-inhibitory response (Low-Low or High-High) would generally predict low overt aggressive behavior in the boys. On the other hand, a pattern of low aggressive test response and high aggression-inhibitory response *or* a high aggressive response and a low aggression-inhibitory response (Low-High or High-Low) would, by and large, be associated with strong overt aggressive responses. Although the predictive power of each of the factors taken singly, thus, would be close to zero, their configural validity would be quite substantial (for the variables given on p. 297 the phi-coefficient for the relationship between the configural score and the overt aggression variable, dichotomously scored, was found to be .38). By the way, these relationships can be detected and intuitively understood by inspection of Figure 6.

The reported results may, of course, also be taken to indicate that the general linear model is not very adequate in the present instance. As a further illustration it can be mentioned that a linear additive combination of five different aggressive and aggression-inhibitory test variables in a multiple regression equation for the sample as a whole predicted the boys' overt aggressive behavior very poorly ($Y = b_1 X_1 + b_2 X_2 \cdots + b_5 X_5 + c$, where Y is the overt aggressive responses). Although this method tends to capitalize heavily on chance variation, the multiple correlation (R) amounted to only .34, accounting for roughly 12% of the variance in Y. The F value for the multiple R did not even approach significance ($F = 1.02$, $df = 5$ and 38). Furthermore it may be pointed out that a linear factor analysis conducted on a selection of the projective test variables did not produce a very meaningful or easily interpretable factor structure. The conclusion to be drawn from the preceding discussions and analyses would seem to be that such powerful linear methods as multiple regression and factor analysis in many cases may be of little value, when not guided by theoretical considerations. Strictly speaking, this conclusion is rather self-evident and only a current tendency toward overconfidence in these and similar linear methods makes it desirable to point out their limitations under particular conditions.

From a slightly different methodological viewpoint the results of the present study may be said to indicate a need of considering the influence of *moderator variables* (Guion, 1967; Saunders, 1956). Moderator effects exist when the relationship between two variables is dependent on the level of some other variable. In the study reported very marked such effects were present: the relationship between projective aggressive responses (ProjA) and overt aggressive behavior (OA) was in fact reversed for the two levels of aggression-inhibitory tendencies (see Figure 6). Due consideration to such theoretically meaningful moderator variables is, in my opinion, a very important prerequisite of future research in the field of aggression. As implied in previous statements (p. 296 and Olweus, 1969), however, there are definitely no theoretical grounds for expecting moderator effects in all types of situations. An example of lack of moderator effects will be given in a later section.

Part of the present study may also be used to illustrate another point of theoretical and practical interest. It concerns the question of the relationship between an observable variable (Levels I and II) and the underlying theoretical variables (Levels III and IV), as touched upon in the introductory section and later (p. 272). This point will be elucidated chiefly by reference to Figure 6. (In the detailed research report [Olweus, 1969, chap. 10], however, the conclusions were based on and received strong support from several statistical analyses.) On close inspection of the left part of the diagram in Figure 6, it will be seen that all boys who have a low score on the projective test variable (ProjA) are obviously not equivalent as regards overt aggressive responses (OA). As a matter of fact, roughly half of the boys with a low aggressive test score (e.g., below a score of 9) were low in overt aggressive behavior, while the other half scored much higher on this behavior dimension. As predicted—and that is also evident in the figure—the boys with high inhibitory tendencies, as assessed from the projective test, were those who displayed most aggressive behavior with peers. This result led to the conclusion that some boys earned a low aggressive test score because of weak habitual aggressive tendencies, while others with a low score in all probability had strong habitual aggressive tendencies which were, however, inhibited in the testing situation. This conclusion is, in fact, a good illustration of the point that a particular value or position in an aggressive variable is not necessarily an indication of one and the same strength in the underlying aggressive tendencies. In the present case it may even be concluded that boys with approximately the same low score in the aggressive test variable were highly different with regard to motivational dynamics and also from a predictive point of view.

Another way of formulating the implications of these results is to point out that a relative absence of aggressive responses in the test or other similar situations does not necessarily indicate weak aggressive tendencies or impulses. In the case of the *overtly aggressive subgroup with high inhibitory tendencies and low aggressive test scores* it is natural to think of psychoanalytic conceptions of defense mechanisms, particularly of a reaction formation type: the strong activated aggressive tendencies are blocked by still stronger anxiety or guilt reactions, resulting in nonaggressive responses in a number of situations. The previous conclusion may also be substantiated by some data from Megargee (1966) in a study of highly assaultive juvenile delinquents (mean age 15 years). In this study it was possible to differentiate between two types of extreme offenders, an undercontrolled type and a chronically overcontrolled type. The latter category, which may be regarded as a more pronounced variant of the personality type under consideration in my study, was found to manifest a number of reactions and behaviors, in test responses as well as detention behavior, indicative of strong self-control and inhibitions. At the same time, however, they had committed extremely violent acts, often at apparently slight provocations, suggesting the presence of very strong underlying aggressive tendencies (my interpretation). The relevant subgroup in my study seems to have the same motivational dynamics as Megargee's overcontrolled type but it is obviously less extreme: the boys could (so far) express a good deal of their strong aggressive tendencies in certain relatively safe contexts, as with peers. In conclusion, then, Megargee's data (although not his theoretical analysis) seem to be generally consistent with the formulations presented here. Incidentally, although no relevant data are available, Becker's (1964) analysis of parent-child relations clearly suggests that boys in the present subgroup as well as offenders of the overcontrolled type have been reared by parents who combine hostility toward the child with restrictiveness (see p. 279). It may also be pointed out that Megargee's undercontrolled type, as a rule with a long record of previous assaultive behavior, very likely would be represented by an extrapolation along the line connecting the means of the two subgroups with low inhibitions in Figure 6.

Just one more implication should be spelled out. It was previously stressed that a particular value in an observable variable is not necessarily a safe indicator of one and the same strength in a particular theoretical variable. A somewhat similar line of reasoning can be pursued with regard to the boys' overt aggressive behavior in the present investigation. As is evident from Figure 6, boys characterized, for instance, by frequent aggressive interactions with peers, that is, boys who manifest relative homogeneity in overt aggressive behavior, are quite heterogeneous with respect to aggressive and aggression-inhibitory responses in the projective test. In view of this circumstance, it is not surprising that many studies using extremeness of aggressive and nonaggressive behavior as a basis for forming groups have produced confusing results. Of course, this argument is not limited to the area of aggression; it may also apply to studies of groups which are extreme in such variables as popularity, self-esteem, and achievement.[4] Some implications of the

4. Incidentally, the risks associated with such a research approach may be counteracted for instance by taking a whole pattern of variables into account in the selection procedure or by examining if the extreme groups can be divided into several fairly homogeneous subgroups.

present study dealing more specifically with projective testing and research are pointed out in the original research report (Olweus, 1969, chap. 13).

After these rather involved analyses in terms of the conceptual scheme presented, you might legitimately ask the question: Is it really necessary to use such a complicated theoretical framework? Cannot the relationships reported and other data be explained in a simpler and more parsimonious way? It is definitely my conviction that all central aspects of the conceptual scheme need to be taken somehow into consideration—at least if more precise predictions and explanations are aimed at. As previously mentioned, there is a paucity of empirical research taking all these components into account, and accordingly, it is impossible for the time being to make a more conclusive assessment of the necessity and utility of such a conceptual scheme. Indeed, the majority of studies in the area of aggression have only dealt with comparisons of whole groups, and differentiation into subgroups, for instance according to habitual inhibitory level, has rarely occurred. And as is well known, a circumscribed pattern of group means can often be explained in several divergent ways, permitting no adequate comparison of alternative theoretical formulations. But I am convinced that, as more investigations become directed toward the study of relatively precise relationships, for example, those involving individual differences or comparisons of subgroups, the need for complex conceptual schemes will become more salient. According to my expectation, the limitations of simple conceptualizations including only situational determinants, for instance, will then become quite obvious. By the way, the utility of fairly complex conceptualizations is in fact also suggested by common-sense analysis of everyday experiences and situations, as in the example previously discussed (p. 267). So, in my view, there is not much hope that future conceptual schemes of aggression will be any simpler than the present one.

Perhaps it should also be pointed out that certain aspects of the relationships between the theoretical variables have not yet been specified in detail in the conceptual framework. It has seemed suitable to leave some of these questions relatively open while waiting for additional data. In particular, much more research is required involving systematic variation of the situational values (A_s, I_s) for individuals with different patterns of habitual tendencies (A_h, I_h). Up to now, my own research efforts have of necessity been largely focused on the development of methods for estimating the individual's habitual aggressive and aggression-inhibitory tendencies. As previously demonstrated, this does not imply a neglect of the situational activation values; indeed, these components were shown to play a decisive part in the formulation of the assumptions. But it may also be of interest to subject the situational aspects to systematic variation in the form of experimental manipulations. Several such studies are now being projected.

AN AGGRESSION INVENTORY FOR BOYS

Instead of giving an outline of these projects I shall direct my attention to the development of a multifaceted aggression inventory for boys which has proved to be quite successful. A detailed research report is now in the course of preparation (Olweus, 1973) and here I will confine myself to a few relevant aspects.

The projective technique described in the previous study was found to have substantial predictive power as well as theoretical relevance. Nevertheless, there are certain disadvantages associated with this type of projective instrument, particularly regarding the scoring of the response material, which may make their use less attractive in large-scale investigations. No doubt the scoring system can be made sufficiently precise but it takes considerable time to train a scorer to thorough mastery of the scoring system. In addition, the scoring of individual protocols is rather time-consuming even for an experienced scorer. In view of such practical and time-economic considerations I was of the opinion that a self-report technique, which is easily administered and scored, should be tried out as one of the instruments in a large-scale project on aggression among 12- to 14-year-old boys.

In this context it was considered of theoretical as well as methodological interest to study the relationship between inventory data and overt aggressive behavior dimensions of the type employed in the previous investigation. As a background for this research it may be mentioned that severe criticism has been leveled against inventories in general as instruments for personality measurement (e.g., Becker,

1960; Mischel, 1968). It has been repeatedly pointed out that very few investigations show clear, substantial relationships between self-report data and other independent data, for instance, behavior ratings or actual behavior. A statement by Mischel (1968, p. 80) may be quoted as typical: "Results of this kind, and the previously reviewed data, typify the usual associations obtained between attitude and behavior measurements: some correspondence, but not very much, and never enough to warrant the assumption that verbal statements about behavior mirror the relevant behavior."

In view of this and similar opinions the present research may be regarded as a general inquiry into the adequacy and validity of young boys' self-report data in a particular personality sphere. From this viewpoint a central research question may be formulated as follows: "Are boys of this age able and willing to describe their behaviors and reactions accurately in the area of aggression?" Seen from a somewhat different angle, the present research is a direct outgrowth of the author's conceptual scheme and deals primarily with certain theoretical and methodological issues in the field of aggression. In particular, the inventory was constructed with the aim of obtaining estimates of the subjects' habitual aggressive and aggression-inhibitory tendencies.

When constructing the present inventory it was considered desirable to get at least a few different aspects or facets of aggressive behaviors and impulses represented; an instrument of the global or omnibus type should be avoided. These facets represented a certain variation in the situations to be responded to as well as a limited number of response modes, such as physically aggressive responses, verbally aggressive responses, and aggressive thoughts and feelings. No attempt was made, however, to accomplish a complete cross-classification of situations and response modes, as certain combinations appeared rather artificial. Furthermore, a scale for the measurement of aggressive inhibitions—mostly items concerning reactions presumably motivated by anxiety and/or guilt—was constructed. Finally, it seemed desirable to include a scale of items referring to the subject's tendency to "say positive things about himself," potentially a social desirability or defensiveness scale. The final inventory comprised a total of 62 items, 6 of which were fillers. Each item consisted of a statement or a question and five or seven response alternatives, representing different frequencies of occurrence or different degrees of applicability.

Two separate but similar samples, comprising 98 (Sample A) and 86 (Sample B) boys respectively, both with a median age of 13 years, were used in the present study. The majority of boys came from middle-class or lower-middle-class families. For the boys in Sample A a great number of data were collected, including peer ratings, school grades, and teacher data on adjustment. For Sample B, however, only inventory data and a selection of peer ratings were gathered.

Factor Analysis of Inventory

In order to examine whether the inventory items could be grouped into a limited number of psychologically meaningful, more comprehensive categories, or "dimensions," factor analyses of the inventory responses were performed on both Sample A and Sample B. The factor analytic program employed (Jøreskog, 1963) performs an approximate image factor analysis (see, e.g., Kaiser, 1963), using squared multiple correlations of each variable with the remaining ones as (lower bound) estimates of communality. The factors obtained were orthogonally rotated, according to the varimax criterion (Kaiser, 1958).

The factor analysis on Sample B was conducted with the primary aim of examining the factorial invariance (see Armstrong & Soelberg, 1968; Harman, 1967), that is, the extent to which the factor structure obtained in Sample A could be identified in another, similar sample. By and large, the data analyses indicated a fairly similar factorial structure in Samples A and B, possibly with one exception (Factor III, see below), and five factors were subjected to psychological interpretation. In view of the results obtained it was considered defensible and desirable to construct composite variables, by means of unweighted summation of items with a factor loading above a certain level (as a rule ≥ .35). These composite variables—simple, linear combinations of five or more items—may thus be regarded as relatively comprehensive "dimensions," covering a certain domain of responses, self-reports of behaviors, or inner reactions.

The five main factors will now be briefly described and exemplified. The items with high loadings in Factor I all concern verbal aggressive behavior directed to an adult who criticizes or is unfair to the boy. The composite variable will be referred to as *Verbally aggressive responses.* Examples: "When an adult is unfair to me, I get angry and protest." "When a teacher criticizes me, I tend to answer back and protest."

The items belonging to Factor II have reference to physically aggressive responses (fighting) directed against peers. The corresponding composite variable is called *Physically aggressive responses.* Examples: "When a boy teases me, I try to give him a good beating." "I fight with other boys at school."

The items grouped under Factor III all concern inner aggressive reactions or impulses. Two of them seem to be related to revengeful feelings and the remaining ones pertain to the intensity of a subject's temperament. The composite variable is designated *Aggressive impulses.* It should be pointed out, however, that some of the items included in this composite variable obtained low factor loadings in Sample B. Examples of this composite variable are: "I am often so upset that I feel like smashing things." "I think of taking somebody down who is stuck-up and cocky."

In the main, Factor IV comprises items indicative of intropunitive reactions in response to conflicts with an adult and items involving expressions of a bad conscience. The corresponding composite variable is called *Aggression-inhibitory responses.* Examples: "When an adult is annoyed with me, I mostly feel that I am at fault." "I say and do things that I really regret afterwards."

The items belonging to Factor V concern somewhat disagreeable but commonly experienced happenings or feelings, for example, being unhappy or scared, or receiving criticism. Some of these items chiefly have reference to peer relations, others, to relations with adults. Essentially, the factor was interpreted to indicate a subject's tendency to say positive things about himself. The composite variable, consisting of nine items, is designated *Positive self-reports.* Examples: "The boys at school never say nasty things about me." "I never get scolded by adults."

The product-moment correlations between the five main composite variables are presented in Table 1, the values for Sample B being given within parentheses. By and large, the results were quite

TABLE 1
Intercorrelations of Composite Variables

II	III	IV	V	Composite Variable
.26 (.30)	.31 (.36)	−.30 (−.08)	−.04 (−.03)	I Verb. aggr.
	.44 (.28)	−.33 (.01)	.16 (−.04)	II Phys. aggr.
		−.14 (.23)	−.04 (−.11)	III Aggr. imp.
			−.25 (−.35)	IV Aggr.-inh.
				V Pos. self-rep.

NOTE: The values in parentheses refer to Sample B. For Sample A (N = 98) r values (product-moment correlations) of .20 and .26 are significant at the .05 and .01 levels respectively (two-tailed test). For Sample B (N = 86) the corresponding values are .21 and .27.

similar in the two samples, possibly with the exception of Composite Variable IV, Aggression-inhibitory responses, which correlated slightly negatively with the three aggressive scales in Sample A but approximately zero in Sample B. The three aggressive composite variables, Verbally aggressive responses, Physically aggressive responses, and Aggressive impulses, showed positive intercorrelations, with a mean value around .35. These three scales, representing different facets or aspects of aggressive responses, thus formed a cluster. And it is worth underlining that the aggression-inhibitory scale was found to be fairly independent of the aggressive scales. It is furthermore of interest to note that the composite variable Positive self-reports—closely related to conventional social desirability scales—did not correlate significantly with any of the aggressive composite variables. The only significant correlation for this variable was obtained with Aggression-inhibitory responses (−.25 and −.35 in Samples A and B respectively). These generally low correlations and the results from the factor analyses converge to the conclusion that the data contained in the main aggressive and aggression-inhibitory scales of the inventory cannot be thought of as merely or chiefly reflecting some sort of response set or a social desirability dimension.

Peer Ratings

Up to now, it is chiefly the internal structure of the inventory that has been examined. In sum, the results obtained so far may be considered meaningful and promising. It should be possible, however, to demonstrate reasonable relationships with other, independent classes of data, such as peer ratings of actual behavior, before confidence can be attached to an inventory of the present type. An examination of such relationships will presently follow but first some data about the peer ratings will be given. It should be stressed, however, that these data are of interest in their own right, not only as "criteria" for the inventory.

In the present investigation four 7-point rating scales were used, two of them involving overt aggressive responses. One of these scales concerned the boy's tendency to start fights with peers, and it was, in fact, identical to the overt aggressive variable (OA) in the previous investigation. Here the term *Start fights* is employed. The other one was focused on the boy's tendency to give verbally aggressive responses, that is, to answer back and protest against a mildly criticizing teacher. This was called *Verbal protest*. A third rating variable concerned the extent to which a boy tended to be the target for other boys' physical attacks. This variable was designated *Aggression target*. The fourth variable was called *Popularity with peers* and needs no particular explanation.

In general, three or four boys selected at random from each class were used as raters. In Sample B only the two variables concerning physically aggressive and verbally aggressive responses were rated. The average of the judges' ratings constituted a boy's value for the variable in question.

The degree of homogeneity, expressed as the average intercorrelation between pairs of raters, as well as the total reliability, that is, the reliability of the mean ratings, was found to be quite satisfactory for the two variables concerning overt aggressive responses. As expected, the corresponding measures were somewhat lower for the popularity variable and, especially in a few classes, for the variable Aggression target. (For a discussion of different aspects of the reliability of ratings, see Olweus, 1969, chap. 6.) The intercorrelations of the four rating variables are summarized in Table 2.

The two variables concerning overt aggressive behavior obviously go together, as manifested in a correlation of .61 in Sample A and .65 in Sample B. These data may be interpreted to suggest a consider-

TABLE 2

INTERCORRELATIONS OF RATING VARIABLES
(Sample A; $N = 98$)

Verbal protest	Aggression target	Popularity	Variable
.61	.13	.08	Start fights
	.12	.17	Verbal protest
		−.43	Aggression target

NOTE: In Sample B ($N = 86$) only two rating variables, Start fights and Verbal protest, were used. Their intercorrelation was .65. r values (product-moment correlations) of .20 and .26 are significant at the .05 and .01 levels respectively for $N = 98$ (two-tailed test).

able degree of consistency of overt aggressive behavior, for two different response modes, physical and verbal, and two kinds of situations, involving interactions with peers as well as with teachers. Of course, this correlation may to some extent be due to rater biases of different kinds, but the negligible correlations between these two variables and the Popularity variable clearly indicate that the association cannot in any case be explained by reference to some simple overall evaluative dimension. This desirable fact, in combination with the previously mentioned reliability data, strongly suggest that the ratings of overt aggressive behavior to a large extent reflected relevant behavior in the boys assessed. This conclusion is further supported by the circumstance that the correlation between these two variables and the variable Aggression target only amounted to .13 and .12 respectively. The raters obviously could make a clear distinction regarding the direction of aggressive responses: there was no association between the extent of being the target of other boys' attacks and a boy's own aggressive behavior. Finally it may be noted that there was a rather strong negative correlation between the Popularity variable and the variable Aggression target. This relationship clearly seems to make sense: the disliked boys tend to become the target of other boys' attacks.

Some data concerning the *stability of ratings* on two scales, Start fights and Verbal protest, may also be reported. In another investigation (unpublished), using a comparable sample of four sixth-grade classes ($n_1 = 17$; $n_2 = 16$; $n_3 = 17$; $n_4 = 14$), ratings by two samples of raters from each class were obtained on two different occasions, separated by an interval of 6 months. On the first occasion three boys from each class served as raters; on the second one the ratings were obtained from two different boys selected at random from the remaining boys in each class. The mean ratings were correlated (product-moment correlations) separately for each class. For three of the classes, the correlations were surprisingly high, the mean coefficient being .80 for Start fights and .81 for Verbal protest, thus indicating a very high degree of stability of the behavior assessed. It should be noted that the high correlations cannot be explained by reference to any memory effects, as no rater occurred on more than one occasion. In the fourth class much lower correlations were obtained, .34 and .21 respectively. Closer inspection of the data revealed a somewhat restricted range of scores for this class, making the rating task more difficult for the raters. Judged on an overall basis, however, the data suggest that the behavior in question may be quite stable in samples of this age and composition. These results in combination with the previously mentioned reliability data also indicate that raters may be excellent "instruments" for recording behavior, at least under certain conditions and in certain domains.

The rating data may also be examined from a theoretical perspective. In the previously reported study the boys' overt aggressive behavior (OA) was, by and large, assumed to be positively related to their habitual aggressive tendencies (A_h). Because of the generally low aggression-inhibitory activation value (I_s) of the peer situation it was thus assumed that boys with stronger habitual aggressive tendencies would start fights with peers more frequently than boys in whom such tendencies were weaker (pp. 288–290). This assumption was made for boys with lower as well as with higher habitual aggression-inhibitory tendencies (I_h). It is quite natural to make the same assumption for the variable Start fights in the present investigation. The second rating variable concerned the boys' tendency to give verbally aggressive responses against a mildly criticizing teacher (Verbal protest). It might be supposed that the aggression-inhibitory activation value (I_s) for this type of interpersonal situation should be generally higher than for the peer situation. This, in turn, could result in a somewhat obscure relationship between the amount of overt aggressive responses (Verbal protest) and the boys' habitual aggressive tendencies (A_h), in particular for boys with higher habitual aggressive inhibitions (I_h). In the present study, however, the correlation between the variable Verbal protest and the variable Start fights was found to be quite substantial, close to .60 in both samples, for boys with higher as well as with lower aggression inhibitions, according to the inventory scale. Correlations of this size have, by the way, also been obtained in two additional samples of the same age. These results thus suggest that the majority of boys experienced this type of interaction with a teacher as a basically safe situation: in general, they have been accustomed to the teacher for a long time and they may be assumed to have a good knowledge of what the teacher is willing to tolerate in the form of verbal protests and opposition; besides, the general level of tolerance in regard to such behavior may be considered fairly high among Swedish teachers. In sum, it seems reasonable to conclude that situations involving verbal protest against a mildly criticizing teacher were appraised to have rather low aggression-inhibitory activation values (I_s) by the majority of boys in the samples investigated. Accordingly, it is natural to assume a largely positive relationship between the boys' verbally aggressive behavior and their habitual aggressive tendencies (A_h). Positive correlations between the two dimensions of overt aggressive behavior may then also be expected.

These two variables of overt aggressive behavior, representing two different combinations of situations and response modes, thus have proved to be substantially associated, suggesting a certain degree of psychological equivalence of these two combinations in terms of the present conceptual framework. This consistency as regards overt aggressive behavior, however, should perhaps not be overemphasized. Each variable very likely contains specific components not covered by the other one.

Relationships between Inventory Scales and Peer Ratings

The two sets of data, the composite variables from the inventory and the peer ratings of overt aggressive behavior, may now be related to each other. The main interest, of course, is centered on the relationships between the peer ratings and the aggressive composite variables, taken separately and in combination. In addition, a more generalized aggressive behavior dimension was formed by summing the two peer rating variables. The data for the remaining two inventory scales are also given in Table 3, which summarizes the main findings.

From Table 3 it is evident that the composite variable *Verbally aggressive responses* predicted peer ratings of Verbal protest quite well, the mean correlation for the two samples being slightly below .50. Correlations of approximately the same magnitude were obtained between *Physically aggressive responses* and its natural counterpart, Start fights. The latter rating variable could to some extent also be predicted from the inventory variable *Verbally aggressive responses* and the same was true for the Verbal protest in relation to *Physically aggressive responses*. Both of these composite variables, however,

TABLE 3

Correlations between Selected Inventory Variables and
Ratings of Overt Aggressive Behavior

	Ratings of Overt Aggressive Behavior					
Inventory Variable	Start fights		Verbal protest		Start fights (z) + Verbal protest (z)[a]	
	A	B	A	B	A	B
I Verb. aggr.	.25	.18	.51	.46	.43	.36
II Phys. aggr.	.48	.41	.39	.26	.49	.37
Verb. aggr. (z) + Phys. aggr. (z)[a]	.46	.37	.57	.45	.58	.42
III Aggr. imp.	.16	.02	.10	.08	.15	.06
Verb. aggr. (z) + Phys. aggr. (z) + Aggr. imp. (z)[a]	.40	.28	.45	.36	.48	.36
IV Aggr.-inh.	−.05	−.12	−.14	−.08	—	—
V Pos. self-rep.	.06	−.05	−.07	.14	—	—

Note: The correlations reported are product-moment correlations. For $N = 98$ (Sample A) r values of .20 and .26 are significant at the .05 and .01 levels respectively (two-tailed test). For $N = 86$ (Sample B) the corresponding values are .21 and .27.

[a] A notation of this type signifies that the individual variables were given equal weight in the composite variable, that is, they were z transformed before summation. It should be mentioned, however, that in most cases essentially the same results were obtained when the individual variables were entered into the composite variables without z transformation.

obtained clearly higher correlations with their "own" behavior dimensions, thereby giving evidence of discriminant validity (Campbell & Fiske, 1959). Still higher correlations were found when these two composite variables were linearly combined to predict the general aggressive behavior dimension, Start fights (z) + Verbal protest (z). The average of the correlations for Sample A and Sample B amounted to .58, the highest value being .58.

The composite variable *Aggressive impulses* manifested very low correlations with the behavior variables and could not, accordingly, add to the "validity" in linear combinations with the other two aggressive composite variables. The conceptual and psychometric status of this scale must be considered somewhat unclear for the time being.

The two remaining inventory scales both correlated insignificantly with the rating variables. It is of particular interest to note the negligible correlation between the *Aggression-inhibitory response* variable and overt aggressive behavior, a finding that parallels the results obtained in the previously reported study employing the projective technique. This implies that it is quite possible for a boy to have a high habitual aggression-inhibitory level and yet to display a good deal of overt aggressive behavior, a fact that was demonstrated in the previous study by reference to Figure 6.

As the boys gave responses about typical behaviors and reactions in the inventory and, moreover, took the inventory in their usual classrooms in an atmosphere of relaxation, there was probably only slight activation of the boys' habitual aggression-inhibitory tendencies in this situation. Consequently, it is natural to assume fairly similar relationships between the aggressive inventory variables and the overt aggressive dimensions for boys with lower as well as with higher aggression-inhibitory levels (I_h; see also Olweus, 1969, p. 163). Preliminary analyses have also given no evidence of marked moderator effects. The correlations for boys with higher and with lower levels of inhibitory tendencies, according to the scale of Aggression-inhibitory responses, seem to be fairly similar: they are positive and of approximately the same magnitude as the correlations for the total sample. As an example it may be mentioned that the correlation between Physically aggressive responses and Start fights was found to be .55 for boys with lower levels of aggression inhibitions from Sample A ($n_L = 51$) and .45 for boys with higher inhibitory levels ($n_H = 47$). The correlation for the whole sample ($N = 98$) was .48, as seen from Table 3.

Perhaps it needs emphasizing that the previous results should not be taken to signify that boys with lower and higher levels of aggression inhibition are similar regarding modes of functioning or internal dynamics. The reported data only indicate that similar patterns of results may be expected for such groups if certain constellations of situational activation values are present. For other constellations quite divergent patterns may be obtained, which was also empirically demonstrated in the previous study.

The Aggression-inhibitory response scale has no natural counterpart in overt behavior. The construct validity of this scale, however, has been highlighted by data from other sources such as adjective check-list ratings, teacher data on adjustment, and school grades.

It may also be noted that the pattern of correlations in Table 3 was very similar for the two samples, A and B, although the coefficients for Sample B were slightly lower. This consistency lends additional support to the results from the factor analyses.

Summing up a few central points, it may be generally asserted that the main inventory scales seem to be theoretically meaningful and also adequate from a psychometric point of view. Two of the aggressive scales, Verbally aggressive responses and Physically aggressive responses, were shown to have substantial predictive power with regard to ratings of overt aggressive behavior. A linear combination of these two scales could predict the general overt aggressive behavior dimension still better, the mean correlation for two samples being .53. This implies that the present inventory scales—without utilization of multiple correlation techniques—could predict overt aggressive behavior as accurately as school grades or college marks can usually be predicted on the basis of intelligence tests. These results thus compare favorably with the "validity" coefficients typically reported in the field of psychology in general and in the personality sphere in particular. On the basis of the results obtained it may be generally maintained that boys of this age are both able and willing to describe their behaviors and reactions with considerable accuracy in the area of aggression, at least under the given conditions.

OVERVIEW AND CONCLUSIONS

Some more general implications of the empirical research and the analyses presented will now be discussed, after a brief summary of some central findings. In the first empirical study, using the projective technique, markedly different relationships were obtained between the projective aggressive responses and overt aggressive behavior for boys with different levels of aggression inhibitions. For boys with low inhibitory levels the correlations were clearly positive, while they were markedly negative for boys with higher inhibitions. In the inventory studies, on the other hand, clear positive relationships were found between two aggressive scales and overt aggressive behavior for boys with low as well as with high inhibitory levels. As regards boys with low inhibitions the correlations with overt aggressive behavior were thus positive and high both for the projective aggressive responses and the inventory scales. For boys with higher inhibitions the correlations were of approximately the same magnitude but in reverse directions, that is, negative for the projective data and positive for the inventory scales. From an empirical point of view these two studies may be said to have demonstrated that under certain conditions the boys' overt aggressive behavior can be predicted with considerable accuracy from the projective test material as well as from the inventory data.

Prediction, however, is not enough and cannot substitute for understanding and explanation in the area of aggression. Although the relationships may seem fairly intricate when the results from these two and other studies are simultaneously considered, they are not hopelessly complicated. In attempting to clarify the nature of these relationships it may be generally helpful to conceptualize the data in terms of stimulus situations, response modes, and subjects, as in Endler and Hunt (1968), for instance. However, still greater advantages seem to be gained in going one step further and using a theoretical formulation by which the different constellations of stimulus situations, response modes, and personality dispositions can be interpreted and understood in terms of theoretical variables. In such an approach a great number of aspects can be tied together and unified by a small number of basic concepts.

In the present paper a conceptual scheme for the determination of aggressive responses has been presented, involving situational and habitual components with regard to both aggressive and aggression-inhibitory tendencies. Furthermore, the individual's cognitive appraisal of the situation is included, although this aspect has not yet been subjected to systematic investigation. In my view, the present analyses and empirical results as well as data from a number of other studies strongly suggest the importance of taking all these aspects into simultaneous consideration.

As previously emphasized, the present conceptualization implies a critique of theoretical formulations chiefly involving situational determinants. Similarly, it stands in opposition to trait theories both by its relative stress on situational components and by the fact that an aggressive response is conceived to depend on the interaction of at least *two* central tendencies, not only one trait of aggressiveness. Some points of view in this connection will be briefly discussed.

As is well known, trait conceptions consider the individual to be made up of certain stable and broad predispositions that presumably lead to similar reactions and behaviors over a wide range of situations. Accordingly, generally positive correlations between aggressive responses in different situations may be expected on the basis of a trait formulation of aggressiveness. When turning to the research literature for evidence, a good deal of support for such a position may be found. For instance, only one factor accounted for nearly all the variance in a peer-rating measure concerning a variety of different aspects of aggression in several studies of third-grade children (Walder, Abelson, Eron, Banta, & Laulicht, 1961). Similarly, Endler and Hunt (1968) found that overall individual differences in the "trait of hostility" contributed as much as 20% of the total variance (for men), as inferred from the responses to an inventory, a contribution that was much greater than in the case of anxiousness. Moreover, the high correlations between the two peer-rating variables in the present investigations as well as the substantial stability of these ratings over time are indications of considerable consistency, in some respects at least. On the other hand, I will immediately call attention to the previously reported finding of a *negative* correlation between aggressive responses in the projective test and overt aggressive behavior for boys with higher inhibitory levels. Also, in the Endler and Hunt (1968) data, roughly 25% of the total variance was accounted for by the three first-order inter-actions, signifying that the subjects reacted (or reported to react) differently in different situations or with different modes of response. Furthermore, some data about highly controlled personality types, in more or less pronounced form (see the discussion on pp. 300–301) cannot be easily reconciled with a trait-theoretical formulation.

The totality of these results may give a confusing impression. In my view, however, some of these inconsistencies are only illusory and may be resolved, for instance, by application of the present conceptual scheme. Among other things, this implies making a distinction between consistency on a theoretical plane and con-sistency in the form of positive correlations between aggressive *responses*. As evident from the previous analyses there may be grounds for *not* expecting positive correlations between aggressive responses in different situations, in particular for individuals with high aggression-inhibitory levels. Moreover, such "lack of con-sistency" may be regarded as quite consistent from another point of view, namely, that the results are in good agreement with theoretical expectation. Accordingly, it may be generally considered of greater importance to search for "theoretical consistency" than for con-sistency from a trait-theoretical point of view. And, of course, if a reasonably comprehensive and specified conceptual framework is formulated, it will also be possible—by consideration of the con-stellation of theoretical components—to predict the type of em-pirical relationships to be expected. Such an approach may help to remove some of the conceptual dilemmas and empirical incon-sistencies that presently plague the field of aggression.

SUMMARY

A general conceptual scheme for a condensed representation of psychological theories and their elements is introduced, exemplified, and discussed, with particular emphasis on the area of aggression. Some definitional problems in connection with the term aggression or aggressive response are then pointed out and the author's own working definition is stated. The issue of short-term causation of aggression or aggressive instigations is examined and briefly reviewed, as is the question of the development of more stable aggressive reaction tendencies in an individual.

The previous considerations lead up to the presentation of the author's own conceptual scheme for the determination of aggressive responses, a scheme that includes situational and habitual components, both as regards aggressive and aggression-inhibitory tendencies. An empirical application of the conceptual framework—concerning the relationship between aggressive responses in a newly constructed projective test and ratings of overt aggressive behavior in 12- to 14-year-old boys—is described. Two theoretically derived predictions were tested by means of correlational analyses and received strong support: the coefficients were about +.60 for boys with lower aggression inhibitions and about −.50 for boys with a higher inhibitory level. Some of the more important implications are pointed out. The results obtained can be viewed as an example of configural or pattern effects, which is also demonstrated by means of an analysis of variance technique (omega squared). Moreover, the findings or parts of them are discussed in terms of moderator effects and in relation to conceptualizations of overcontrolled and undercontrolled personality types.

The development of the author's multifaceted aggression inventory for boys is then outlined. The results of two factor analyses on two separate samples are briefly reported; five factors were subjected to psychological interpretation. As expected, two of the inventory scales correlated quite substantially with independent data on overt aggressive behavior in both samples.

The paper is concluded with an overview and some general implications, particularly in regard to the individual-versus-situation controversy in psychology.

REFERENCES

Amsel, A. The role of frustrative nonreward in noncontinuous reward situations. *Psychological Bulletin*, 1958, **55**, 102–119.

Amsel, A. Frustrative nonreward in partial reinforcement and discrimination learning: Some recent history and a theoretical extension. *Psychological Review*, 1962, **69**, 306–328.

Armstrong, I. C., & Soelberg, P. On the interpretation of factor analysis. *Psychological Bulletin*, 1968, **70**, 361–364.

Bandura, A. *Principles of behavior modification.* New York: Holt, Rinehart and Winston, 1969.

Bandura, A., & Walters, R. H. *Social learning and personality development.* New York: Holt, Rinehart and Winston, 1963.

Barnett, S. A. On the hazards of analogies between human aggression and aggression in other animals. Review of *On aggression*, by Konrad Lorenz. *Scientific American*, 1967, **216**, 135–138.

Becker, W. C. The matching of behavior rating and questionnaire personality factors. *Psychological Bulletin*, 1960, **57**, 201–212.

Becker, W. C. Developmental psychology. *Annual Review of Psychology*, 1962, **13**, 1–34.

Becker, W. C. Consequences of different kinds of parental discipline. In M. L. Hoffman & L. W. Hoffman (Eds.), *Review of child development research*. Vol. 1, New York: Russell Sage, 1964.

Berkowitz, L. *Aggression: A social psychological analysis*. New York: McGraw-Hill, 1962.

Berkowitz, L. The concept of aggressive drive: Some additional considerations. *Advances in Experimental Social Psychology*, 1965, **2**, 301–329.

Berkowitz, L. (Ed.) *Roots of aggression*. New York: Atherton Press, 1969.

Berkowitz, L., & Holmes, D. S. A further investigation of hostility generalization to disliked objects. *Journal of Personality*, 1960, **28**, 427–442.

Boelkins, R. C., & Heiser, J. F. Biological bases of aggression. In D. N. Daniels, M. F. Gilula, & F. M. Ochberg (Eds.), *Violence and the struggle for existence*. Boston: Little, Brown, 1970.

Bronfenbrenner, U., & Ricciuti, H. N. The appraisal of personality characteristics in children. In P. Mussen (Ed.), *Handbook of research methods in child development*. New York: Wiley, 1960.

Brown, J. S., & Farber, I. E. Emotion conceptualized as intervening variables— with suggestions toward a theory of frustration. *Psychological Bulletin*, 1951, **48**, 465–495.

Buss, A. H. *The psychology of aggression*. New York: Wiley, 1961.

Campbell, D. T., & Fiske, D. W. Convergent and discriminant validation by the multitrait-multimethod matrix. *Psychological Bulletin*, 1959, **56**, 81–105.

Clark, R. A. The effects of sexual motivation on phantasy. In D. McClelland (Ed.), *Studies in motivation*. New York: Appleton-Century-Crofts, 1955.

Clemente, C. D., & Lindsley, D. B. (Eds.). *Aggression and defense. UCLA Forum in Medical Sciences*, 1967, No. 7.

Dollard, J., Doob, L., Miller, N., Mowrer, O., & Sears, R. *Frustration and aggression*. New Haven: Yale, 1939.

Endler, N. S., & Hunt, J. M. S–R inventories of hostility and comparisons of the proportions of variance from persons, responses, and situations for hostility and anxiousness. *Journal of Personality and Social Psychology*, 1968, **9**, 309–315.

Feshbach, S. The function of aggression and the regulation of aggressive drive. *Psychological Review*, 1964, **71**, 257–272.

Feshbach, S., & Singer, R. D. *Television and aggression*. San Francisco: Jossey-Bass, 1971.

Feshbach, S., Stiles, W. B., & Bitter, E. The reinforcing effect of witnessing aggression. *Journal of Experimental Research in Personality*, 1967, **2**, 133–139.

Guion, R. M. Personnel selection. *Annual Review of Psychology*, 1967, **18**, 191–216.

Harman, H. H. *Modern factor analysis.* Chicago: University of Chicago Press, 1967.

Hartmann, H., Kris, E., & Loewenstein, R. M. Notes on the theory of aggression. In *Psychoanalytic Study of the Child, 1949.* Vols. 3 & 4. New York: International Universities Press.

Hays, W. L. *Statistics for psychologists.* New York: Holt, Rinehart and Winston, 1963.

Hinde, R. A. The nature of aggression. *New Society*, 1967, **9**, 302–304.

Hoffman, P. J., Slovic, P., & Rorer, L. G. An analysis-of-variance model for the assessment of configural cue utilization in clinical judgment. *Psychological Bulletin*, 1968, **69**, 338–349.

Holt, R. R. Ego autonomy re-evaluated. *International Journal of Psychoanalysis*, 1965, **46**, 151–167.

Holt, R. R. (Ed.) *Motives and thought: Psychoanalytic essays in honor of David Rapaport.* New York: International Universities Press, 1966.

Holt, R. R. Beyond vitalism and mechanism: Freud's concept of psychic energy. In B. Wolman (Ed.), *Historical roots of contemporary psychology.* New York: Harper & Row, 1967.

Horst, P. Pattern analysis and configural scoring. *Journal of Clinical Psychology*, 1954, **10**, 3–11.

Jøreskog, K. G. *Statistical estimation in factor analysis.* Uppsala: Almqvist & Wiksell, 1963.

Kagan, J. Thematic apperceptive techniques with children. In A. Rabin & M. Haworth (Eds.), *Projective techniques with children.* New York: Grune & Stratton, 1960. Pp. 105–129.

Kaiser, H. F. The varimax criterion for analytic rotation in factor analysis. *Psychometrika*, 1958, **23**, 187–200.

Kaiser, H. F. Image analysis. In C. W. Harris (Ed.), *Problems in measuring change.* Madison: University of Wisconsin Press, 1963.

Kaufmann, H. Definitions and methodology in the study of aggression. *Psychological Bulletin*, 1965, **64**, 351–364.

Klein, G. S., Barr, H. L., & Wolitzky, D. L. Personality. *Annual Review of Psychology*, 1967, **18**, 467–560.

Lorenz, K. *On aggression.* New York: Harcourt, Brace, 1966.

Meehl, P. E. Configural scoring. *Journal of Consulting Psychology*, 1950, **14**, 165–171.

Megargee, E. I. Undercontrolled and overcontrolled personality types in extreme antisocial aggression. *Psychological Monographs*, 1966, **80** (3, Whole No. 611.)

Miller, N. E. The frustration-aggression hypothesis. *Psychological Review*, 1941, **48**, 337–342.

Mischel, W. *Personality and assessment.* New York: Wiley, 1968.

Murstein, B. I. *Theory and research in projective techniques (emphasizing the TAT).* New York: Wiley, 1963.

Olweus, D. *Prediction of aggression: On the basis of a projective test.* Stockholm: Skandinaviska Testförlaget, 1969 (Box 461, S-12604 Haegersten 4, Sweden).

Olweus, D. Development of a multi-faceted aggression inventory for boys. In *Reports from the Institute of Psychology*. Bergen, Norway: University of Bergen, 1973, in press.

Orne, M. T. Hypnosis, motivation, and the ecological validity of the psychological experiment. In W. J. Arnold & M. M. Page (Eds.), *Nebraska Symposium on Motivation, 1970*. Lincoln: University of Nebraska Press, 1971. Pp. 187–265.

Patterson, G. R., Littman, R. A., & Bricker, W. Assertive behavior in children: A step toward a theory of aggression. *Monographs of the Society for Research in Child Development*, 1967, **32** (5, Whole No. 113).

Saltz, G., & Epstein, S. Thematic hostility and guilt responses as related to self-reported hostility, guilt, and conflict. *Journal of Abnormal and Social Psychology*, 1963, **67**, 469–479.

Saunders, D. R. Moderator variables in prediction. *Educational and Psychological Measurement*, 1956, **16**, 209–222.

Schafer, R. *Psychoanalytic interpretation in Rorschach testing: Theory and application*. New York: Grune & Stratton, 1954.

Scott, J. P. *Aggression*. Chicago: University of Chicago Press, 1958.

Siegel, A. E. Film-mediated fantasy aggression and strength of aggressive drive. *Child Development*, 1956, **27**, 365–378.

Spielberger, C. D. (Ed.) *Anxiety and behavior*. New York: Academic Press, 1966.

Walder, L. O., Abelson, R. P., Eron, L. D., Banta, T. J., & Laulicht, J. H. Development of a peer-rating measure of aggression. *Psychological Reports*, 1961, **9**, 497–556.

Wheeler, L. Toward a theory of behavioral contagion. *Psychological Review*, 1966, **73**, 179–192.

Zigler, E. Learning, development, and social class in the socialization process. In Melvin H. Marx (Ed.), *Learning: Interaction*. London: Collier-Macmillan, 1970.

Chronological List
of Contents of the Nebraska
Symposia on Motivation

1953 (Vol. 1)

Brown, J. S. Problems presented by the concept of acquired drive, pp. 1–21.

Harlow, H. F. Motivation as a factor in new responses, pp. 24–49.

Postman, L. J. The experimental analysis of motivational factors in perception, pp. 59–108.

Nowlis, V. The development and modification of motivational systems in personality, pp. 114–138.

Newcomb, T. M. Motivation in social behavior, pp. 139–161.

Mowrer, O. H. Motivation and neurosis, pp. 162–185.

1954 (Vol. 2)

Farber, I. E. Anxiety as a drive state, pp. 1–46.

Atkinson, J. W. Exploration using imaginative thought to assess the strength of human motives, pp. 56–112.

Ritchie, B. F. A logical and experimental analysis of the laws of motivation, pp. 121–176.

Festinger, L. Motivation leading to social behavior, pp. 191–219.

Klein, G. S. Need and regulation, pp. 224–274.

Nissen, H. W. The nature of the drive as innate determinant of behavioral organization, pp. 281–321.

1955 (Vol. 3)

Maslow, A. Deficiency motivation and growth motivation, pp. 1–30.

McClelland, D. C. Some social consequences of achievement motivation, pp. 41–65.

Olds, J. Physiological mechanisms of reward, pp. 73–139.

Peak, H. Attitude and motivation, pp. 149–189.

Young, P. T. The role of hedonic processes in motivation, pp. 193–238.

Rotter, J. B. The role of the psychological situation in determining the direction of human behavior, pp. 245–269.

1956 (Vol. 4)

Beach, F. A. Characteristics of masculine "sex drive," pp. 1–32.
Koch, S. Behavior as "intrinsically" regulated: Work notes towards a pretheory of phenomena called "motivational," pp. 42–87.
Marx, M. H. Some relations between frustration and drive, pp. 92–130.
Miller, D. R., & Swanson, G. E. The study of conflict, pp. 137–174.
Seward, J. P. A neurological approach to motivation, pp. 180–208.
Solomon, R. L., & Brush, E. S. Experimentally derived conceptions of anxiety and aversion, pp. 212–305.

1957 (Vol. 5)

Morgan, C. T. Physiological mechanisms of motivation, pp. 1–35.
Lindsley, D. B. Psychophysiology and motivation, pp. 44–105.
Rodnick, E. H., & Garmezy, N. An experimental approach to the study of motivation in schizophrenia, pp. 109–184.
Wittenborn, J. R. Inferring the strength of drive, pp. 191–259.
Sears, P. S. Problems in the investigation of achievement and self-esteem motivation, pp. 265–339.
Osgood, C. E. Motivational dynamics of language behavior, pp. 348–424.

1958 (Vol. 6)

Bolles, R. C. The usefulness of the drive concept, pp. 1–33.
Estes, W. K. Stimulus-response theory of drive, pp. 35–69.
Spence, K. W. Behavior theory and selective learning, pp. 73–107.
Littman, R. A. Motives, history and causes, pp. 114–168.
Eriksen, C. W. Unconscious processes, pp. 169–227.
Malmo, R. B. Measurement of drive: An unsolved problem in psychology, pp. 229–265.

1959 (Vol. 7)

Schneirla, T. C. An evolutionary and developmental theory of biphasic processes underlying approach and withdrawal, pp. 1–42.
Hess, E. The relationship between imprinting and motivation, pp. 44–77.
Cattell, R. B. The dynamic calculus: Concepts and crucial experiments, pp. 84–134.
Levin, H., & Baldwin, A. L. Pride and shame in children, pp. 138–174.
Whiting, J. W. M. Sorcery, sin, and the superego. A cross-cultural study of some mechanisms of social control, pp. 174–195.
Janis, I. L. Motivational factors in the resolution of decisional conflicts, pp. 198–231.

Logan, F. A. The free behavior situation, pp. 99–128.
Edwards, A. L. The assessment of human motives by means of personality scales, pp. 135–162.
Mandler, G. The interruption of behavior, pp. 163–219.
Schachter, S., & Latané, B. Crime, cognition, and the autonomic nervous system, pp. 221–273.

1965 (Vol. 13)

Kendler, H. H. Motivation and behavior, pp. 1–23.
Leeper, R. W. Some needed developments in the motivational theory of emotions, pp. 25–122.
Premack, D. Reinforcement theory, pp. 123–180.
Hunt, J. McV. Intrinsic motivation and its role in psychological development, pp. 189–282.
Campbell, D. T. Ethnocentric and other altruistic motives, pp. 283–311.
Guilford, J. P. Motivation in an informational psychology, pp. 313–332.

1966 (Vol. 14)

Holt, R. R. Measuring libidinal and aggressive motives and their controls by means of the Rorschach test, pp. 1–47.
Burke, C. J. Linear models for Pavlovian conditioning, pp. 49–66.
Masling, J. Role-related behavior of the subject and psychologist and its effects upon psychological data, pp. 67–103.
Dethier, V. G. Insects and the concept of motivation, pp. 105–136.
Helson, H. Some problems in motivation from the point of view of the theory of adaptation level, pp. 137–182.
Malamud, W. The concept of motivation in psychiatric practice, pp. 183–200.

1967 (Vol. 15)

Berlyne, D. E. Arousal and reinforcement, pp. 1–110.
Scott, J. P. The development of social motivation, pp. 111–132.
Katz, I. The socialization of academic motivation in minority group children, pp. 133–191.
Kelley, H. H. Attribution theory in social psychology, pp. 192–238.
Pettigrew, T. F. Social evaluation theory: Convergences and applications, pp. 241–311.

1968 (Vol. 16)

Grossmann, S. P. The physiological basis of specific and nonspecific motivational processes, pp. 1–46.
McClearn, G. E. Genetics and motivation of the mouse, pp. 47–83.
Levine, S. Hormones and conditioning, pp. 85–101.

Flynn, J. P. Patterning mechanisms, patterned reflexes, and attack behavior in cats, pp. 125–153.

Hutchinson, R. R. The environmental causes of aggression, pp. 155–181.

Calhoun, J. B. Disruption of behavioral states as a cause of aggression, pp. 183–260.

Olweus, D. Personality and aggression, pp. 261–321.

Alphabetical List
of Contents of the Nebraska
Symposia on Motivation
by Author

Dethier, V. G. Insects and the concept of motivation. 1966, **14**, 105–136.

Deutsch, M. Cooperation and trust: Some theoretical notes. 1962, **10**, 275–319.

Donaldson, M. Preconditions of inference. 1971, **19**, 81–106.

Edwards, A. L. The assessment of human motives by means of personality scales. 1964, **12**, 135–162.

Ekman, P. Universals and cultural differences in facial expressions of emotion. 1971, **19**, 207–284.

Elkind, D. Cognitive growth cycles in mental development. 1971, **19**, 1–32.

Epstein, S. The measurement of drive and conflict in humans: Theory and experiment. 1962, **10**, 127–206.

Eriksen, C. W. Unconscious processes. 1958, **6**, 169–227.

Estes, W. K. Stimulus-response theory of drive. 1958, **6**, 35–69.

Exline, R. Visual interaction: The glances of power and preference. 1971, **19**, 163–206.

Falk, J. L. The behavioral regulation of water-electrolyte balance. 1961, **9**, 1–33.

Farber, I. E. Anxiety as a drive state. 1954, **2**, 1–46.

Festinger, L. Motivation leading to social behavior. 1954, **2**, 191–219.

Flynn, J. P. Patterning mechanisms, patterned reflexes, and attack behavior in cats. 1972, **20**, 125–153.

Grossman, S. P. The physiological basis of specific and non-specific motivational processes. 1968, **16**, 1–46.

Guilford, J. P. Motivation in an informational psychology. 1965, **13**, 313–332.

Harlow, H. F. Motivation as a factor in new responses. 1953, **1**, 24–49.

Heckhausen, H. Achievement motive research: Current problems and some contributions towards a general theory of motivation. 1968, **16**, 103–174.

Heider, F. The Gestalt theory of motivation. 1960, **8**, 145–172.

Helson, H. Some problems in motivation from the point of view of the theory of adaptation level. 1966, **14**, 137–182.

Hess, E. The relationship between imprinting and motivation. 1959, **7**, 44–77.

Hilgard, E. R. The motivational relevance of hypnosis. 1964, **12**, 1–44.

Holt, R. R. Measuring libidinal and aggressive motives and their controls by means of the Rorschach test. 1966, **14**, 1–47.

Hunt, J. McV. Intrinsic motivation and its role in psychological development. 1965, **13**, 189–282.

Hutchinson, R. R. The environmental causes of aggression. 1972, **20**, 155–181.

Janis, I. L. Motivational factors in the resolution of decisional conflicts. 1959, **7**, 198–231.

Katz, I. The socialization of academic motivation in minority group children. 1967, **15**, 133–191.

Kelley, H. H. Attribution theory in social psychology. 1967, **15**, 192–238.

Kelly, G. A. Europe's matrix of decision. 1962, **10**, 83–123.

Kendler, H. H. Motivation and behavior. 1965, **13**, 1–23.

King, J. A. Ecological psychology: An approach to motivation. 1970, **18**, 1–33.

Klein, G. S. Need and regulation. 1954, **2**, 224–274.

Orne, M. T. Hypnosis, motivation, and the ecological validity of the psychological experiment. 1970, **18**, 187–265.

Osgood, C. E. Motivational dynamics of language behavior. 1957, **5**, 348–424.

Peak, H. Attitude and motivation. 1955, **3**, 149–189.

Pettigrew, T. F. Social evaluation theory: Convergences and applications. 1967, **15**, 241–311.

Pfaffman, C. The sensory and motivating properties of the sense of taste. 1961, **9**, 71–108.

Postman, L. J. The experimental analysis of motivational factors in perception. 1953, **1**, 59–108.

Premack, D. Reinforcement theory. 1965, **13**, 123–180.

Pribram, K. H. Reinforcement revisited: A structural view. 1963, **11**, 113–159.

Rapaport, D. On the psychoanalytic theory of motivation. 1960, **8**, 173–247.

Ritchie, B. F. A logical and experimental analysis of the laws of motivation. 1954, **2**, 121–176.

Rodnick, E. H., & Garmezy, N. An experimental approach to the study of motivation in schizophrenia. 1957, **5**, 109–184.

Rogers, C. R. Actualizing tendency in relation to "motives" and to consciousness. 1963, **11**, 1–24.

Rotter, J. B. The role of the psychological situation in determining the direction of human behavior. 1955, **3**, 245–269.

Sarason, S. B. The contents of human problem solving. 1961, **9**, 147–174.

Schachter, S., & Latané, B. Crime, cognition, and the autonomic nervous system. 1964, **12**, 221–273.

Schneirla, T. C. An evolutionary and developmental theory of biphasic processes underlying approach and withdrawal. 1959, **7**, 1–42.

Scott, J. P. The development of social motivation. 1967, **15**, 111–132.

Sears, P. S. Problems in the investigation of achievement and self-esteem motivation. 1957, **5**, 265–339.

Sears, R. R. Dependency motivation. 1963, **11**, 25–64.

Seward, J. P. A neurological approach to motivation. 1956, **4**, 180–208.

Solomon, R. L., & Brush, E. S. Experimentally derived conceptions of anxiety and aversion. 1956, **4**, 212–305.

Spence, K. W. Behavior theory and selective learning. 1958, **6**, 73–107.

Taylor, D. W. Toward an informational processing theory of motivation. 1960, **8**, 51–79.

Teitelbaum, P. Disturbances in feeding and drinking behavior after hypothalamic lesions. 1961, **9**, 39–65.

Toman, W. On the periodicity of motivation. 1960, **8**, 80–95.

Vinacke, W. E. Motivation as a complex problem. 1962, **10**, 1–46.

Walker, E. L. Psychological complexity as a basis for a theory of motivation and choice. 1964, **12**, 47–95.

White, R. W. Competence and the psychosexual stages of development. 1960, **8**, 97–141.

Subject Index

Author Index

340